GW00853420

מצפורה

ArtScroll Judaiscope Series

Seasons of
the Soul

Seasons of

Collected from the pages of
The Jewish Observer
by

Rabbi Nisson Wolpin,
Editor

the Soul

Religious, historical, and philosophical perspectives on the Jewish year and its milestones

Published by

Mesorah Publications, ltd

in conjunction with
Agudath Israel of America

FIRST EDITION
First Impression ... January, 1981

Published and Distributed by
MESORAH PUBLICATIONS, Ltd.
Brooklyn, New York 11223

Distributed in Israel by
MESORAH MAFITZIM / J. GROSSMAN
Rechov Bayit Vegan 90/5
Jerusalem, Israel

Distributed in Europe by
J. LEHMANN HEBREW BOOKSELLERS
20 Cambridge Terrace
Gateshead
Tyne and Wear
England NE8 1RP

ARTSCROLL JUDAISCOPE SERIES / "SEASONS OF THE SOUL"
© *Copyright 1981*
by MESORAH PUBLICATIONS, Ltd.
1969 Coney Island Avenue / Brooklyn, N.Y. 11223 / (212) 339-1700
The essays in this volume have been adapted from articles
that have appeared in the pages of
THE JEWISH OBSERVER
published by Agudath Israel of America.
Copyright and all rights reserved by The Jewish Observer, *New York City*

No part of this book may be reproduced in any form *without written permission from the copyright holder,*
except by a reviewer who wishes to quote brief passages in connection with a review written for inclusion
in magazines or newspapers.

THE RIGHTS OF THE COPYRIGHT HOLDER WILL BE STRICTLY ENFORCED.

ISBN
0-89906-852-9 (hard cover)
0-89906-853-7 (paper back)

סדר בְּמִסְגֶּרֶת
חֶבְרַת אַרְטְסְקְרוֹל בֶּע"מ

Typography by Compuscribe at ArtScroll Studios, Ltd.
1969 Coney Island Avenue / Brooklyn, N.Y. 11223 / (212) 339-1700

Printed in the United States of America by Moriah Offset

Table of Contents

Contributors to this volume
(in order of their appearance)

Maharal of Prague — Rabbi Yehudah ben Bezalel Loewy זצ"ל, a seminal figure in the last 500 years of Jewish thought, who was Rav of Prague in the late 16th century.

Sefas Emes — Rabbi Yehudah Aryeh Leib Alter זצ"ל, Gerrer Rebbe in late 19th, early 20th Century, whose teachings on Talmud and Chassidic discourse on Torah were recorded and posthumously published in volumes bearing the name *Sefas Emes.*

Rabbi Yehudah Leib Orlean זצ"ל was the director of the Beth Jacob Teachers' Seminary of Cracow and a distinguished educator and writer in prewar Poland.

A. Scheinman is an American who is currently studying in a Jerusalem Yeshivah.

Rabbi Eliyahu Dessler זצ"ל was a leading thinker and teacher of *Mussar* in the previous generation. *Michtav Me'Eliyahu*, based on his lectures, became a classic in its field.

Rabbi Nisson Wolpin is editor of both *The Jewish Observer* and this volume.

Rabbi Mendel Weinbach is a dean at Ohr Samayach Institutions/Joseph and Faye Tanenbaum College of Judaic Studies, and an author of several books on Judaic topics.

Rabbi Chaim Dov Keller is a Rosh Yeshivah of Telshe Yeshivah in Chicago.

Alexander Zusha Friedman זצ"ל was a prominent leader of the Agudath Israel movement in Poland and a prolific writer and author. Among his best known volumes is *Der Torah Kvall* on Torah.

Rabbi Zalman Sorotzkin זצ"ל, the Lutzker Rav, was a leading figure of Jewry in Europe and Israel during the mid 20th-Century.

Rabbi Menachem Rokeach a former vice president of Igud HaRabonim (Rabbinical Alliance of America), is a frequent contributor to various Jewish journals.

Rabbi Ralph Pelcowitz is the spiritual leader of the Congregation Knesseth Israel in Far Rockaway, N.Y.

Y. Yechezkieli, writer of note, was educated in pre-World War II Europe and lives in Israel today.

Rabbi Moshe Barkany studied at Mesivta Torah Vodaath and Beth Medrash Govoha of Lakewood, N.J., and is currently principal of Yeshivah Gedolah of Montreal.

Rabbi Yitzchok Hutner זצ״ל, late Rosh Yeshivah of Mesivta Chaim Berlin/Kolel Gur Arye in Brooklyn and Jerusalem, was an outstanding thinker and leader of the present generation. Some of his writings on Torah philosophy are published in the five volume *Pachad Yitzchok.*

Rabbi Yaakov Feitman, principal of the Rabbi Jacob Joseph School in Staten Island, N.Y., is a well known writer and educator.

Rabbi Joseph Elias, a noted lecturer and writer, is Menahel of Yeshivah Rabbi Samson Raphael Hirsch Girls' High School and the Rika Breuer Teachers' Seminary. He is a member of the editorial board of the Judaiscope Series, and author of the ArtScroll *Haggadah.*

Rabbi Avrohom Chaim Feuer, writer and lecturer of note and rabbi in Miami Beach, Florida, is author of the translation and commentary of the ArtScroll *Tehillim.*

Rabbi Samson Raphael Hirsch זצ״ל, the father of modern German Orthodoxy, was a fiery leader, brilliant writer and profound educator, who changed the face of Frankfort-am-Main during the mid-19th Century.

Rabbi Nosson Scherman, well-known educator, writer, and lecturer, is general editor of the ArtScroll Series, and editor of *Olomeinu,* Torah Umesorah's magazine for children.

Rabbi Yisroel Alter זצ״ל, the late Gerrer Rebbe, was an outstanding leader of Chassidic Jewry, especially well known for the guidance of his followers during the years of reconstruction and rehabilitation in Israel after World War II. His Chassidic writings were published as *Bais Yisroel.*

Rabbi Zev Hoberman is Rosh Yeshivah of Shaarei Torah of Rockland County, N.Y. His essays on Torah thought were published as *Zev Yitrof*.

Rabbi Moshe Sherer is president of Agudath Israel of America and co-chairman of Agudath Israel World Organization.

Rabbi Elkanah Schwartz is rabbi of Congregation Kol Israel in Brooklyn.

Rabbi Nachman Bulman, founding editor of *The Jewish Observer*, leading educator, thinker, and lecturer, heads an American Torah community in Migdal HaEmek in Israel.

Yehuda Leib Gersht זצ״ל was an educator, thinker, and writer of great distinction, in pre-war Poland. He continued his work in *Eretz Yisrael* until his death.

Rabbi Fabian Schonfeld is the spiritual leader of Young Israel of Kew Garden Hills.

Dr. Isaac Breuer זצ״ל is considered the spiritual heir of his grandfather Rabbi Samson Raphael Hirsch and was recognized as a leading thinker and ideologist of Torah Jewry during the mid-20th Century.

Rabbi Paysach Krohn was ordained by Mesivta Torah Vodaath and is a practicing *mohel*.

Rabbi Shmuel Borenstein זצ״ל, the Sochaczover Rebbe, was a highly respected leader of Chassidic Jewry at the turn of the century whose writings on Talmud and on Torah were published under the title *Shem MiShmuel*.

Rabbi Moshe Weitman is dean of the Torah Academy for Girls in Far Rockaway, N.Y. His "Sefirah Thoughts" is based primarily on the *Bnei Yissachar* of the *Rebbe*, Reb Tzvi Elimelech of Dinov זצ״ל.

Rabbi Aryeh Kaplan is a widely published author, translator, and lecturer, whose works include *The Torah Anthology*, an English Translation of *Yalkut MeAm Loez*.

Rabbi Menachem Mendel Schneersohn the *Lubavitcher Rebbe*, leads his worldwide community of thousands of followers from his headquarters in the Crown Heights section of Brooklyn, N.Y.

Rabbi Alter Ben Zion Metzger, lecturer and author, is a professor of Judaic Studies in Yeshiva University's Stern College for Women.

Rabbi Mordechai Gifter, a leader of contemporary Torah Jewry, is Rosh Yeshivah of Telshe, in Wickliffe, Ohio, and a member of the Moetzes Gedolei HaTorah (Council of Torah Sages), the policy making body of Agudath Israel of America.

Moreinu Yaakov Rosenheim צ״ל a leader of German Jewry, was one of the architects of the World Agudath Israel Movement, and served as the chairman of the Agudath Israel World Organization for many years.

The essays in this book first appeared as articles in
The Jewish Observer,
a monthly journal of thought and opinion
published by Agudath Israel of America.
The Editorial Board of **The Jewish Observer** *is chaired*
by Dr. Ernst L. Bodenheimer

Seasons of the Soul

These are the seasons (mo'adim) *of HASHEM ... that you are to declare in their seasons (Vayikra 23:4). Mo'ed — a season, an appointment, a rendezvous with the Divine.*

W E ARE ACCUSTOMED to the consecration of place. A site becomes sacred because an extraordinary event had occurred there; or because it was reserved for communion with G-d; or both. We remove our shoes in awe for Mount Moriah, which was selected as the place for the *Bais HaMikdash*, where man can reach for the Divine. Its specialness stems from (among many other factors) G-d's designation of it to *Avraham Avinu* as "the place that I will show you" and Avraham's readiness to offer his only son as a sacrifice to G-d on the mountain. And so this spot, as the sacred Temple Mount, has remained sacred to this very day.

By the same token, a place can become holy because it is dedicated to a holy pursuit. Our *shuls* and *batei midrash* are consecrated, reserved for sacred pursuits — mundane conversations or vulgar activities are prohibited on their premises.

Time, too, is effected by the events that occur within its specific frames. The initial day of rest, when G-d abstained from His creative endeavors, made the seventh day a sacred segment of time. And so it is every seventh day. Strictly a day of commemoration? By no means. Every week is a cycle within time and every *Shabbos* is a return to that period that G-d had originally endowed with a tranquility akin to that of the World-to-Come — a perfect day of rest on that very first *Shabbos* day. Every completion of the *Shabbos* cycle is a return to that blessed station in time ... not unlike a traveler's return to his point of embarkation as he circles an island in the space of his existence.

◆§ The Infinite Variety Within Time

As the earth spins on its tilted axis and progresses along its elliptical tour of duty around the sun, it turns its cheek toward the glowing orb from a different vantage point day after day. Thus each day is of slightly different duration from the preceding one; no two days exactly the same in length.

This is not happenstance, but a reminder of the distinctiveness inherent in each day. It is as if the sunrise-sunset table in the daily newspaper is telling us, "Check me out and remind yourself how you are a creature of time. Today is not a duplicate of yesterday, nor will it be repeated tomorrow. Each day is separate, unique."

The singularity of each unit of time tells man that time — indeed, the seconds that flicker by — is the very substance of life. And its passage is death. For no second can be recaptured once it has passed, nor can it ever be repeated.

There are ways, however, that moments can be preserved, perpetuated, and extended into eternity. The divinity implanted in each moment offers a potential of eternity, if it is but unlocked and developed. Should man sidestep the ephemeral — refuse to be seduced by the glittery attractions of self-indulgence, destruction, or whimsy — and utilize his time for *mitzvos*, fulfillment of G-d's eternal commands, and live by the dictates of His infinite wisdom, then he succeeds in directing time and energy toward a Divine purpose, and unlocks the secret of eternity in the transitory.

The very difference within each passing day cries out, saying: "I offer you an unrivaled opportunity to serve G-d in a way as yet unexperienced, and never again to be experienced. Yesterday — Tuesday — sang out with the potential of the third day of the week, when the Levites in the Temple chanted a song that celebrated that day's inherent character *(tiferes)*. Today, Wednesday, is a totally different day, with a purpose all its own, and a song that proclaims the particularity of the fourth day *(netzach)*. Tomorrow? another day, of yet different character, and a song to match" (see Overview to *Zemiroth*, ArtScroll ed.).

Man is a creature of time. A prisoner of time? Perhaps. But he is also the only one of G-d's creatures that can overcome time, grab its elusive moments and perpetuate them, extend them to that world beyond time.

In the daily *Shacharis* prayers, in advance of the *Shema*, we praise G-d for "creating light and fashioning darkness ..." concluding with "*Yotzer HaMeoros* — Who created the luminaries." We offer a praise to G-d for structuring the passage of time — day following night following day — a phenomenon that can be charted as a result of the luminaries that G-d hung into space.

But this blessing on the creation of luminaries says more — it praises G-d for man's potential to release the transcendental lights imbedded into the events of each passing day — the lights of every single day, markedly distinct from that of the next — lights that man is enjoined to release.

◄§ The Various Dimensions of Time

The human personality is complex beyond imagination. Man's capacity for good and evil, creativity and destruction, intellectual analysis and intuitive projections — the full range of human emotions from ecstacy to despair — all of these have a place in the Divine scheme; each has a way in which it can be utilized to recognize G-d and serve Him. When this takes place, and love becomes sublimated to love of G-d, or hostility becomes expressed in "those who love G-d despise evil" *(Tehillim 97:10)*, then a Divine spark within the individual is fanned into a blaze of glory.

There are times inherently endowed with the ability to provoke such responses. Did not *Shlomo* advise us that there is a "time to plant and a time to uproot ...; a time to weep and a time to laugh; a time of grief and a time of dance" *(Koheles 3:2,4)*.

Not only do occasions arise for the myriad gestures within the human range of activity; not only do events occur that provoke the infinite possibilities of human emotions. *The times are times* "to weep ... to laugh ... to seek ... to lose ... to love ... to hate" (ibid. vs. 4,6,8). The times become tempered, colored, molded, stamped, indelibly marked by the events of major significance that occur within them. And the times themselves are thus permanently endowed.

☐   The children of *Yaakov Avinu* were redeemed from slavery in Egypt and emerged as the Nation of Israel on the 15th of the month of Nissan, and the day became *Zman Cheiruseinu* — the Time of Redemption. As the Jew passing through his year enters the third week of Nissan, he encounters the season of redemption. Should he avail himself of the spiritual stimuli of the time, he finds himself unusually responsive to yearnings for spiritual freedom. With a fullness of realization, he may say "on this night I and my ancestors were freed from bondage in Egypt ... *I*, now join my ancestors in experiencing a spiritual liberation."

☐   It was on Shavuos, in the year 2448 after Creation, that the Torah was given. The heavens were opened and for one electrifying hour on that day, inhabitants of lowly regions were raised to unrivaled heights where they shared the wisdom of Divine intellect. Every year thereafter, the heavens part on the same Sixth of Sivan, releasing rays of illuminating wisdom. If he but wills it, man can absorb these rays in a *Kabalas HaTorah* of his own. It is *Zman Mattan Toraseinu* — the Time When Torah is Given — as it was and always will be exactly fifty days from the second day of Pesach. The day of the calendar tells man this, and asks him, "Are you ready to seize the passing day and grasp it before it slips by?"

And so are the Three Weeks — from the Seventeenth of Tammuz through the Ninth of Av — days of destruction, tears and mourning, followed by weeks of comfort, hope and reconstruction — capped by the freshness of renewal — Rosh Hashanah — the New Year ... as it ever was and always will **be**.

⃒ Of Time and Space

The relentless passage of time, and inexorable passage of man through time, are phenomena of interplay between life and death ... emotions, intellect, and the spirit ... the timebound and the timeless. Space, the physically finite, was presented as a metaphor for the setting through which man passes, only to return again to stations of significance. It is also one of the elements that contributes to the spiritualization of time, to be sublimated in turn by the sanctity of time.

The Torah associates each of the *Shalosh Regalim* — the Pilgrimage Festivals — with a season of the soil: Pesach, *Chag HaAviv* is the Festival of Spring; Shavuos is *Chag HaKatzir* the Festival of Reaping; and Succos is *Chag HaAssif*, the Festival of Harvest. Each of these seasons, in which man tends to become earthbound through his involvement in agrarian pursuits, also offers a release from the mundane, because tied to each is an experience that elevates tilling the soil to an experience of developing the soul. Pesach is the beginning of the *Omer* count, when the barley offering was brought in the *Bais HaMikdash;* Shavuos is the time when the Two Breads were brought, also initiating the season, extending through Succos, of bringing *bikkurim*, the first fruits.

Each of these festivals is a special time of communion with G-d, when the the pilgrim approaches the *Bais HaMikdash*. By virtue of the *korban re'eyah* (the special sacrifice mandated for the occasion) he does "not see G-d empty-handed." By the same token, he does not *leave* empty-handed, but is enriched by the blessings of spiritual bounty and material plenty that were bestowed on him to take home. Indeed, the journey served to focus on Torah and *avodah* (Divine service) as central to Jewry's existence — so that *aliyah l'regel* became a means of strengthening one's *Yiras Shamayim*.

In our contemporary *galus*, the occasion of a *regel* finds us distant from the Temple Mount, or even if within view of its sacred stretches, painfully aware that they are no longer graced by the *Bais HaMikdash*. The festival is also in *galus*. Together — the Jew and the *Yom Tov*, the appointment with G-d and the individual's celebration of it — suffer an alienation, and both yearn for the restoration of Divine sovereignty in the Holy Land when "our mouths will be full of laughter". Every festival is an occasion of the Jew's appointment with the divinity of *Eretz Yisrael* and the sanctity of Jerusalem: when that attitude of holiness is present, the festival is marked by celebration; when it is absent, the festival is marked by yearning.

◆§ Seasons of History

> *"Remember the days of yore, understand the years of each generation"* (Devarim 32:7).

A Jew never leaves the immediacy of his history; he is reminded of it day after day in his Grace and prayers, by his *tefillin* and his *Shema* with their recollections of the Exodus from Egypt. And he encounters its full scope in the annual cycle of the calendar. History is an expression of Torah's decisive influence in the national existence of the Jewish People, and the festivals and fast days are the milestones in its development. As the seasons of the land are celebrated in the passage of the months of the year, so are the seasons of our peoplehood commemorated in the rituals that raise their meaning from the accidental to the sanctified. And these are Torah, for they are the days of celebration, of contemplation, and mourning for the nation's collective soul.

The springtime, summer, and autumn of the Jewish nation are in Pesach, Shavous, Succos. The winter of its suffering and the oppressive heat of its defeats are preserved in the Four Fast Days. And its triumphs over tyrranical circumstances are found in the solstice of Chanukah, and the heady blossoming of the Purim victory.

Indeed, as we continue to endure the *galus*, this frigid winter of our peoplehood, we may find greater affinity with the *galus* festivals, and find them more conducive to incisive comment. But even Pesach, the festival of liberation, has its *Yom Tov Sheini shel Galus* — its second day, of rabbinic origin, celebrated only in the Diaspora. It is our task to heighten our sensitivity to all the special days and their sacred emanations.

It was the practice of Rabbi Nachum of Chernobel to light candles in his Chanukah menorah.

"But Rebbe," one of the Chassidim questioned, "don't many authorities consider olive oil preferable for the menorah?"

"Yes," the Rebbe replied. "But after a candle has burned out," he added, pointing to the drippings on his window sill, "it leaves an impression."

With the flames of all our festivals and fast days — some leaping high, some flickering, some burning low — shadows may abound, obstacles obstruct; but after they have passed, the impressions are still there.

◆§ A Word About This Book

In these pages are essays that have appeared in *The Jewish Observer*, a monthly journal of thought and opinion. They approach the *mo'adim* from a variety of vantage points, based on the insights of Chassidic masters and their followers, the teachings of great thinkers of the Hirschian school and their disciples, the profound reflections of teachers of Mussar and towering figures of the rabbinate and the yeshivos and their *talmidim*. Some are translations from Hebrew, German, or Yiddish, others are original essays based on the insights presented in past generations. While no season is treated exhaustively in these pages, we believe that the reader will not pass through any of them without some lasting, illuminating impressions.

"These are the seasons of G-d" — as He created them — "that you are to declare in their times" as interpreted by His children. So our Sages teach. The means they saw and imparted to us provides beauty, flavor, and holiness to the Jew's *Seasons of the Soul.*

Nisson Wolpin

⩙ Yomim Noraim /
Days of Teshuva, Days of Awe

> the spirit of holiness evoked by the
> festivals ... achieving a sense of vision ...
> the pivotal role of awareness ... the
> conversion of sin to merit ... the "little"
> deeds that make a big difference ...
> carrying the burdens of society ...
> restoring the individual's place in G-d's
> world ... the shock therapy of Yom
> Kippur ... the season of awe and the
> sovereignty of G-d

So Great is Teshuvah

*Selections from the writings
of Maharal of Prague
based on midrashic references
to teshuvah*

*Wisdom was asked: What is the result of sin? It replied that
man's sins will forever pursue him. In response to the same
question Prophecy replied: The soul that sins must die.
When Torah was asked the result of sin, the Torah declared:
Let the sinner bring an offering and he will find atonement.
And finally, the Holy One, Blessed is He, was asked, What
of the sinner? He replied, Let him do teshuvah and he will be
forgiven (Talmud Yerushalmi).*

⋙ The Teshuvah Mystique

THIS AGGADAH explains to us the mystique of *teshuvah*.
From the point of view of reason, the sinner should not be able
to simply erase his deeds by *teshuvah*, for how can one undo an
act which has already been done? Nevertheless, reason notwithstanding, *teshuvah* is offered to us as a direct function of the
Almighty. While Prophecy maintains that evil and doers of evil
must be removed from Creation, and the Torah — the instrument
for man's perfection — insists on an actual *deed* to undo evil, it is
the Almighty alone who grants the gift of *teshuvah* whereby the
emotion of repentance alone eradicates an evil deed.

◄§ A Paradox

It appears paradoxical that *teshuvah*, which has no weight in the judgment of a human tribunal, is yet fully acceptable before the Heavenly Tribunal. But there is good reason for this difference. A human tribunal has jurisdiction over man's evil deeds alone: it does not have the competence to judge goodness, since what appears to be a proper act may be a cloak for evil. The Almighty alone can plumb man's heart. This tribunal is therefore restricted to judging whether or not a man was guilty of an evil act. It cannot measure *teshuvah*; it is unable to evaluate the authenticity of what is essentially a deeply-rooted emotional experience. The Heavenly Tribunal sees man in his totality; it can measure evil and evaluate goodness and therefore has jurisdiction over all of man's actions, a competence which even Wisdom and Prophecy do not possess.

◄§ Repent One Day Before Death

Let each man repent one day before his death, Rabbi Eliezer tells us. But how is man to know when he is to die? his disciples asked him. And Rabbi Eliezer replied: Let him then be engaged in teshuvah each day of his life, lest he die the following day; he will thus pass his life in a constant state of teshuvah (Talmud).

This being the case, why did not Rabbi Eliezer simply state that one should be constantly engaged in *teshuvah*? Had he stated it thus, we might have been led to believe that if man has not been in a constant state of *teshuvah*, then *teshuvah* before his death would be of no avail. He therefore states: Let every man repent one day before his death, in order to make it clear that even if man has sinned all his days, the gates of *teshuvah* are open to him until his dying day. This is so because death itself is essentially a return to G-d, and if he has experienced *teshuvah*, then his return to G-d is so much more complete.

◄§ Love and Fear

Rabbi Chama the son of Chanina said: So great is teshuvah that it brings healing to the world (Talmud).

When man repents, he returns to his original state of purity, and the entire world returns to its original state. This is what Rabbi Chama means when he tells us that *teshuvah* brings healing to the world, for it restores the world to its pristine state.

There appears to be a contradiction between two passages

from the prophet Yirmiyah on the matter of *teshuvah*. In one instance (3:14) he declares, in the name of G-d, "Return, my rebellious children ... " which suggests that by the very act of *teshuvah* they are already healed. In another passage (3:22) he declares, "Return, my rebellious children, and I will heal you...," indicating that after *teshuvah* they must yet be healed. In fact, however, the two passages refer to two different types of *teshuva*. When man returns out of love of G-d he is already healed, since his expression of love has brought him to his destination. But if he returns out of fear of G-d, he has not yet come all the way, and he has need of G-d's help to bring him to complete healing.

ᵈ§ Communal Teshuvah

> *Rabbi Levi said: "So great is teshuvah that it can bring man up to the Heavenly Throne." Rabbi Yochanan points out that it can bring him up to the Throne, but not actually to the Throne itself. But how can Rabbi Yochanan say this when he has himself pointed out that teshuvah has the power to set aside a negative command of the Torah?*
>
> *How is this so? If a man should divorce his wife and she becomes the wife of another man, he may never again take her back as his wife. And yet, Israel has "taken another wife" and the Almighty permits her to return through teshuvah. But this is no contradiction, for when the entire people return, the power of teshuvah propels them to the very Throne, a goal which one man alone is not able to achieve (Talmud).*

Teshuvah returns man to his original state, and his soul — having been hewn from beneath the Heavenly Throne — returns to whence it came. But since we might think that it takes man directly to the Almighty Himself, Rabbi Yochanan points out that *teshuvah* does not take him all the way. The *Gemara* finds this in contradiction to Rabbi Yochanan's own declaration that *teshuvah* has the power to set aside a negative command of the Torah, which obviously would mean that it returns man to the Almighty Himself. The *Gemara* therefore concludes that in this respect there are two levels of *teshuvah*, the personal and the collective. Man by himself, through *teshuvah*, can climb up to the Heavenly Throne, but no further. But when Rabbi Yochanan tells us that *teshuvah* can set aside a *mitzvah*, he is speaking of *Klal Yisrael*, of the power of collective *teshuvah*, which can bring the people of Israel directly to the G-d of Israel.

◄§ Teshuvah and Geulah

> *Rabbi Yosi HaGlili said: So great is teshuvah that it brings Geulah (Redemption) to the world. As it is written: "And a Redeemer will come to Zion and to those among Yaakov who return from sin." Why will the Redeemer come? — because of those who return from sin (Talmud).*

By the act of *teshuvah* man separates himself from the *yeitzer hara* (the inclination to evil) and thereby becomes free. Since man is normally ruled by the *yeitzer hara*, and *teshuvah* frees him from that rule, his act of self-redemption is an act of *Geulah*, which brings closer the Redemption of *Klal Yisrael*.

It is for this reason that the Jubilee year, when the bondsman is released from his obligations, is proclaimed on Yom Kippur, on the day when man is released from the *yeitzer hara* and he gains freedom for his body as well as his soul.

◄§ Meritorious Wrong-doing

> *Resh Lakish said: So great is teshuvah, that deliberate acts of wrong-doing are reckoned to have been committed without intent. As it is written: "Return, O Israel, to the L-rd your G-d, for you have stumbled in your sin." The Prophet speaks of intentional sin and yet calls it "stumbling." But, is this Resh Lakish's opinion? — has he not said that teshuvah transforms intentional acts to merits? There is no contradiction, for when teshuvah is stimulated by fear of G-d, man's sins are deemed to have been without intent, but when this teshuvah is motivated by love of G-d, then his sins are reckoned as merits.*

It is perfectly clear why intentional acts are considered — after *teshuvah* — as though they were without intent. *Teshuvah* elevates man to a higher degree of spirit wherein he is no longer capable of his previous wrong-doing, which is now looked upon as having been without intent.

But — how are we to understand that *teshuvah*, even if motivated by love of G-d, can transform evil into merit? The answer lies in the fact that it was man's wrong-doing which took him far from G-d. When he is overwhelmed by feelings of regret coupled with love for G-d, it then becomes evident that his very acts of wrong-doing served to bring him back to his G-d, and they are now reckoned as merits. But while all this is undoubtedly so, one should not attempt to probe the depths of these teachings.

In the Light
of the Holy Days

Selections from the writings
of the Gerrer Rebbe
Rabbi Yehudah Leib Alter זצ״ל

Moshe Told the Festivals of G-d
to the Children of Israel (Vayikra 23:44)

WHY does the Torah find it necessary to stress the fact that *Moshe Rabbeinu* taught the Jews concerning the festivals? The explanation may be that the Jews at Mount Sinai attained the highest degree of spiritual illumination and holiness, but then forfeited it when they sinned at the Golden Calf. On the festivals, however, they are able to return to their earlier eminent position — and this was made clear to them by *Moshe Rabbeinu* who had had no part in the sin of the Golden Calf and had remained on the lofty heights from which the people had descended.

⋙ Evocations of Holiness

On every festival the Almighty awakens anew a spirit of holiness among the Jews; hence the Torah speaks of the Festivals of G-d as *"mikraei kodesh* — evocations of holiness," for on them a call for holiness goes out to man. *Moshe Rabbeinu* ordained, in turn, that on these festivals the Jews should study all matters concerning the holy days — so that, in response to G-d's call, they should do *their* share to awaken in themselves the special spirit of the festival. *"Draw me, and we will run after You" (Shir HaShirim* 1:4) — when a moment of closeness to Heaven offers itself, we must in turn bestir ourselves with ever greater vigor and resolve to grasp it.

◆§ In Memory of the Going Out from Egypt

The three festivals, which are meant to give us such a profound understanding and illumination, reflect the role of our three Patriarchs, each of whom laid out a particular road to the recognition of G-d — that is why we speak of the "G-d of our Fathers." However, all the festivals are *zeicher leyetzias Mitzrayim*, "in memory of the going out from Egypt" because it was only then — with the revelation of G-d's presence in Egypt and at the Sea of Reeds — that the message of the Patriarchs found an echo in the souls of the Jews. In later times the full recognition of G-d's rule on the various festivals came with the Jews coming up to the *Bais HaMikdash* "whence they drew *Ruach Hakodesh.*" On the other hand, one who treated the festivals with disdain was declared by our Sages to be like an idol-worshiper — for he turned his back on the revelation of G-d that every festival brings.

◆§ The Body Sleeps; the Heart is Awake

Even in exile, we may seek strength from the festivals, for their inner essence is with us at this time, too, even though we cannot go up to the *Bais HaMikdash* and bring the required sacrifices. As the *Midrash* explains the verse, *"I am asleep, but my heart is awake" (Shir HaShirim* 5:2), "I am asleep," unable to bring sacrifices in the *Bais HaMikdash*, "but my heart is awake" in the synagogues and study halls. The building of the sanctuary and the bringing of the sacrifices in the desert was a matter of *Na'aseh*, doing, and we forfeited this ability through our sins — the *yeitzer hara* (evil impulse) very readily attached itself to the outward and visible aspects of life. But the *Nishma*, the inner attachment, remains with us forever, and it is even possible that nowadays, in exile, we can attain a greater closeness to the holy days because what is unobtrusive and hidden is of particular value.

◆§ Lasting Goodness

It is the special spiritual light, revealed to us only on the holy days, that causes us to call them *Yomim Tovim*, "good days" (when we ask in our prayers that "Thou shouldst satisfy us with

Thy goodness", we mean that we should be able to carry some of the light of the "good days" into the rest of the year). In fact, the *tefillos* speak of "festivals *for* happiness, holy days and seasons *for* rejoicing" rather than "festivals *of* happiness, holy days and seasons *of* rejoicing," because these occasions are meant to generate happiness and rejoicing for the days that follow.

◄§ Fear of Sin Leads to Acquisition of Wisdom

As pointed out, all festivals are in memory of the Exodus from Egypt which provided the foundation for them. The sequence of events at the birth of our people can be understood in the light of the *Mishnah's* statement that a person's fear of sin must precede his acquisition of wisdom. This statement explains why we put *tefillin* on the arm, opposite the heart — showing restraint of our actions and of the emotions of our heart — before we put them on our head; and it also explains why the Exodus from Egypt, replacing enslavement to Pharaoh with the acceptance of G-d's rule, had to precede the receiving of the Torah's divine wisdom. The same point is made by our Sages in stressing that the first passage of *Shema* precedes the second one because the acceptance of the yoke of Heaven, expressed in the first passage, must come before acceptance of the *Mitzvos* expressed in the second passage. Therefore, too, Pesach is considered the first of the festivals, followed in turn by Shavuos and finally by Succos which represents the total absorption in a Torah existence.

◄§ Redemption — Drawing Near

We may say that in the first quoted verse from *Shir HaShirim*, "Draw me" refers to Pesach, for the Jews were taken out from Egypt with a strong hand, even though they were not yet fully ready; "and we will run after You" refers to the crossing of the Sea of Reeds, when the Jews rushed into the sea, disregarding the dangers. The verse continues: "The king brought me into his chambers," this refers to Shevuos, when we entered the halls of Torah; "let us rejoice and be joyful" refers, finally, to Succos. Pesach, the redemption from Egypt, marked the beginning of the elevation of the Jewish people to its ultimate height.

◄§ Reawakening by Retelling

"Whoever tells more about the Exodus from Egypt becomes better thereby" — because through the retelling, the forces of redemption are reawakened in the community of Israel and in the soul of every Jew. We say in the *Haggadah* that if we had not been redeemed from Egypt we would have been forever enslaved; it follows, on the other hand, that the blessing of redemption is also lasting, forever and without limitation. The Almighty did "great things, beyond all understanding, and miracles, beyond all counting," as we say in our prayers; the impact of these deeds is indeed unlimited — spreading throughout the generations if only we go on and on dwelling on them (hence, also, the obligation to remember them "all the days of your life").

At the time of the Exodus, G-d told us, "I took you out from the land of Egypt to be your G-d," — the redemption from Egypt led to the acceptance of the Torah and of the Kingdom of Heaven; therefore, the more we bring again to life the redemption from Egypt, through our retelling, the more we also attain of Torah, and once again, bring upon ourselves the Kingdom of Heaven. Thus, through the telling of the Haggadah year after year, we are given ever anew the opportunity to free ourselves from the hands of the yeitzer hara and to lift ourselves up to the point where, in the end, we will bring the coming of Moshiach when the Almighty will once again reveal Himself as our G-d.

Rabbi Yehudah Leib Orlean ז״ל

Senses for Spirituality

*The teshuvah period is the time
to reflect on the development
of man's sensitivity to the Divine.
The martyred author notes
some of the obstacles
and ways to overcome them*

OVER HEAVEN AND EARTH, over stars and seas, over mountains and valleys, over birds and fish the Divine glow shines. From the tiniest plant to the tallest cedar tree, from the weakest insect to the most heroic beast, all of existence bespeaks the Glory of its Creator. From them all His endless loving-kindness and limitless power shines forth. From each of them His might and energy stream forth. Everywhere His Creation and supervision are apparent. Everything utters a song of praise to the eternal King, to the Creator and Ruler of the world.

It is true that *Hashem* concealed His endlessness, His light and greatness, together with the creation of the world. It is true that He limited our vision and narrowed our intellectual grasp. He does however send us His rays through the weave of the heavens, through the furrowed earth, through His formed creatures. Even in the dark and coarse world, He made it possible for us to sense the Divine Breath which is blown through all of creation. For this, one only needs a free heart, an open eye and a healthy ear.

Lift your eyes on high and see Who created these (Yeshayah 40:26). A mere look into the heavens; one glance upon the world, and the strength and majesty of the Creator will be revealed for you!

Why then does Mankind not stand in awe of His might? Why do we not hide in the clefts of rocks in fear of His greatness? Why are men so immodest and unrestrained? Why do they not experience a sense of gratitude for the hidden Benefactor? Do then people lack souls and hearts, eyes and ears? Do they lack the capacity to see and hear, to feel and grasp the creation and sovereignty of the Creator?

No! We were not born incapacitated. We *do* enter the world with all our senses. But the senses need further development. It is from our nourishment that they must grow to maturity. With the nourishment with which we feed the newborn child we first open his eyes; we first enable him to see. The sight organ is there; but its function is initially exceedingly weak. To be effective it first needs to be greatly strengthened.

⫷§ The Development of Senses

With the growth of the child, however, the usual nourishment no longer suffices. The physical food requires the help of psychic and spiritual cooperation. The development of the senses becomes dependent not only on food, but also upon the mood and the state of consciousness which accompanies the food. The constantly crying infant will remain anemic and sickly despite the best nourishment. The knowledge of food possession in itself partially stills hunger. The glance of the eye upon the food in itself partially satisfies the stomach. Nourishment, mood and knowledge are then all important factors in the normal functioning of Man's physical organs.

Upon closer observation of the effect of food one first sees how strong an impact the psyche and the intellect have in the matter; how close a contact there is between body and spirit. The undernourished person will not seek elsewhere the cause for his dulled vision or hardness of hearing. He will surely consider it a natural result of his inadequate self nourishment.

Why then do we complain over the blindness of our deeper sense of vision? Why do we wonder over the weakening of the delicate sensitivity of the heart? Why do we not see the real reason for the dulling of the more refined hearing?

The senses which reach physical completeness at the normal age of maturity do not come then to the end of their development. In this stage their function continues. However, their habitual nourishment is entirely insufficient to enable them — via contact with the physical world — to sense creation's hidden power; to see the Creator's widespread benevolence; to hear His stern command for life.

To the contrary. Through onesided nourishment the senses became constantly duller. And less capable of their most important function. If one moves a single limb only, the second must stiffen. If one exerts only one kind of energy, another energy potential loses its strength.

Thus it is also with the development of the senses. To strengthen material vision the body needs to be nourished with bread, mood, and knowledge. The pleasure derived, or better stated, the close interaction between the three factors makes the nourishment richer and more effective.

In order, however, to develop an eye for spiritual vision, each food needs an admixture of a refined mood and higher knowledge. The pleasure derived, the interaction between the physical, psychic and intellectual, needs to be finer and more delicate. Every nourishment which is accompanied by the most elementary acknowledgment to the eternal Benefactor; which is imbibed together with a *brachah* for the Creator and Ruler of the world, is capable of developing the eye for spiritual vision in addition to material vision. In such an instance we have before us another consciousness and another experience. Not the knowledge of food-possession alone operates here, but rather does the knowledge concerning the heavenly Bread-Giver come to expression here. It is not the joy of the bodily pleasure which makes the bread satisfying; but rather the good fortune to be capable of gratitude to the Eternal One. We have before us a deeper experience and a higher knowledge.

Further, to develop the eye for spiritual vision, every activity — not only the intake of food — needs to be accompanied by this type of mood and mental perception. Such development of spiritual perception results from the practical *mitzvos*, which encompass all of life; which exalt every single activity to G-d. Thereby are body and soul nourished together; thereby both the physical and spiritual powers of sight are cultivated together.

◢§ Leading Man to His Creator

The more frequently the human organism is nourished with such food, the stronger are its actions tied to the deeper experience and higher knowledge, the more capable does it become to sense the nearness of the Creator to Creation. Not Man's food-nourishment alone nor the poet's mood alone, nor the philosopher's probing of nature's reality alone, bring one close to G-d; but rather *the most precise interaction between deed, emotional sensation and thought leads Man to his Creator.*

Mere actions, without intending to fulfill the will of G-d; without the feelings of gratitude to the Benefactor; without submission before the King of the Universe, make the heart fat, besmudge the eyes, and dull the ears for sensing the greatness of the Creator which is manifest in creation: *The heart of this people is fattened, his ears are made heavy and his eyes are besmirched."* (*Yeshayah* 6:10)

A. Scheinman

Why Confess?

*The role of "Vidui"
in the
teshuvah experience*

TWO OF THE basic elements of *teshuvah* (repentance) are well
known — remorse for past misconduct and a commitment not
to repeat the offensive behavior in the future. But not everyone is
aware of the importance of the third element — *vidui*, confession
of the sin. Yet, the *Rambam* in both *Sefer HaMitzvos* and *Yad
HaChazakah* puts major emphasis on *vidui*. In *Mitzvah 76* he
says: "We are told to confess our sins which we have sinned to
the Almighty, and to enumerate them as part of our repentance."

In *Yad HaChazakah* (*Hilchos Teshuvah* 1:7) he writes:
"Should a person intentionally or unwittingly transgress any
command in the Torah, be it a positive or negative command,
when he repents from his actions, he is required to confess, as is
written (in the Torah) ... " Again one's impression is that *vidui* is
not ancillary to the *teshuvah* experience but rather one of its major aspects. What, then, is the deeper significance of *vidui*?

◄§ Cain's Punishment

When Kayin (Cain) killed his brother Hevel (Abel), he was
punished twice. He was made into a nomad ("You shall be a
wanderer on earth"), never finding rest for his tortured soul; and
he, too, met a violent end (see *Rashi* on *Bereishis* 4:15). Why did
he suffer two punishments for one sin?

It is axiomatic that G-d's retributions are meted out *midah k'neged midah* — that is, measure for measure. Any suffering a person endures is meant to somehow correspond to the sin. While people accept this concept in regard to punishments of supernatural scope, such as the Deluge of Noach's time, and the drowning of the Egyptians and The Splitting of the Sea at the Exodus, it is equally true in regard to even the smallest measure of suffering one experiences, no matter how much it may seem to be part of a natural chain of events. This is obvious in the countless explanations of the *Chazal* as to how specific transgressions cause different diseases and demises. (The reader is also referred to Rabbi Dessler's essay on Purim in *Michtav M'Eliyahu* wherein he explains the obligation of recognizing the Divine process in "natural" occurrences.)

Rabbi Yechezkel Levenstein, the late *mashgiach* of the Ponovezher Yeshiva in Bnai Brak, pointed out that until the most recent generations, people died mainly from plagues or bacterial diseases. The people themselves had been perfectly healthy, except for the effects of attacks from outside forces, such as microbes and disease-bearing bacteria; only then did they succumb. Today, we find that it is not the "outside forces" that claim human lives; rather, man falls victim to the products of his own body. His system becomes filled with excesses — be they cholesterol clogging the arteries, or malignant cells crowding out the vital organs, interfering with their life-sustaining processes — which finally kill him.

"How closely this reflects the shift in spiritual patterns," reflected Reb Yechezkel. "For many generations people were apparently "healthy" in the spiritual sense, yet a sudden assault by a Shabsai Tzvi or a wave of *Haskalah* (in its early stages) came and claimed hundreds of thousands of souls, paralleling the physical situation. Today the problems arise from within us. While we are able to cope with destructive forces from the outside, spiritual debilitation takes place as a result of the little 'extras' that accumulate over the years, quietly starving the 'heart' of its necessary 'oxygen', slowly disabling the vital 'organs.' Until one day, the seemingly healthy organism crumbles away."

◆§ Galus as Atonement

When a person commits an *aveirah*, he inflicts a spiritual wound on himself. The injury can be healed — by a process called *kaparah*, forgiveness. People generally are unwilling to accept the thought that they suffer defects, so instead of embarking on the time-consuming and laborious path of *teshuvah* and *kaparah*, they apply a touch of cosmetics to disguise the wound, and continue on with life as usual. But covering up a wound permits the infection to fester further, requiring even more cosmetics, plus a generous dousing of perfume to mask the foul odor emanating from the wound. Thus they continue to fool themselves and others, not realizing that if they continue this way, they will succumb from the progressive rotting away of their flesh.

The Prophet describes the phenomenon: "They pull the sin with cords of naught, like wagon ropes, the transgressions" (*Yeshayah* 5:18). *Malbim* explains this to mean that every time a person commits an *aveirah*, he becomes saddled with two "wagon loads". One is the transgression itself, pulled by "heavy ropes" — for the individual most likely had a strong desire to commit the illicit act. The second wagon is loaded with rationalizations and excuses; these are held by flimsy strings — "cords of naught." He does not really believe its freight of explanation at all, but just pulls it along because it covers for his shortcomings.

Thus the otherwise religious Jew may indulge in various practices that are destructive of time or violate Torah standards of conduct. He shrugs off the ill effects claiming, "After all, I *do* have to make a living," or "Isn't it important to be worldly?" Or other such rationalizations. Once a person has saddled himself with the "*mitzvah*" of pursuit of comforts at all costs, or worldliness, he discovers many *hiddurim* (enhancements) in the *mitzvah* which affect countless aspects of his life — from minor matters to major goals and values — doing further violence to the Torah quality of his life ... The cords of rationalization introduce many new aspects to his initial foray into violation of Torah.

With this insight into the effects of a transgression and its ramifications, one can better understand the punishments that were imposed on Kayin for having murdered his brother. His atonement for the act itself was that he, too, was killed. Kayin, however, had gone one step further. He rationalized his crime, saying, "Am I my brother's keeper?" He attempted to remove the horrid crimson stain of fratricide by painting it over, instead of eradicating it. For this he suffered the punishment of "being a wanderer," demonstrating that man's soul can have no respite from its inner turmoil until it comes to grips with its condition. "You will have no rest," says G-d, "until you face your transgression squarely." Thus, the wanderings of his body were reflective of his soul's inner tortures.

This may well be the intention of the statement by Rabbi Yehuda brei d'Reb Chiya: "Exile atones for half of a sin" (*Sanhedrin* 34a), the "half" referring to these rationalizations and self-deceptions that require *galus* for forgiveness.

Vidui performs this function: *it forces a person into the realization that he has indeed sinned*. It is the necessary first step in *teshuvah*, for as long as a person deludes himself, thinking that he has not sinned, he will never come to *teshuvah*.

Another *Midrash* relates that as soon as Kayin confessed: "My sin is too great to bear" — the curse of wandering was removed from his head, demonstrating the interfacing between *galus* and *vidui*. Kayin either was to come to grips with his *aveirah* through *vidui*, or he was forever doomed to wander the length and breadth of the earth, a fugitive from the haunting truth (*Vayikra Rabbah* X).

◀§ Rationalization of Sin

Recognizing the pivotal role of awareness of the sin in *teshuvah*, we gain a new understanding into two of the punishments that the Torah has meted out. The first is the imposition of exile for some cases of unintentional murder. In a sense, this punishment is the same as Kayin's. For just as Kayin attempted to exonerate himself with his excuse of "Am I my brother's keeper?", so too, does a person guilty of manslaughter tend to deceive himself that the lack of premeditation frees him of guilt. Yet the awesome truth remains: Man is responsible for the results of his every action that he can control, and it is his duty to insure that no harm emanate from what he does. Not having been faithful to his duty, he remains a shedder of blood, premeditated or otherwise. It is the haunting inner cry of, "The voice of your brother's blood calls out to me," that forces him into exile where he must come to grips with his sins (*Midrash Tanchuma HaYashan*).

The *korban asham* is another "punishment" with a similar purpose. Every category of *korban* has a specific thrust to it, designed to bring about a specific atonement for a specific type of falling. For instance, the various types of *korban chattos* atone for transgressions of the harshest type — acts that earn the perpetrator *koreis* (cutting short of one's lifespan) when committed intentionally; the *korban olah* atones for having missed an opportunity to perform a positive command; the *korban shlomim* brings the owner closer to G-d. By contrast, the *korban asham* seems to be required for a random collection of sins, with no commonality of weakness to them. They are: perjury under oath in monetary matters; use of Temple funds for personal benefit; doubt regarding unintentionally committing an *aveirah* that when definitely done would require a *chattos;* and having had relations with a half-freed slave woman who was betrothed to someone else. (There are two more *ashomos* — *nazir* and *metzorah*, but they are of a different category.)

Perhaps one can find one common factor among them: *The relative ease with which people absolve themselves of guilt in all these "aveiros."* Be it perjury, or embezzlement, or doubt whether one has sinned altogether, or even "semi-adultery" — a person manages to avoid thinking too much about it. And that is why he is required to bring a *guilt-offering* — to realize the full extent of his guilt! The entire procedure, from setting aside the lamb for the purpose of the *korban* through the completed ritual, dramatically reminds the *asham*-bringer that he is indeed guilty.

The *Talmud* relates that Rabba bar bar-Chana once came upon the spot where Korach had been swallowed up in the earth. Great quantities of smoke were billowing forth. Upon listening closely, he heard voices in the abyss proclaiming: "Moshe is true, his Torah is true and we are liars!" A strange combination of punishments, but very fitting indeed.

Which other sinner had ever constructed such a grand edifice of spurious arguments, rationalizing his actions, as did Korach?

1. He argued with seemingly infallible logic that just as a completely blue *tallis (kulo techeiles)* should not (to his reasoning) require the requisite blue *tzitzis*-thread, so too "A nation that has been proclaimed holy by G-d has no need for a special holy caste."

2. He marshalled proofs from the Torah itself that under the laws of inheritance he was entitled to the positions of power that he had coveted.

3. His designs were reinforced by the knowledge imparted to him by *Ruach HaKodesh* (Divine inspiration) that his progeny would be leaders of *Klal Yisrael*. All these "proofs" were, of course, projections of his inner desire for power.

His punishment reflects the duality of his crime. The fires of *Gehinnom* can purge him of the sins of strife and contention; but to rid his soul of those layers and layers of rationalization, he must proclaim, "Moshe is true, his Torah is true ...," until the day *Moshiach* comes, when knowledge will cover the earth and there will be no more possibility for falsehood.

◆§ Cleanse Yourselves

This, then, is our preparation for the day of judgment. In those precious few moments when we stand silently in the presence of our Maker, we bend our stiff necks and we utter: "*Ashamnu* — We are guilty!" (Guilty? — of what? I *daven* three time a day — never miss! ... My *kavanah* — well lacking, more often than not ... My record for honesty is unimpeachable — but off the record ... *Ashamnu*, indeed!) "*Bagadnu* — we rebelled." (Rebelled against G-d! what an extreme, unforgivable breach of fidelity! That surely does not apply to a Sabbath observer like me. I adhere to the very letter of the law, comes *Shabbos*. My hands are absolutely tied — except for picking up a recent newspaper or best seller lying around the house; and an occasional lapse into stock-market banter, but *rebel* against G-d's sovereignty. ... On the other hand: *Bagadnu* ...)

Slowly and painfully a few strips of the self-righteous veneer peel away, and each layer removed brings the confessor one measure closer to G-d ...

Every year during the *avodah* in the Yom Kippur service, we close our eyes for the moment and travel back centuries ... to that awesome place called the *Bais HaMikdash*. We see the *Kohen Gadol* at the pinnacle of his glorious sanctity standing before us, donned in his eight vestments.

In a voice that echoed through the Land of Israel ("His voice was heard in Jericho") he would proclaim: " ... כי ביום הזה יכפר עליכם לטהר אתכם מכל חטאתיכם לפני ד' "Today you will be forgiven all your sins. ... " But he would add one point, and demand: "תטהרו ... Cleanse yourselves!"

Yomim Noraim

Adapted by
Rabbi Nisson Wolpin

The Anatomy
of Teshuvah

Rabbi Eliyahu Dessler זצ"ל
analyzes the compelling mitzvah
of these Days of Awe

HOPEFULLY, we strive to do what is right. Fortunately, there
are times when we succeed ...

Wishfully, we attempt to match rightness of action with
purity of motive. Unfortunately, we do not succeed very often.

We *daven*, but our prayer is motivated by habit. We give
vast sums to charity, but we do so in anticipation of flattering
recognition (or to get our arms untwisted). We honor our festivals
most lavishly, but in a measure proportionate to our wardrobes'
needs and our digestive systems' capacities; the holiness of the
festival is too often lost on us. Even our Torah study is frequently
an exercise in mental gymnastics and serves as yet another format
for gaining recognition. Our inner motivations seldom match our
exterior activities.

The older generation has been accused of "phoniness" by its
children. This inconsistency between thought and action seems to
bear out the validity of the accusation, and to make mockery of
our style of adherence to Torah. Yet our rabbis accepted this
situation, and enjoined us to "ever should a man engage in the
study of Torah and the performance of *mitzvos,* even if not for its
own sake, for from *shelo lishmah* — selfish motives — one
graduates to *lishmah* — purity of motive."

The exterior act, though hollow of a heartfelt drive to serve one's Creator, works inwardly. The *Rambam* reassures us that "deep inside every Jew resides the yearning to be counted among his people, to perform *mitzvos* ... only his momentary desires prevent him from doing so." This deep-seated yearning lies waiting for an awakening.

Furthermore, the *Sefer haChinuch* points out, "Man's actions forever mold the inner man, for one's heart hearkens to the actions of his hands." Repeated performance of *mitzvos*, as lacking in genuine existential experience as it may be, eventually finds union with the broad inner yearning to do right, and individual actions some day find that ultimate justification of being *lishmah* — pure in motive.

This enjoiner of "ever should a man ... " applies to a great number of performance areas in Torah and *mitzvos*, but to one field it cannot apply — to the prime *mitzvah* of the season of awe: the doing of *teshuvah* — repentance for wrong-doing. To be sure, *teshuvah* is complex, and involves outward expressions of confession and remorse as well as an inner experience; but there is no parallel performance on two levels: the exterior action separate from the inner conviction. While one can give charity without dedicating one's generosity to G-d's command and still fulfill that command, *teshuvah*, by contrast, *must* begin from within. Then, generating outward, it should find expression as prescribed. *Teshuvah* as such refers to the inner experience, not to its outward expressions.

◄§ The Source of Teshuvah: The Initial Recognition

What is the starting point of *teshuvah*? *Teshuvah* must entail a remorse for wrongs perpetrated; this should be coupled with a resolution to never again repeat the offense; and these both must stem from a stark realization that whatever premise, whatever outlook on life, whatever lack of thought caused one to err, was totally false, and must be uprooted from one's personality. The deeper this initial realization, the more profound is the regret that results, and that much stronger is the resolve toward the future. And the greater the totality of the *teshuvah*. Should this initial recognition be shallow, however, consisting of only a momentary pang of regret, inspired by a mere shift in temperment — should it be a mere emotional reaction to a favorable circumstance, but be totally lacking in soul-searching recognition of the folly of sin — then *teshuvah* has not taken place.

Emotional conditions do have their place in the *teshuvah* situation for they serve as a preparation for *teshuvah*. These conditions soften the shell of indifference that encases the heart — the *timtum halev* — but this alone is not *teshuvah*.

◂§ Teshuvah: Its Mark

So, these are the wellsprings of *teshuvah:* a moment of truth when worthiness and folly exchange positions, and a new perspective on life emerges ... But what are the results of *teshuvah?* What are its ramifications, and how far do they reach? On one hand, we know that time alone does not obliterate the stain of a sin. The thievery or slander, the blasphemy or malice of years gone by may be lost to the conscious awareness of the individual, but transgressions of the past share a vivid presence with today's occurrences in the world of the soul. The spiritual world retains the full freshness of events of years past in the same way that the memory of the conscious mind does not release the imprint of any tragic dimensions of experience, for sin is the trauma of the soul. And further, there is no fading by time in the world of the spirit where all events — past, present and future — share concurrence.

Teshuvah, indeed, does open a new page, but is the stain of the sin ever truly erased? Or does it live on, awaiting the inevitable purging of retribution?

Our *Chazal* present us with a wide range of comments regarding *teshuvah*. Rabbi Meier said: "Great is *teshuvah!* For the sake of one man who repents, he and the entire world are forgiven!" So great is the impact of a total *teshuvah* that the individual and all in his sphere of influence are now offered a new status, unencumbered by errors of the past ... Full erasure, to be sure.

By contrast, we are told that should a man betroth a woman on the condition that he is a *tzaddik* — a fully righteous man — the betrothal is valid, even if he is a *rasha gamur*—thoroughly wicked — because we may assume that he decided to do *teshuvah*. As a *rasha gamur* he undoubtedly included some offenses "between man and man" in his repertoire of sins. These can never be erased without the forgiveness of the people who were wronged, nor without the return of any material loss suffered through his misdeeds. Yet his status as a *tzaddik* is justified without remaking his past on the sole basis of his decision to do *teshuvah*, and this decision is enough to fulfill the conditions of his betrothal.

A momentary resolution is apparently potent enough to endow a person with a new perspective on life, and in accordance with the meaning of the word *teshuvah*, it implies an "about face" in his outlook, and a new direction in his life. Obviously, the imprint of years of misdeeds cannot be summarily erased with this decision alone ... This is surely minimal *teshuvah* and can only have consequences for the future, but not retroactively.

What, then, makes one type of *teshuvah* more effective than another?

◄§ The Resolution

Basic to *teshuvah*, of course, is the firm resolution to abandon one's past. It must be so strong that the *Yode'ah Ta'alumos* — He who fathoms the hidden depths of our hearts — can testify that the *ba'al teshuvah* will not return to his earlier patterns of behavior. This resolution must be present in fullest potency in every occasion of *teshuvah*. For as no man in his right mind would repeatedly lend money to a borrower who always promises payment, but never pays, so would the *Yode'ah Taalumos* refrain from continually granting clemency to a deliverer of promises, who never delivers what he promises. Thus, the new status is granted only to the man who is firm and reliable in his resolve to turn the new leaf. This resolve is the constant factor in every *teshuvah*.

Remorse is the factor that can appear in a great range of degrees, and effects a different kind of *teshuvah* in accordance with its nature and its intensity. Remorse can form the foundation for resolution, and it can bolster it. Remorse can be the factor that converts deliberate transgressions of the past into unintended errors. Remorse can be the touchstone that transforms a vice into a virtue, and produces a *mitzvah* where once an *aveirah* left its mark. In its searing self-criticism, in the wake of its propelling guidance, remorse changes a man, his future and his history.

◄§ Remorse and the Awe-struck

In the context of our society, which is so involved in unshackling itself from any bonds of guilt-feelings, it seems bizarre to glorify regret for wrong-doings. Yet, in *teshuvah*, remorse must be more than a passing state of mind. It must be an unending process, elevating the individual as it spirals in its intensity.

Remorse, of course, does occur in varying shades of intensity. Visualize for a moment the disappointment experienced at carelessly missing a green light. The miscalculation that so resulted can cost the driver a minute of time. Too bad, but soon forgotten. By comparison, think of missing a commuter train as a result of buying a newspaper, with the ensuing inconvenience of a fifteen minute wait, the telephone calls and explanations that must then take place. Then consider the errors of poor judgment that result in a bad investment, an unwise real estate purchase, or a disastrous personal involvement. How much greater is the self-blame and recrimination that accompanies errors of the greater magnitude, even if they are more understandable in their commission. Still the man who commits them feels foolish — even ridiculous — as he views the scope of his lost opportunity and the pettiness of the momentary distraction that stood in his way. The regret is proportionate to the magnitude of the error committed.

In the mundane world of day-to-day affairs, the lesson to be learned is gleaned from the mishap, and it is hoped will be applied to future situations. But eventually the past is forgotten because, after all, we cannot relive our past, so why apply psychic energy where it is only wasted?

In spiritual affairs, we can relive our past, so we do focus attention on our errors. From the perspective of remorse, a lost opportunity to act with fidelity to Torah looms large, and an act of selfishness which was contrary to Torah is of only fleeting value — if any. Pitting one against the other enlarges the loss of an opportunity of faithfulness to Torah to an act of defiance against G-d's will, and reduces the little act of self-service to an ugly one of self-defeat. With this new assessment of the past error, the pangs of regret grow into pains of remorse; and in a spiraling pattern, this heightened sensitivity to what had transpired makes the act of defiance against one's Creator seem rebellious and the motive that brought it into being seem even uglier. Deeper regret brings forth a newer perspective, which in turn gives basis to the ba'al teshuvah's further regret.

This process involves more than an intellectual change. A metamorphosis in personality also takes place. A new being emerges from the teshuvah process, and by the standards of his newly gained insights into the awesome majesty of Torah, his transgressions of yesterday that resulted from his previous outlook can only be considered errors of judgment, not acts of defiance. The healing powers of the regret factor in *teshuvah* have been set into motion, changing past as well as future.

⋖§ Remorse and the Love-struck

There is another type of remorse that works an even greater transformation upon the spiritual make-up of the *ba'al teshuvah*. In this instance the keystone is a sense of marvel at the forgiving powers of the Almighty: What folly it was to sin against so magnanimous a Creator! Then, through growing awareness of His loving-kindness, the *ba'al teshuvah* comes to view his own transgressions as acts of petty foolishness. No gain can be reaped from defying such a Master. Such defiance is not only pointless but truly intolerable, and yet our Master not only tolerates, He forgives! This enlarges the sensation of gratitude, which gives rise to one of even greater significance — love. And to wrong one's beloved is a wrong one regrets most profoundly ... . As the sense of having wronged grows, the sense of regret deepens, the gratitude and awesome respect for the Forgiver assume even vaster proportions; and so does the love one experiences for Him.

Transgressions become the basis for merits, for the more one accepts the gravity of his sins, the more he is overwhelmed with love for his all-forgiving Master. On the lofty pedestal where the *ba'al teshuvah* stands, the most righteous can never gain a foothold. The *tzaddik* who has never sinned can never know the love that grows from a first-hand encounter with the Almighty's forgiving powers.

⋖§ ⋖§ ⋖§

Volumes have been written advising one on how to perform the *mitzvah* of *teshuvah*. Many more volumes could be written on the personal agonies and triumphs of the *ba'al teshuvah* — his attempts, his faltering, his victories.

Teshuvah in its fullest glory is more than an awesome challenge. It is the imperative of the season of Elul-Tishrei. And it is the enviable opportunity of one's lifetime.

Rabbi Mendel Weinbach

The Little Fellows

A shofar's blast ... a still small voice ... the trembling of angels ...
THE SCALES MUST BE BALANCED!
A whispered response:
Alter the dimwit ... Dr. Isaacs ... Old Man Haimson ... the little fellows who somehow make a big difference.

ALTER ... you'd hardly imagine one calling him a *mashgiach*. He never rose above the rank of *shammos* to the *shammos* in the Williamsburg *shtiebel* where so many spent their evenings studying the Torah. None of a *mashgiach's* intellectual gifts had been bestowed upon this dimwitted caretaker — but no *mashgiach* guarded his charges with more passionate dedication. Alter would not return to his rented room until the last *masmid* had departed and the *shtiebel* could be locked for the night. None of a *mashgiach's* moral and psychological strategies were at Alter's disposal — but he managed unparalleled efficiency in making his point. A *chavrusa* surrendering to the urge to steal a few minutes of gab over the *Gemara* about the hard day at the office suddenly found the lights above them extinguished ... and Alter mumbling something about the *shtiebel* not providing precious electricity for *schmoozers*.

DR. ISAACS ... guess you'd call him a general practitioner who was a specialist in *chessed*. The Rosh Yeshiva wouldn't think of using another doctor. He knew how to appreciate such a patient, too, and showed it by taking him into his office ahead of everyone else in the waiting room. One day he didn't. That was the time Mottel, the *kabtzon* who always came around to the Yeshiva for handouts, arrived in the waiting-room first. Dr.

Isaacs invited him in and asked the Rosh Yeshiva to wait his turn. When his turn finally came, one of the *talmidim* who had accompanied the Rosh Yeshiva asked the doctor why he always passed over his wealthiest clients to favor his master but had reverted to following the rules for lowly Mottel's sake. "If I let Mottel wait," explained Dr. Isaacs, "he is certain to think that the reason I am doing so is because I treat him free of charge, and don't feel that he deserves to come ahead of paying patients. No need to add pain to poverty, is there?"

OLD MAN HAIMSON ... hardly seemed like the hero type. But heroes and knaves are not limited to battlefields and stages. They can flourish in even the unlikely setting of a half-empty *shul* on Simchas Torah eve. This is a *shul* in a dying section and a petty man has gained leadership of the few *minyanim* of Jews who had not yet moved away. *Atta Horaissa* had been sold, and its buyer gave the president the privilege of handing out the honors of saying the verses that launch an evening of Torah celebration. The crowd was small enough for each man to recite a *pasuk*, but petty men will seek to settle scores at even such a moment of spiritual elevation. Berel, the unfortunate family-less friendless *schlimazel*, rubbed the president the wrong way. So he was bypassed. The slight was not lost upon the small congregation, but who had time for demanding justice when the long-awaited *hakafos* were about to begin? Well, Old Man Haimson, who appeared to be the last man in the world to even be aware of what's going on, suddenly came up with a request that *Atta Horaissa* be sold a second time. What *shul* president would pass up an opportunity to effortlessly gain a few more dollars for the congregation's depleted treasury? Old Man Haimson won the bidding with a respectable sum and asked the president to honor Berel with the very first *possuk*.

... *Little fellows tipping the scale up there?*

Remember what Yoseif told his father, Rabbi Yehoshua ben Levi, about his vision of heaven as he momentarily stood on the threshold of death:

> "*I saw a topsy-turvy world. Those who are on top in this world are lowly up there, while those on the bottom here are on top up there.*"

Little fellows?

It's all a question of perspective.

Rabbi Chaim Dov Keller

Is the Jew
Losing His Identity?

*The role of
the individual
on the
Day of Judgment*

*This day the world was conceived; this day will He bring to
judgment all the creatures of all the worlds whether as
children or as subjects ... (Rosh HaShanah Machzor).*

O N THE DAY of Rosh HaShanah the world attained
fulfillment with the creation of Man. Therefore on this day
each year, Man must stand before the Divine bar of judgment to
give an accounting of himself. It must be determined if he is that
Man for whom all of Creation was designed and who was its
ultimate goal; or if he has fallen short of Divine expectations.
And this judgment before which man must stand is two-fold. He
stands judged as a *son* of the Almighty and as His *subject.*

The implication of his role as a subject involves man in the
human establishment. He must serve as one cog in the great
machine of Mankind which must subject itself in totality to the
King of kings, the Master of all the worlds. Just as a human king
maintains his dominions by virtue of the myriads of his faithful
servants, no single one of whom is indispensable to the royal
scheme of things, so must each man find his proper place as a part
of a greater community of mankind whose purpose is the glory of
G-d.

Yet our Sages teach us that being a part (no matter how important) of an all-inclusive whole is not the sum of human experience and human responsibility. Man is something more than a soldier, more even than a general in the army of humanity which must be the army of the Lord. He is a *son* — and, in a sense, an *only son*. Each child in a family, no matter how large it is, is not looked to by a wise father for what he will add to the family power or for what measure he may enhance the family prestige, but is considered as an end in himself.

A king may lose a soldier, a company, or even a division. He may feel saddened at the loss, but the war has not been lost, the throne still stands. But if a father loses a child, there is little comfort in the fact that the family still remains; a *world* has been destroyed. This world that was the lost child has vanished, never to return. What comfort that there are other worlds?

◄§ Man Was Created as an Individual

> *Therefore was a single man created, to teach you that whoever destroys one Jewish soul, the Torah considers as having destroyed a whole world, and whoever sustains one Jewish soul the Torah considers as having sustained a whole world ... Therefore each person should say, "For me was the world created!"* (Sanhedrin 37a).

The whole human race descended from one man. Therefore it follows that not only does each man have the potential of reproducing a whole world, but in a truer sense each man *is* a whole world. I, with *my* psychological makeup, *my* intellectual capacity, *my* spiritual powers, am unique. There is no other quite like me. My world does not exist for another as his does not exist for me. Up until a certain point I am one of many. But from that point on I am one — alone with my G-d.

It is in this inner, truer role as an inimitable individual that each of us must stand before the bar of Divine justice on Rosh Hashanah—and give his accounting as a child of the Almighty.

The secret of the truly great man lies in his ability to maintain that delicate balance between his responsibility toward his fellow man, as a member and leader of the community, and the responsibility to develop his own potential as an individual.

The contemporary scene boasts great organizations; great men, however, are all too scarce. In Jewish life the trend is toward *organized* philanthropy, *organized* social work, *organized* synagogue activities and *organized* education. The "leaders" are the executives — the organization men who, by dint of technical know-how and clever jockeying, can push themselves to the top of the heap, much as does any executive in any other American industry. Progress is measured in statistics — numbers of dollars raised, numbers of students enrolled, numbers of members, size of buildings.

We Jews have an old rule handed down to us by our Sages אין בכלל אלא מה שבפרט which rendered freely states: *There is no more in the group than there is in the individual.*

One thousand zeros will still equal zero — although they take up more space on paper.

Unless we Jews here in America wish to surrender our historic role as a unique people and assume the non-identity of a nameless mass of statistics, directed by a benevolent bureaucracy, we must concentrate on being men, not only members.

The Torah envisions Man as one who *personally* gives to the poor and feels their anguish and their need; who helps his fellow *personally* and shares his burdens; who prays *personally* and feels the closeness of G-d; who learns *personally* and experiences the exhilaration which only Torah study can give to the earthbound soul.

It is the crying need of the hour to provide our Jewish youth with a frame of reference in which they can develop as useful members of the Jewish community and as loyal citizens of society at large without losing their identities as individuals with G-d given talents and propensities and the G-d-commmanded duty to develop them.

When religion is removed from the heart and relegated to the synagogue; when *tzeddakah* becomes an organized industry; when the study of Torah is delegated to a small group; and when the rabbi ignores the individual spiritual needs of his congregants to devote himself to "social justice" — then we are in danger and it is time for rediscovering our individual selves.

As we prepare ourselves to stand before the Heavenly bar of judgment on Rosh Hashanah, let each of us reflect on himself as an individual so that he may clearly determine where he stands in his own relationship with G-d. Only out of this individual introspection can come the restoration of the glory of *Klal Yisrael*.

Alexander Zusha Friedman

The Mitzvah
of Tochachah

*Admonition as a tool
for safeguarding
and improving society*

◂§ An Unpopular Mitzvah

ONE TORAH COMMANDMENT which contemporary Man finds it most difficult to tolerate, is that of *tochachah* (admonition); namely, the obligation placed upon every Jew who sees his fellow commit a wrong, to draw the latter's attention to the character of his deed, and to admonish him over it. The modern nose "wrinkles up" in the matter, as if to say: "It isn't proper to interfere in the affairs of others, to impose upon others one's personal views on how they ought to conduct themselves and how they ought to live." The modern, "unrestrained" world has adopted as its motto the conventional dictum: "Must I be the *Ribono Shel Olam's* Cossack?" Or, "Why must I probe the soul of another?" These and similar utterances convey the attitude of our "refined" and "ethically sensitive" world — a world which, as is known, scrupulously adheres to the dictates of good taste and propriety.

It is therefore fitting for us to seek the clearest possible insight, for ourselves and our children, into the exalted foundations of human love and social well-being, on which the *mitzvah* of *tochachah* rests.

▸§ Admonition — The Result of True Brotherhood

What does the Torah command us?

"You shall not hate your brother in your heart — you shall surely admonish your fellow and you shall not bear sin over him" (Vayikra 19:17).

It is clear then that the *mitzvah* is specifically based on friendship and brotherhood. When you see your friend doing something improper, whether in his behavior towards his fellow man, or in acts which are between man and G-d — do not allow your anger, which is the result of his wrongdoing, to enter your heart. You are rather to point out his failing to him and to admonish him over it (the root of *tochachah* means to point out, to prove, as well as to admonish). For, only through your unwillingness to bear his wrongdoing in your heart, through your desire that he not repeat his sin a second time, do you attest to your love for him.

In truth, the daily events of life demonstrate that it is precisely nearness and friendship which lead to greater penalty for wrongs committed. The father punishes his child the more often, because it is his child -- who is nearer to him than any other person, and whom he loves more dearly than all others. It is for this reason that he wants his child to walk in the right path and not to do wrong. To a stranger, all this does not matter, for it is not his affair. And therefore, the Torah — which desires for every Jew to see his fellow as one who is closest to him; as one who is his brother (since they are both children of the same Father) — obligates Jews to behave towards one another like brothers; to *react* to each other's wrongdoings.

The modern view in the matter is characterized by a sense of cold estrangement. "Let every one do as he wishes. It is no concern of mine. Isn't he a stranger to me?" Certainly such an approach has nothing to do with friendship and brotherhood. For *those* feelings compel a sense of mutual responsibility and concern.

Only through this very distinction are we enabled to reconcile the seeming discrepancy in the teachings of our Sages, who in one instance point to baseless hate as the reason for the destruction of the *Bais HaMikdash*, but in another ascribe the Sanctuary's destruction to the lack of mutual admonition. For both were only aspects of the same cause, and they each led to the other. The prevalent hate, the widespread sense of mutual estrangement, brought it about that none should be concerned over the lot of another, and that none should draw the other's attention to his misdeeds. Had friendship and brotherhood prevailed, the necessary result would have been the presence of mutual admonition.

◄§ The Safeguard of a Society's Well Being

If we were to probe deeply into the essence of the *mitzvah* of *tochachah* we would see that it is intended to advance the pursuit of both individual and societal perfection. For a society can only achieve betterment if its members are prepared to bend an ear to criticism of its evils. Similarly, the individual can ascend the ladder of self-improvement only if he views words of admonition as a mark of friendship intended only for his good. The person who seeks perfection will always willingly draw his friend's attention to any of the latter's misdeeds because he wants his friend to do the same for him. However, one who prefers a life of licentiousness is unwilling to address criticism to his fellow, so that the latter might not restrain his libertinism.

Modern mankind — which so dislikes criticism — seems to have a secret agreement: "Let us not disturb one another! I will not trouble you, and you are not to trouble me." How wonderfully idyllic libertinism becomes. ...

The way of Torah, however, must be entirely different. For the Torah seeks to lead mankind to an utterly different kind of "agreement"; to one which would replace the mutual tolerance of libertinism by the mutual tolerance of admonition. To the contrary! "I will not permit you to do wrong so that you should similarly restrain me from wrong." For one always sees another's blemishes more clearly than his own. Mutual admonition, therefore, is a means of mutual assistance and protection.

The lack of patience that modern Man exhibits for admonition recalls to mind the well known anecdote:

A blind man and a sighted man ate *kreplach* together. Out of fear that his companion would eat more than his fair share, the blind man suggested that they each take one *krepl* at a time simultaneously. The other agreed. After a few minutes the blind man pounced on his erstwhile dinner partner and began pummeling him.

When asked for an explanation, he replied simply: "If I took two *kreplach* and you failed to protest, then you must have taken three *kreplach* at a time .... Otherwise, you would have shouted at me for taking two at a time ...."

The "blind" man of our day does not react on becoming aware of some minor misdeed of his friend so the latter might not react to a weightier wrong on his part. He is agreeable to his friend's eating two *kreplach*, so that the latter might permit him to eat three at a time.

Not for naught did our Sages ascribe the Sanctuary's destruction to the absence of mutual criticism. For a society founded on the silent consensus to maintain libertinistic tolerance must disintegrate, since it lacks the primary foundation of ethical existence.

◆§ Self Perfection

Admonition addressed to another necessarily leads to self-perfection, if only in the given area of concern. For he who addresses admonition does not want his criticism to be hurled back at himself. Indeed, our Sages teach us that before one says to his fellow: "Remove the splinter from between your teeth," he ought to make certain that the latter be unable to retort: "Remove the beam from between your eyes." And since no one wants to make of himself a target for such "compliments," he will therefore strive for self-perfection.

Thus another motive presents itself for our generation's abhorrence of the rod of admonition. Its members do not want to be thereby bound in their own behavior ... . They do not want to base their lives on purity and ethical norms, so as to be worthy of addressing admonition to others. They constantly fear, therefore, that another might say to them: "Remove the beam from between your eyes."

The Torah, however — which desires that Man constantly strive for self-improvement and personal perfection — demands that we should address admonition to each other — as a means for self-improvement. In the *mitzvah* of *tochachah* a double wording is used, "admonish shall admonish," implying an additional commandment:

"Make sure that you improve your own mode of life sufficiently for you to be worthy of admonishing others. Remove the beam from between your own eyes so that you might have the right to tell your friend that there is a splinter in his teeth."

◆§ Admonition Must Never Shame Another

And since the foundations of the *mitzvah* of *tochachah* are love for another and the desire for self-perfection, the performance of the *mitzvah* must always correspond to those foundations. The purpose of admonition must be solely the improvement of .. s target, never his embarrassment or degradation. The one admonished must always feel convinced that whoever admonishes him has no aim other than his good. Indeed, the matter is precisely formulated in the *halachah:*

> If one sees his fellow having committed a sin or having followed an evil path — it is a *mitzvah* to return him to the good, and to inform him that he had committed wrong through his evil deeds — as it is said: 'You shall surely admonish you friend.' Whoever admonishes his friend, whether in matters that are between themselves, or in matters that are between his friend and G-d, should do so in private. He should speak gently, with mild language, and should let his friend know that he speaks only for the latter's good, in order to lead him to the life of the World-to-Come ... Whoever admonishes his friend should not speak to him so harshly as to embarrass him, for it is said: " ... You shall not bear sin over him." Upon which the Sages commented: "One might think that he should admonish another even if the latter's face is altered — it is therefore taught: 'You shall not bear sin over him'. We learn from this that it is forbidden to shame an Israelite, and all the more (is it forbidden to do so) publicly." Even though one who shames another does not incur *malkos* (the penalty of stripes), all the same it is a great sin (to do so). Thus did the Sages say: "He who causes his friend's face to turn white (with shame) has no share in the world to come" (*Rambam, Hilchos Dayos,* 6:7-8).

Side by side, then, with the paramount obligation to utter admonition, far-reaching assurances are prescribed to make certain that one who is admonished shall not suffer or be shamed thereby. For otherwise, the purpose of the *mitzvah* would not be served. And if, on occasion, the *halachah* does permit the utilization of sharper means of *tochachah*, even to the extent of public embarrassment of another *(Rambam ibid.)*, it does so only where thrice-repeated, gently uttered, admonition — in matters that are between man and G-d — has been to no avail. For in such an instance, the matter affects the desecration of the Divine Name, and therefore has educational significance for the given surroundings.

◄§ The Extent of the Mitzvah

The significance attached by the Torah to the matter of *tochachah* is illustrated by the *halachah* which treats of the prescribed extent of the *mitzvah*:

> *And so, a person is constantly obligated to utter admonition till the sinner strikes him and says to him: "I will not listen." And whoever has the capacity to prevent (sin) and fails to do so is held liable for the sins of those whom he could have prevented from committing wrong (Rambam ibid.).*

The requirement that a person be prepared even to be struck by the sinner, and his being held responsible for the latter's wrongdoing, demonstrates the importance which the Torah ascribes to the matter of *tochachah*, namely, that it sees *tochachah* as the foundation of the ethical existence of a society and the means for its improvement.

From a Yom Kippur derashah
by Rabbi Zalman Sorotzkin זצ"ל

The Tablets
and the Golden Calf

The shattering
of the Luchos
reflected in the
Kol Nidre Service

*"We go to the Bais HaKnesses [on Yom Kippur eve] and it
is the custom that the chazan removes a Sefer Torah and
recites Kol Nidrei" (Rosh).*

THIS IS ONE of the few references we find to the custom of
removing a *Sefer Torah* from the Ark before *Kol Nidrei*.
Others are silent on the subject — perhaps because they could find
no basis for it. But, since the *minhag* is now so widely practiced, it
would be useful for us to discover its origins.

Yom Kippur was set by the Torah on the tenth of Tishrei,
since it was on that day that *Moshe Rabbeinu* came down from
Sinai with the second *luchos* (tablets) and informed his people
that the Almighty had forgiven them for the sin of the Golden
Calf. Each year, on that day, the *ais ratzon*, the time of grace, is
reawakened, and for that reason the tenth of Tishrei was fixed for
all generations as a day of forgiveness.

Viewed in this light, we can see the *minhag* as a recapitulation of Moshe's return to the people, bringing with him the Torah
and G-d's forgiveness.

• The *chazan* opens the Ark, symbolizing the opening of the Heavens.

• He removes a *Sefer Torah*, symbolizing the second *luchos*.

• *He goes down from the bimah* to the people, symbolic of Moshe's descent.

• *"Ohr zarua latzaddik* (Light is sown for the righteous)" is recited, symbolic of the rays of light which emanated from Moshe, and recalling Moshe's success in prevailing upon the Almighty to undo His oath, so that He might forgive the people.

• The congregation calls out: "Forgive this people's sin."

• The *chazan* replies: "And G-d said, 'I have forgiven, as you prayed I would,' " symbolic of Moshe's announcement to his people.

All this is followed by the *Shehecheyanu*, praising G-d for having brought us to the Day of Atonement, and for the high level in which the people find themselves in prayer and fasting — as compared to their normal level, symbolizing finally, the contrast between the status of the people when Moshe came down with the first *luchos* — dancing around the Golden Calf — and the contrite manner in which he found them when he brought down the second *luchos*.

◄§ Some Questions

There a number of questions which may be raised in regard to the breaking of the *luchos* by Moshe.

• Moshe was told by G-d to go down to his people because they had made a Golden Calf. Nevertheless, he took the *luchos* with him, most likely, to give them to Israel even though they had sinned. But what he saw changed his mind. He saw the Calf — of which he already knew — but he saw also that the people were dancing around the Calf. At that point he decided to break the *luchos*. But why was the dancing around the Calf more disturbing to Moshe than the making of the Calf itself?

• Why did the Almighty permit Moshe to take down the *luchos*, knowing that the people were not in condition to receive them — was it His purpose that Moshe should break them?

• By what right did Moshe break the *luchos*, which were the handiwork of G-d; and why did G-d Himself congratulate Moshe for breaking them?

• Moshe ruled that since an estranged Jew could not be given a portion of the *Korban Pesach*, one could certainly not give the entire Torah to those estranged from the true G-d. But, would it not have been a better course of action if Moshe judged only those actually guilty in the affair of the Calf, convinced the others to go back to their G-d, and *then* to have given them the *luchos* — why instead did he break them?

• The Torah eulogizes Moshe with these words: "And there arose no *navi* (prophet) in Israel like Moshe whom G-d knew face to face, by virtue of the signs and wonders ... and the strong hand, and the great fear which Moshe generated before the eyes of all of Israel." The Sages tell us that the "strong hand" is a reference to Moshe's breaking the *luchos*, and it is characterized in a similar vein to the wonders that Moshe performed before the Egyptians. What was the strength Moshe had manifested in breaking the *luchos*?

• Moshe called out, "Whoever is loyal to G-d, come to me!" in order to filter out the unfaithful; and "all the men of Levi rallied to him." But where did the majority of the people stand? With Moshe? — why did they fail to come to his aid to root out the evil which had spread in the camp? With the Calf-worshipers? — why did they permit the men of Levi to wipe them out? And how did Moshe manage to prevail with one tribe against eleven others?

• Moshe returned to G-d and said: "This people has committed an immense sin; they have made for themselves a god of gold." From this it would appear that before Moshe descended the Mount, he did not think that the sin of the Calf was quite so terrible — they had made a god of base metal. Only when he learned that it was formed of gold did he consider that a grave sin had been committed, but what difference does it make if people make their gods of base metal or of gold?

◂§ Some Answers

Certainly, there is no difference between one false god and another, but — there is a great difference between those who *believe* (even in false gods) and those who do *not* believe. The believers are looking for a god, and while they stumble, they may one day be brought to serve the true G-d. But the *kofrim* (the non-believers) are not looking for a god; they believe only in themselves and they serve — only themselves. The believers have at least a belief in a power greater than themselves; they believe that man has some responsibility, that he must exercise some restraint on his passions. The others have no standards of behavior other than those imposed upon them by society, and when these restraints are removed for a moment, they are capable of the most vicious acts.

When Moshe was told by G-d that his people had made a molten image, he felt that they had only been slightly diverted from the proper path to G-d; that they retained their belief in a higher power and their belief that man must restrain his instincts. He felt that the *luchos*, "written by the Finger of G-d" would quickly motivate them to return to the true G-d. But as he approached the camp and he saw the people dancing around the Calf in a spirit of abandon, as the Torah tells us: "And they arose and made sport," an expression which the Sages tell us connotes sexual immorality and a relaxation of moral restraint, he realized that the people had gone too far for the *luchos* to have any effect upon them. He expressed his re-evaluation of their sin with the words," ... they have made for themselves a god of gold" — gold being the currency with which man can indulge all of his inclinations to evil, and which opens the door to a complete rejection of the true G-d and the abandonment of all moral restraint.

A Compromise?

While he realized that the bulk of his people was not involved in the rebellion against G-d, he saw them standing by, watching what was happening, yet failing to protest the action of their brothers. He knew that it was simply a matter of days perhaps before they would all be sucked into rebelliousness. When they saw that Moshe had come down from Sinai with the *luchos*, written by G-d, they were cast into confusion and turmoil. Perhaps, they conjectured, they could evolve a middle path, a compromise between the *luchos* and the Golden Calf. The Golden Calf would assure them "happiness" in *Olam Hazeh*, (this world) and the *luchos* would gain them *Olam Haba* (the world-to-come). (In our own time there are Jews who are *rodfei shalom*, pursuers of peace, who would compromise, who would reconcile "the good life" with the demands of Torah; who go to the *Bais HaMidrash* each day, and send their children to schools where their *emunah* is destroyed.)

Moshe saw that such compromise could only lead to a complete break by the people away from the G-d who had taken them out of Egypt. He understood that he could do but one thing; that he had to act with a "strong hand." Before the eyes of his people he shattered the *luchos*. When the people saw what Moshe had done — Moshe, who had been their faithful leader and had pleaded their cause before the Heavenly Throne, had shattered the *luchos* because of the Golden Calf — they regained their moral sense. Indeed, they offered no resistance when Moshe, with the men of Levi, rooted out the evil that was among them, and destroyed the Calf. It was perhaps for this reason that the Almighty permitted Moshe to take the *luchos* with him, knowing that his drastic act would save the people from an irreparable break with their G-d. And it was this act of Moshe which brings the Torah to say of him: "And there arose no *navi* in Israel like Moshe because of 'the strong hand' which he demonstrated before the eyes of all of Israel."

◆§ In Our Generation

Although in our generation, which has climbed to such great cultural heights, there are none among Israel who practice idolatry in a base sense, there are all too many among us who dance around the "Golden Calf", whose lives consist of an endless and self-defeating pursuit of physical pleasures, and who know no restraint.

When the rabbi comes down to his people on Yom Kippur night, *Sefer Torah* in hand, he must be able to discern the nature of the sounds he hears. If he hears cries of, *"Forgive us"*; expressions of regret for past sins and a resolve to come closer to G-d, then he knows the people are ready for the Torah, and that the Almighty will forgive their sins.

But if he hears the sounds of pagan festivity, the echoes of singing and dancing around the "Golden Calf", then he must muster the strength of Moshe Rabbeinu, he must show "the mighty hand," to shatter the *luchos*, as it were, and to make his people realize how dangerously close they are to breaking the last threads that tie them to their G-d. And it is only with such forcefulness and daring that he can rescue his congregation from "the evil decree."

Rabbi Menachem Rokeach

King Over All The Earth!

*... so the Jew
proclaims his Creator forever,
but especially
during Tishrei*

THROUGHOUT THE YEAR, every Jew attempts to echo King David's yearning: "My soul pants for you, O G-d; my soul thirsts for ... the living G-d" *(Tehillim* 42:2,3). With *"Modeh Ani,"* the very first words a Jew utters upon awakening, he expresses gratitude for the restoration of his *neshamah* — the daily repetition of the initial: "And He blew into his nostrils a soul of life" *(Bereishis* 2:7).

During the *Yomim Noraim* — the Days of Awe — the focus is even stronger, beginning with the *Slichos* cry of "*haneshama lach* — the soul longs for you," shaking off the dross accumulated during a year of mundane activity.

The longing of the soul is deeper than words can express. On Rosh Hashanah this longing becomes overwhelming, impossible to contain. It is then communicated through the *shofar,* with the wordless sobbing of the *teruah.* This instrument, unassisted by the organs of speech, possesses expansive capacities of expression ... Upon completing one hundred fifty chapters of praise to G-d, King David concludes his Psalms on the note: "Praise Him with the sounds of the *teruah;* every soul praise the L-rd!" — leaving what had been left unexpressed and unuttered to the *shofar,* the vehicle of the soul. The cries resounding from this instrument, in turn, penetrate the soul which is attuned to receive the *shofar's* message. "The sounds of the *shofar* hast thou heard, my soul" (*Yirmiyah* 4:19).

The task of the Jew, however, is not fulfilled by exalting expressions of the soul, leaving its partner, the body, to its earthly instincts. The struggle between body and soul is a continuous one and the spiritual forces are charged with the responsibility of emerging in full control, as Isaiah said: "He gives a *neshamah* to the people who are on 'top' of the earth" (42:5) — expressing the expectation that the *neshamah* reigns supreme.

◄§ The Goal: Harmony

Rather than suppress the physical aspects of the Jew, the Torah sanctifies them, leading to the creation of a balanced personality. "I have created a *yeitzer hara* (evil inclination), and I have created the Torah as its antidote" (*Kiddushin* 30b). When the *malachim* attempted to prevent Moses from receiving the Torah, he challenged them with the argument: "Do you have a *yeitzer hara* among you?" Since they did not, the Torah was obviously not designed for them.

The two morning *brachos*, "*Asher Yotzar*" referring to man's bodily functions and "*Elokai Neshamah*" referring to the soul, are to be pronounced in sequence, according to the *Tur*, indicating that harmony should prevail between the two. The first *brachah* clearly states that man is prepared to stand before G-d because of the faithful function of his organs. The Midrash (*Tanchuma, Shemini* 8) points out that the words "*chalulim chalulim*" in that benediction have the same numerical value (248) as the number of positive commands in the Torah, further demonstrating the spirituality of man's physical nature.

This is in stark contrast to the world at large, which either pursues a hedonistic existence of soul-denial or unrealistic religious goals of body-denial.

◄§ The Torah's Fulcrum

One can find an allusion to the delicate balance of the physical and spiritual at the core of the Torah, if one would count the Torah's passages, words, and letters to determine the respective mid-points of our Written Law. Among our rabbis are those known as *sofrim*, for having made this count, and each of the midpoints they determined testifies to the physical-spiritual symbiosis.

The letter ו, *Vav* in the word גָּחוֹן, *gachon (Vayikra* 11:42) divides the Torah in two when the letters are counted. In that portion, the Torah forbids the eating of snakes and other creatures that transport themselves on their bellies ... The words דָּרֹשׁ דָּרַשׁ, *darosh darash (Vayikra* 10:16) mark the middle of the Torah when counting words. In this context Moses instructs the *kohanim* not to fail to eat the *Rosh Chodesh* offering ... The place indexed as the middle of the Torah in sentences *(Vayikra* 8, end of *pasuk* 7) relates how "Moshe clothed the *ephod* on his brother Aaron, the High Priest." (See *Torah Temimah Vayikra* 13:33.)

In the first instance, the Torah deals with the laws of *kashrus* as one aspect of avoiding detrimental involvement in the material. Indeed, the dietary laws elevate the dining table to that of a "table before G-d" *(Yechezkel* 41:22). The Jewish table — kosher in atmosphere as well as in ingredients — is then likened to an altar. One of the signs of *kashrus*, the split hoof, suggests the objective of raising the consumer above ground level, similar to the hoof itself, which raises the animal from the ground. A creature that moves on its belly is the antithesis of an animal bearing signs of *kashrus*.... In the count of the letters of the Torah, the *vav* of *gachon* is in the exact center of the Torah. By adhering to the dietary laws the Jew reaches the core of the Torah.

At the other end of the spectrum is the consumption of food from an offering in the *Bais HaMikdash*. This is a physical act that obviously brings the Jew to peaks of nearness to G-d, for he eats *kodesh* — literally from G-d's table. This is the middle of the Torah when counting words.

The passage recording Moses' garbing Aaron in the *ephod*, which constitutes "half the Torah" in passages, reinforces the above principle. The *ephod* is one of the holy garments. It covered the lower half of the *Kohen Gadol's* body (see *Rashi, Shemos* 28:6), illustrating that all elements of the physical being are to be immersed in holiness; symbolizing a perfect harmony between the body and the spirit.

The Jewish dining table and the very organs of the body are thus elevated from mere gluttony or frivolity to one of service of G-d. With this transformation, the Jew can exclaim with David, "... And Thy Torah is in my stomach" *(Tehillim* 40:99). With a table of this calibre, the Jew reaches "*chatzi haTorah*" the very center of Torah.

Not only does the body submit to the soul, it joins it in praise of G-d. This offers an insight in Rav Chisda's opinion that prayer is not permitted when there is filth on one's hand *(Berachos* 25a). It is forbidden, he says, for it is written "All my bones shall say: O L-rd who is like Thee!" *(Tehillim* 35:10). A spiritual funcion such as prayer prevades the entire body — to the very tips of one's fingers. The *Shabbos* prayer of *"Nishmas"* expresses this same total involvement. It begins with the extolments of the soul, later joined by the organs of the body, quoting King David: "All my bones shall say ... . "

◆§ The Tishrei Festival Sequence

The sequence of the Tishrei festivals expresses this same theme. The entire season is one of total dedication through *avodah* — service to G-d. By our responses to the urgings of the soul — explains Rabbi Shlomo Zevin *(Le'Torah Ul'mo'adim)* — articulated with *"haneshamah lach,"* we bring about *"vehaguf shelach* — the body is also Thine." The concept is expressed in the very benediction of sanctification of the day for each of the *Yomim Noraim:* "King over all the earth." By sanctifying one's earthly elements — the parts of one's body — and declaring them as part of the Heavenly Kingdom, G-d is crowned as King of all earth as well.

Specifically: on Rosh Hashanah, the pivotal *mitzvah* of the day is the *shofar,* which articulates in the language of the soul; no organs of the body share in this expression. Yom Kippur follows, with its emphasis on fasting, purging the body of stain. Once both the *neshamah* and the body are purified, Succos follows with a harmonious sanctification of both together. On Succos, the bodily needs, such as eating and sleeping, are strongly accentuated. One enters the *succah* with one's entire body. During this same holiday, the *arba'ah minim* (four species) stress the place of the bodily organs in the service of G-d (as will follow). The culminating emphasis is reached on Hoshana Rabbah, when honor is given to the *aravah* — symbol of the lip — the organ used in prayer and study; for speech is the result of the combined effort of body and soul: "And He blew into his nostrils a *neshamah* of life and man became a living soul" *(Bereishis* 2:17) — *"a speaking spirit"* (Onkelos).

The *arba'ah minim* are especially rich in their representation of the spiritual potential of man's physical nature. According to the Midrash, the *esrog* symbolizes the heart; the *lulav* symbolizes the spine; the *hadas* resembles the shape of the eye; the *aravah,* the shape of the lips. In concert, they symbolize the envelopment of the body with sanctity, and its subordination to the service of G-d. A closer analysis of the spiritual role of each of these particular organs offers a fascinating insight into the choice of these organs for representation in the *mitzvah* of *arba'ah minim*.

◂§ "With All Your Heart"

Of all the organs of the body, the heart comes nearest to the realm of the soul. — We are commanded to love G-d "with all your heart and with all your soul." — We pray "And purify our heart to serve You in truth." The heart is the seat of emotion. — The Midrash *(Koheles* 1) attributes love and hate, joy and sadness, and a host of additional emotional experiences to the heart. — The *Yalkut* (beginning of *Mishlei)* relates that King Solomon searched for the seat of wisdom and, according to Rabbi Yehoshua, found it to be the heart. No wonder, then, that the *esrog*, symbolizing the heart, has such stringent requirements of beauty, purity, and absence from flaw.

◂§ Eyes and Mouth

The eye and the lip seem more physical; yet they, too, are invested with spiritual qualities. The *Maharal* points this out as a basic contention between the Jewish people and the nations of the world. The Talmud relates that when Bar Kamtza sought to slander the Jews before the Roman Emperor *(Gittin* 56a), he proved their disloyalty by bringing an animal offering on his behalf for sacrifice in the *Bais HaMikdash* to see if it would be accepted. He secretly cut the animal's eyelid — others say the lips — something Jews consider a blemish, but non-Jews do not. The Jews could not explain their refusal of the offering because the issue of what constitutes a blemish was a major point of dispute. The Jews regard the eyes — and the lips — as inner organs endowed with spiritual qualities, a reflection of their own way of life — as distinct from the view of other nations. A defect in these organs is therefore considered crucial to a Jew — but not to a non-Jew. That the king's criterion was not respected was in itself regarded as rebellion. To a Jew, vision and speech are more than physical.

◂§ The Eye: Vehicle of Blessing and Curse

Our sages have always understood the eye as possessing spiritual qualities. Eye-contact with another person is a type of intimacy that allows for the conveying of blessings — or curses: —

Rabbi Eliezer regards having a "good eye" as most important in one's approach to life *(Avos* 2:13). —"The good eye shall be blessed" *(Mishlei* 22:9) — "shall be able to bless" — referring to Moses *(Yalkut):* "And Moses 'saw' ... and Moses blessed them" *(Shemos* 39:43). When Menashe and Ephraim were brought before Jacob for his blessing, his eyes "were dimmed because of age, he could not see, and he brought them to him and he kissed them" *(Bereishis* 48:10). The *Sforno* explains that Jacob's eyes were dimmed, and that since vision is so crucial in bestowing a blessing, he instead kissed them as a means for his soul to cleave to theirs, to invoke his blessing.

By the same token, Balaam always sought vantage points for gazing at the Jews as a prerequisite for cursing them. When his donkey rebuked him for his ambition to curse the Jews, she alluded to them as the pilgrimage festivals *(shalosh regalim).* The performance of this *mitzvah* involves an eye to eye audience with the Almighty, which is meant as an opportunity for receiving G-d's blessings. The *Netziv* explains the festival command "You shall not see My face empty handed" as a reciprocal commitment between G-d and His people. (The passage in *Shir HaShirim* 2:9: "He looks through the window, peering through the lattice," is a reference to the *Shechinah* peering through the fingers of the *Kohanim* while they confer their blessings on the Jews — *Midrash Bamidbar.* Also: "Look forth ... and bless ... " in *Devarim* 26:15.) Thus the donkey took Balaam to task for challenging the Almighty's design of blessing the Jews, with his own plan to curse them.

This capacity of the eye is represented by the *hadas.*

◂§ The Worm, The Jew, and The Power of the Lips

The Torah is replete with examples of what constitutes true Jewish power. It is perhaps best expressed in the appellation "thou worm Jacob" *(Yeshayah* 41:14). "Just as a worm's sole power is in its mouth, so is Israel's power in its mouth, by virtue of prayer and Torah study" *(Midrash Tanchuma Shemos* 14:10). Jacob referred to the Land of Israel as "the land which I conquered with my sword and bow" *(Bereishis* 48:22), that is, "with my prayer and supplication" *(Onkelos* and *Tanchuma).* This leads to a compelling lesson regarding Moses' entering the Holy Land.

Moses was prohibited from entering the Land of Israel because he did not sanctify G-d's name by speaking to the stone in order to draw water from it (*Bamidbar* 20:12). The speaking expected of Moses, according to *Netziv*, was not a matter of addressing the stone, but addressing G-d with words of Torah and prayer before the stone. This would have left an indelible impression upon Israel as to the power of words of Torah and prayer. Moses was thus punished by being deprived of entering the Land of Israel, because its conquest essentially depends upon this word of Torah and prayer.

During Succos, on Hoshana Rabbah, the *aravah* is the object of special attention. After completing the Days of Awe and Succos, filled with so much fervent prayer — says the *Sefas Emes* — this symbol of the lips is given a special place of honor: the other three species are laid aside and the *aravah* is held in the hand alone while reciting the special *tefillos* of the day.

◄§ The Core of Service: The Spine

Although the spine is essentially the most physical of the four organs represented by the *arba'ah minim*, it too is close to the realm of the spirit. During divine worship, its outward movements and flexures stem from an inner restlessness. The Talmud relates that Rabbi Akiva would start his daily prayers in one corner and conclude them in another corner, because of his many movements and flections (*Berachos* 31a). The eighteen benedictions in the *Shemoneh Esrei*, we are told, correspond to eighteen vertebral links in the spinal column (*Berachos* 28b). Commentators quote a Midrash that one shakes his body during prayer, as inspiration to *kavanah* — for the purpose of arousing concentrated thought, or as a result of *kavanah* — the unconscious result of deep enthusiastic prayer (*Rama* in *Orach Chayim*, 48). The same applies to bodily movements during Torah study, based on the passage: "And the people saw and moved about trembling" (*Shemos* 20:18, see *Baal HaTurim*).

Says Reb Moni: "All my bones shall say, O G-d, who is like You!" (*Tehillim* 35:10). In this passage David referred to the *lulav*, which is likened to the spine (*Midrash Vayikra* 30:14). When the devout Jew shakes the *lulav* he thinks of involving his entire body, to the last bone, in the service of G-d. Small wonder, then, that the *lulav* was chosen for special mention in the benediction for the *Mitzvah* of *arba'ah minim*, since this species — representing the least spiritual of the four organs — illustrates the extent to which we devote ourselves to G-d.

✒️ All the Earth

The concept of Succos culminating man's acceptance of the Heavenly dominion over his most earthly aspects extends beyond the individual Jew and the entire Jewish nation. In a broader sense, the all-inclusiveness of Succos extends to the nations of the world, for 70 sacrifices representing them were brought in the *Bais HaMikdash* during the Succos week.

The *avodah* (service) of these days, then, is to proclaim the Creator as King over all the Earth, with special emphasis on the material and the earthly. Indeed, this is the ultimate and deepest aspiration: to form an *agudah achas* — one organism possessing complete harmony, reflecting man in control of all his faculties — united in fulfillment of G-d's will.

⮮§ **Succos** / *The Season of Joy*

*from destruction through reappraisal to
celebration ... from the depths
of despair ... in the Clouds of Glory ...
the Kabbalas HaTorah of Yom Kippur to
the Simchah of Succos ... from
understanding to ecstasy ... the plunge
into sacred revelry*

Rabbi Ralph Pelcovitz

Security, Illusion
and Reality

*Reflections on Succos
and its relationship
to the entire holiday season*

SUCCOS IS THE SEASON of *simchah*, the holiday of
authentic joy and true happiness. Succos is a time of harvest,
of ingathering. Were we to follow the normal procedure of
society, the universally accepted practices of mankind, we would
mark this festival with symbols of stability and thanksgiving. We
would invoke G-d's blessings upon our homes and contemplate
our good fortune as we observe our storehouses filled to
overflowing. Instead we leave our homes and dwell in booths and
devote the *Shabbos* of *Chol HaMoed* to the study of *Koheles*, a
book that examines man and his life, finding them to be filled
with vanity! In the midst of *simchah* we ask ourselves: "And of
joy what doth it accomplish?" (*Koheles* 2:2). In the midst of affluence and the security of prosperity, we take up residence in a
flimsy hut with a fragile roof!

Another anomaly. In *Bircas HaMazon*, the grace after meals,
we add a brief petition — "May the All-merciful raise up for us
the fallen Tabernacle (*succah*) of David." We ask for the restoration of the Davidic Kingdom, the Messianic Age. Why only during this *Yom Tov*? Because the prophet Amos refers to the fallen
Kingdom or Kingship as a *succah*? But that is begging the question. The royal *house* would be a far more appropriate phrase

then a royal *booth* or tabernacle. "And He made them houses," the blessing granted by the Almighty to the midwives in Egypt, is interpreted by *Chazal* to mean houses of priesthood and royalty. Why then does the prophet refer to the most illustrious and historic royal house of David as a mere *succah*?

◆§ Beginning With Despair

Succos is the third holiday in the month of Tishrei. Rosh Hashanah, the Day of Judgment; Yom Kippur, the Day of Atonement; and Succos, the Season of Rejoicing — this is the sequence, with each following the other in rapid succession. The Midrash quotes the Psalmist: "You make me know the path of life, in Your presence is fullness of joy," (*Tehillim* 16) and comments that the "path of life" is taught to us during the Days of Awe, while the "fullness of joy" is revealed to us through the experience of Succos, thereby indicating not only a sequence but a cause and effect relationship between the Days of Awe and Succos. A leading teacher of Mussar, Rabbi Eliyahu Dessler, in his *Michtav MeEliyahu*, links the holidays of Tishrei to the preceding months of Tammuz, Av, and Elul, going even beyond the casual connection of the Midrash. He observes that during the three week period beginning with the Seventeenth of Tammuz and culminating on Tishah B'Av, we experience a sustained period of progressive *yiush* of deep despair. This is due not only to our recollection of *churban*, our reliving of the destruction of Jerusalem, but also because we develop a sense of despair about the world and the society in which we live. We are insecure for good cause as we realize that the seeds of destruction that deprived us of our homeland and brought us into exile are still very real and current. This *yiush*, however, is not one of unrelieved anguish, for it actually leads us to the period of comfort which follows closely on the heel of Tishah B'Av. Despair of the world means the shattering of illusions and a re-examination of our reliance upon man. The recognition of reality, of the futility of so much of man's pursuits and illusory success, brings one to a rejection of these illusions — *Olam Hazeh*, this transitory world, hence the beginning of renewal — or what Torah calls *teshuvah*.

The sequence and progression now becomes most logical. The period of *nechamah*, of comfort, follows that of *yiush* ... followed in turn by Elul, the month of repentance ... climaxed by Rosh Hashanah and Yom Kippur. Succos, the festival of *simchah*, is the ultimate destination of this journey — to serve G-d with joy

— and authentic happiness, distilled from the awe and reverence of the *Yomim Noraim*, built upon the foundation of *teshuvah*, provoked and initiated by the seeds of *nechamah*, which in turn were planted and nurtured by the *yiush* of Tammuz and Av!

This thesis opens avenues of thought which shed new light on the concept and character of Succos. Man instinctively seeks security. Strength is usually equated with security, might with majesty and power, and these in turn are considered to be the guarantors of peace. This indeed has ever been the basic philosophy and policy of governments as well as individuals, who also seek security through material means and rely upon physical measures for protection — be they walls, locks, or alarm systems. The State of Israel is no exception to this world-view, just as individual Jews (including Torah Jews, unfortunately) are no different from their gentile neighbors. It is interesting to note how certain writers and commentators lament the de-spiritualization of the Jewish experience, bemoaning the fact that Israel's traditional faith and trust in G-d has been replaced by trust in military hardware. Strange how the world expects us to be different and unique, unfortunately a classic case of favorable but frustrated expectations. Erik Erikson recently wrote that he detected among Israelis "a certain sadness over the necessity to re-enter historical actuality by means of military methods" — a most perceptive observation and hopefully correct, for we *should* be unique and different in our nationhood and statehood!

◆§ And Wisdom Brings Joy

Here then is the Jewish problem — how to *define* strength and power, not only how to *use* it. To know the answer is to know wisdom — *chochmah. The Sefarim* teach us that the letters of *chochmah* (חכמה) also spell *ma koach* (מה כח), "What is strength?" and *koach ma* (כח מה), "What is strength's purpose?" Indeed, what is true strength, and to what avail is strength of man and his arsenals? In *Koheles* (2:26), which we read for excellent and valid reasons on Succos, *Shlomo HaMelech* states: "For to the man that is good in His sight He gives wisdom and knowledge and joy, but to the sinner He gives the task to gather and accumulate." A sinner is one who has missed the mark. He labors under the delusion that amassing and accumulating, be it wealth or weapons, will grant him safety and security. The man favored by G-d, who places his faith and trust in the Almighty, is granted three precious gifts — wisdom, knowledge, and happiness. The man who knows where strength lies possesses true *chochmah* and is therefore blessed with *simchah*. The words of *Koheles* are an amazing reflection of that which we indicated above. The Jew who has experienced the shock of self recognition, beginning with his shattered illusions of the Three Weeks, who began to grope his way back to sanity in Elul and found himself in Tishrei through the Almighty, now logically and reasonably comes home in Succos sensing security under the protective *s'chach* of the *Shechinah*. The succah is not well built nor sturdy, physically; but neither is man and the world he lives in. The *succah* does not protect us too well from the elements, but man has always been vulnerable to nature and its furies. What the Jew does realize in the succah is that peace, both in body and mind, is to be found in the knowledge that strength is not in our exclusive province, nor is security in our power, but both are under the protective shield of the Guardian of Israel.

The selection from *Tehillim* that we read from Rosh Chodesh Elul to the end of Succos becomes perhaps somewhat clearer in the light of all that has been written. "In the day of trouble He will hide me in his *succah*" — a *succah* not a *house*. The phrase in *Ma'ariv* that we recite every *Shabbos* and *Yom Tov* evening should also become more meaningful! "Spread over us the *Succah of thy peace*" — *not a house* of peace, but a *succah*, for a house would be misleading. It could delude one into thinking that the walls and doors are our security. The *succah* creates no such illusions, for we know that we are frail and vulnerable, and yet secure and strong if we but merit the concern and protection of the Almighty.

❧ The Succah of David

The Maharal of Prague in his commentary on *Mesechta Sanhedrin* discusses why all other royal "houses" are so designated, while that of David and Moshiach is called a *succah*. "Every kingdom is called a house so as to indicate its power and strength, akin to that of a house which is stable and strong. The Kingdom of David, however, is referred to as a *succah*, for this kingdom is a divine one, unlike all others; therefore, it is called a *succah* to indicate that it is protected and sheltered from on high." The words of the Maharal illuminate the words of the prophet and answer the question we posed at the beginning of this essay. When the prophet speaks of "The fallen *succah* of David," he reveals to us, and hopefully to the leaders of the State of Israel as well, that our protection and our security is guaranteed only from on high, and that an umbrella of jets may well prove to be a mirage unless it is supplemented by *s'chach*. Peace in the Holy Land is illusory unless it be a *succas shalom* — a tabernacle of peace. All this we can appreciate when we ourselves dwell for seven days in *succos*, read *Koheles*, and experience the *simchah* that is the harvest fruit of Tishrei, but which was actually planted in the months of Av and Elul.

A chassidic Rebbe once said that the *mitzvah* of *succah* is the only one which we can enter into with our body. Every *mitzvah* needs heart in its observance, but unfortunately it is often lacking, for we do our *mitzvos* by rote. The *mitzvah* of *succah* is one where we are sure of the presence of the heart, at least physically. We all have the unfortunate tendency of listening to other people's opinions, following the values dictated by our environment, and being influenced by the world-view of a society that has wandered so very far away from the basic tenets of Torah. On Succos we can hopefully find that our heart is not wanting, as we sit in the *succah* with our total being. With our hearts to guide us, rather than our ears, we may yet be granted a vision of greatness, one that will alter our perspective for the entire year.

Y. Yechezkieli

Adapted by
Moshe Barkany

In the Valley
of Death

Days of judgment, days of joy
in a labor camp

> *The night was heavy with the awe of the Slichos, and*
> *the holy atmosphere of the departed Shabbos still lingered in*
> *the air. The group of Chassidim huddled around the table,*
> *each trying to find solace in his own thoughts, seeking*
> *warmth in a glass of steaming tea.*
>
> *Reb Noach broke the silence: "Tyere brieder! Do you*
> *know how lucky we are? A few moments ago we ripped*
> *open the heavens with our cries of 'Shema Koleinu — Listen*
> *to our voices ... have mercy on us!' There was a time — it*
> *seems like a lifetime ago, but it's only years — when our*
> *mouths were sealed in fear. We had so much to cry for, so*
> *much to beg mercy for in the Nazi labor camp but all we*
> *could manage was a whispered prayer torn from the inner-*
> *most crevices of our hearts."*

HASSAG. It was called a labor camp, but it was a slaughter house — no more, no less. We were the remnants of the Chenstochover Ghetto. Our families had been sent to their death. Only we few remained — like limbs torn from their bodies, writhing with pain, living a life without life.

Our task was the manufacture of bullets — millions of bullets for the mighty Nazi armies. And whenever they suffered a loss or a defeat, the guards exacted their revenge on us, the bullet makers. Day and night we stood over the machines as each piece of metal went through its seven stages of preparation until it was perfected into its death-dealing form ... One machine punched out disks from the sheets of metal. The next one drilled holes in them. Then they were flattened out. A fourth machine rounded them. The fifth polished the metal. At the sixth stop, the gunpowder was inserted, and at the final stage, the sharp penetrating tip was attached to the missile ... In this assembly line, I was a runner, a human conveyor belt.

We, the inmates, also rode a conveyor belt through seven stages of Hell, subjected to punches, reshapings — pieces cut from our very being, crushed by an intolerable load, the marrow drained from our bones. We were only part of a vast mechanism of destruction — destroying and being destroyed at the same time.

ᴥ§ Rosh Hashanah

Yet battered, starving, and decimated as we were, we suddenly found ourselves united in one yearning. Yes, believe me, *tyere brieder,* one yearning enflamed our imaginations, one concern gnawed at our minds: Where would we get a shofar for Rosh Hashanah? We proposed plans, only to discard them. Suggestions were offered, then rejected. Of dreams there was no shortage, but a shofar we lacked.

... A *shul?* We set aside a corner in one of the storage areas. At the noon break, when others lined up at the barrel of watery soup, we crowded the storage corner and quenched our thirst for a chance to empty our souls to G-d. A guard detail was set up to warn our congregation of the ever-present danger of discovery by the dreaded Kapos. There was never a shortage of danger.

Another commodity in generous supply was *chazanim* to lead the *tefillos.* Where else could one find so many men who were capable of melting our hearts with just a few muffled words? Qualified *chazanim* were plentiful ... We were only missing a shofar.

How we begged for a shofar! "Have mercy on us, fellow Jews!" we cried. "Search the rooms of our homes. Tunnel under the plundered synagogue! Try looking in the remains of the Rabbi's house!"

To whom were our "cries for mercy" directed? To those few

fortunate Jews in our camp who had W.W.J. status. As *wirtschaftlich wertfuller Juden* (skilled valuable Jews) they had special talents and consequently enjoyed certain privileges, such as assignment to unguarded factories or performing various personal services for high-ranking German officers. These privileged Jews were approached in secret and exhorted to devote every spare minute to search for a shofar among the ruins of the ghetto. Search they did, often endangering their lives, scrounging through the endless rubble. One group in particular outdid itself — the *Aufräumungs Kommand* — the clean-up squad that was supposed to unearth the vast deposits of buried gold which the Germans were passionately convinced lay secreted under the ground and in the walls of the now-desolate ghetto. While searching for gold, they searched for a shofar — equally in vain.

Then, late in the afternoon of the second day of Rosh Hashanah, when defeat was taken for granted, the miracle came to pass. One group of searchers returned to the camp, and before they even lined up for their meager ration of "soup," the exhilarating news that burst forth from their lips somehow reaching the entire camp: *We have a shofar!*

Somehow or other, perhaps out of an aching yearning we all shared, throngs of Jews began to congregate around the kitchen of the privileged W.W.J. All were seemingly oblivious of the danger of such a gathering. Everyone should have been aware that the hated Kapos were sure to investigate this unusual gathering. No matter. We all gathered, anyway. And suddenly, it materialized right before our eyes! The shofar! — "Who brought it?" "Who will blow it?" There was no time to answer. It was very late. There was barely enough time for the preparatory Psalms, and surely no opportunity to answer "Who?" and "How?"

We recongregated at the *"shul."* The words of the blessings quivered in the air, uttered in a trembling voice, shofar-like, broken and wavering, wailing and sobbing. "... Who kept us alive, preserved us, and brought us to this day ... to hear the voice of the shofar."

Then the piercing blast of the shofar rose to split open the very Heavens. The entire gathering was breathlessly quiet and even the Kapos, the lackeys of Satan, stood petrified at the awesome sound. The voice of the shofar held the entire camp captive.

(Here Reb Noach paused dramatically.)

And who do you think found the shofar? No one would

have believed that it was a coarse, rough-hewn man, an expert shoemaker, whom the Germans actually honored with the title *"Schuster Meister"* — Master Shoemaker. We knew very little about him personally, but we were all aware that he was unsurpassed in the craft of boot-making and that, as a result, his talents were much in demand by the high-ranking German officers.

Who would have dreamed that a simple man, whose life was so assured (comparatively), would risk his life for a shofar for Rosh Hashanah? Yet beneath the humblest of surfaces lie deep reserves of self-sacrifice, especially when involving *Kiddush Hashem*.

We all speculated on how the cobbler succeeded in smuggling out the shofar. Some members of the clean-up squad guessed that he used his special status with the S.S. command to be allowed to search for special materials for his craft among the stores of ghetto plunder, which were kept under particularly heavy guard. Once inside, it was quite simple to slip the shofar under his loose clothing. Simple, but risky, for would he have been apprehended by the guard, few questions would have been asked, and little heed given to the answers. The sentence would have been swift — a rifle bullet on the spot or perhaps a prolonged torture followed by a public hanging. But the cobbler was *not* caught.

"One *mitzvah* brings on the fulfillment of another." Fortified by the success of his first venture, aided by the merit of bringing the sacred *mitzvah* of shofar to so many, he was prepared to steal a *Sefer Torah* from the Germans' storage room and secrete it into Hassag, for our Simchas Torah celebration. How? No one knew yet for sure — but wait, I am jumping ahead.

◄§ Yom Kippur

We were still under the impact of the shofar, when suddenly it was Yom Kippur. We felt no need for special preparations for the Holy Day. Going without meals for a day posed no threat, for fasting was no stranger to the inmates of Hassag ... *Teshuvah?* There were quite a few among us who repented their sins daily, and prayed on behalf of all Jews. Some even made a habit of reciting *Vidui* — the formal confessional of Yom Kippur — every day. After all, staying alive was subject to the whims of any guard. One scholar half-seriously posed Korach's classical question: "Does a house full of *sefarim* require a *mezuzah?*", and then rephrased it in Hassag terms: "Does a year full of fasting and repentance need a Yom Kippur?"

Yet, when Yom Kippur arrived, there was no mistaking it. It was no ordinary day. The intensity was almost tangible in the air. It was undeniably Yom Kippur.

◄§ Succos

Succos, too — the festival which brings farmers and city apartment-house dwellers alike into temporary huts — somehow found its way to Hassag. We discovered an unused corner between two factory buildings. Lumber was piled up, as if in storage, for the succah walls, and somewhat above these walls, branches were unobtrusively stacked for the s'chach. We slid in and out of this temporary dwelling with our treasured crusts of bread, thinking of the protective succos in the wilderness, hoping for the succah of the livyasan.

◄§ Simchas Torah

So we had our Succos in those stolen moments, for the experience of eating in the succah, no matter how makeshift it was, was a genuine experience; but what lavud, which halachic bridging of circumstances, could take the place of a lechayim for the next holiday — Simchas Torah — Joy of the Law? We had no Torah scroll, and joy was absolutely foreign to Hassag. Worse yet, on that date, just one year earlier, we were witnesses to the liquidation of the Chenstochover Ghetto.

Simchas Torah — a day of unbridled joy? Hardly. Yet, Simchas Torah was brought to Hassag by this cobbler, who was so obscure to us that I cannot even recall his name. Here is how it happened:

One day of Chol HaMoed Succos, a whispered message flitted around the camp: the shoemaker had been delayed in his return from the ghetto. When he finally appeared, he did not head for the kitchen for his especially generous portion, but instead hurried into the depths of his hut. What had happened? The impossible — no, the incredible had come to pass for the second time in a month! He had successfully spirited a Sefer Torah out of the clutches of the dreaded Gestapo and smuggled it into our camp. How? He simply rolled it around and around his body, let his loose tunic hang over it, and then walked into the camp. Where he had gotten it from, he adamantly refused to reveal.

Once again, the clean-up squad advanced their pet theory —

that he had found it in the S.S. stores of Jewish properties, from where he had procured the shofar — but they were at least partially wrong. It had not been nearly as easy to get the *Sefer Torah*. The S.S. maintained an extremely heavy guard on their large holdings of Jewish plunder, and were particularly careful with *sefarim* and other religious objects, regardless of their intrinsic value. Our intrepid cobbler decided to bribe one of the guards, but since he was not exactly solvent then, he offered the corporal something that he could never have purchased for *any* sum — a pair of officer's boots! (The Germans seemed to have regarded hand-crafted boots as a singular luxury and thus reserved them for high-ranking officers. Hence, too, the cobbler's privileged status.)

We later found out that he had literally saved the *Sefer Torah* from desecration because a short while later the Gestapo burned all the *Sifrei Torah*, other *sefarim*, and various sacramental cloths and articles in one gigantic bonfire. This one *Sefer Torah* was the sole surviving remnant of the sacred articles of the ghetto. The cobbler selected it because of its small size, for that made it feasible for him to wrap it around his midriff without causing a tell-tale bulge, and later, in camp, its size permitted easy concealment.

We had instituted a regular *minyan* on *Shabbos* in one of the barracks, and it was there, on *Shabbos Chol Hamoed* Succos, that the heroic shoemaker turned to us and demanded: "Who wants to hide the *Sefer Torah?*"

A companion of mine and I decided to assume the responsibility. We immediately removed a board from the head of one of the wooden cots we slept on, and in the hollow under it concealed the scroll.

The news of the *Sefer's* arrival had naturally electrified the entire camp. On Simchas Torah night we held crowded *hakafos* in the cramped run-down shack we called home. These *hakafos* would have been outlandish in any other situation. The *Sefer Torah* remained safely ensconced in its hollow behind the board. We stealthily walked around the wooden cot that contained our sacred treasure. As we passed, we leaned over and kissed the board that lay directly above the *Sefer*.

We knew that if we had carried the *Sefer Torah* in our arms, as in conventional *hakafos*, we would have been running a great risk. Don't think it was our lives that we were protecting! Of course being caught carrying the Torah would have meant sure death, but what value did our lives have, anyway? It would have been worth it! But the scroll would have also been destroyed — G-d forbid! — and this was a loss we would not risk.

And so it went, far into the night. The silent "dancers" held themselves strenuously in check, as the joyous songs surged repeatedly to their lips.

One song echoed softly in our ears. Because of its obvious relevance, we could not contain it within us. And as we walked around the *Sefer*, we were almost deafened by the silent screaming of its chords that enveloped us all:

"Rejoice and be gay on Simchas Torah, because it (the Torah) is our strength and our light ... !"

Reb Noach looked up from his cold glass of tea and peered into the faces of his listeners:

"Do you think I made up this story? Have you ever been at the Gerrer Bais HaMidrash on Or HaChayim Street in B'nei Brak? Well, the Sefer Torah is there, in the Aron HaKodesh. I brought it there after the war. The destruction was terrible, but we survived."

Adapted from the writings of
Rabbi Eliyahu Eliezer Dessler זצ"ל
by Rabbi Nisson Wolpin

Succah Sparks

The temporary shelter of Succos
illuminates man's role
as a tenant on earth
with a lease of limited duration

"You extend Your hand to sinners and Your right hand is outstretched to receive repenters" (Yom Kippur, Ne'ilah Service).

◆§ G-d Teaches, Man Internalizes

A S AN INITIAL STEP in pulling man out of his torpor of alienation from the divine, G-d extends to him an intellectual awareness of His presence; His "hand" prompts the sinner to acknowledge G-d. Ideally, man will internalize the message and integrate it into his emotional make-up. This change is significant: Before, he had *understood* that G-d makes demands of him, but now he will *feel* the urgency of these demands. As the *Talmud* describes it, the apathy that encrusts his heart has been pierced — perhaps with only a 'pin-prick' of regret and concern; but his heart is no longer insulated from his intellectual musings.

In response to man's initial step, G-d widens the tiny aperture in his heart to the dimensions of "an opening of a great hall," and his commitment becomes intensified further. His "right hand" draws the penitent Jew close to Him.

Succah Sparks / 85

First, G-d's hand shakes the indifferent Jew out of his slumbering indifference ... ultimately embracing him fully, and his knowledge becomes part of his personality.

This experience is not limited to Yom Kippur. Daily life is full of such lessons, instructing man in regard to G-d's presence in the world, prompting him to conduct himself in accordance with G-d's will. In fact, we thank G-d in our daily prayers for "Your daily miracles that are with us, Your constant wonders and acts of kindness ... " *(Modim)*. At the outset, this instruction — the never-ending display of G-d's miracles in nature and the super-natural — is perceived on an intellectual level. But once man ponders the lesson and takes it to heart, his awareness becomes heightened and intensified, with G-d's intervening instruction — His "right hand."

⊷§ View From the Succah

Every evening (in the *Hashkiveinu* prayer), we implore G-d to "spread over us Your *succah* of peace ... and grant us good counsel." The soundest advice G-d can grant us is to prompt us to take note of our place on earth, our assigned role in life — and somehow, it seems, this is best conveyed to us from within the *succah*. How does the *succah* accomplish this?

On Succos man is instructed "Leave your permanent home and take shelter in your temporary dwelling." Living in a *succah* is an instruction in the transitory nature of all of life's mundane experiences — a negation of the material *(bitul hayesh)*. For when the Jew in the *succah* ponders life in this thrown-together hut, he realizes that nothing is of permanence in this world. The joys and comforts of the home are inaccessible. And even the modest creature comforts of the *succah* are only of short duration ... And such is life itself: Striving for material possessions, for fulfillment of passions, desires, and petty pleasures becomes revealed as a hollow pursuit. Designs to secure a place for oneself and for future generations are mere fantasy; after all, whatever gains are realized are of little duration and of no intrinsic value. Position? — power? — possessions? — they all are of no substance. If man is to strive for anything of worth, it must be for spiritual attainment, because only in the realm of the spirit do gains have any permanence. Only a spiritual existence can give a man authentic pleasure and lasting satisfaction ... This is the lesson of the *succah*.

~§ The Succah Test

The Talmud foretells that in the end of days, when it becomes obvious that only the Torah way of life is of value, many strangers will clamor for a place among the People of the Torah. "Had You but given us Torah and *mitzvos*," they will argue, "we too would have kept them. Why should we be deprived of a place amidst the Torah Nation?" G-d will offer them the *mitzvah* of *succah*, which they will readily accept. But then the sun will burn hot, and the pretenders will abandon the discomfort of the *succah*, hastily slamming the door behind them (*Avodah Zarah* 3a). Of all 613 *mitzvos*, why will the *mitzvah* of *succah* be selected to test their loyalty to G-d and His commandments?

In truth, the lessons implicit in the *succah* are central to a Torah life. On the surface, they appear to be within everyone's grasp. Who can pretend that fleeting sensual pleasures and makeshift material security endow a life with meaning or purpose? And since it is so, what does one lose by demonstrating this conviction by moving into a *succah*? But the actual test of commitment can be much more taxing than simply voicing agreement to it in principle, for it involves exposure to discomfort and, at times, even pain. The person who has truly negated the material aspects of existence can successfully withstand these challenges. But he who merely voices verbal acquiescence cannot; his move to the *succah* will culminate in a hasty escape, slamming the door behind him.

~§ The Succah and the Clouds of Glory

Indeed, the *succah* is laden with meaning:

☐ The *succah* commemorates the *ananei hakavod* — the Clouds of Glory that accompanied the Jewish people on their forty year trek through the Wilderness.

☐ The Clouds' constant presence was attributed to the merit of Aaron.

☐ The *succah* is also referred to as *succas shalom* — the dwelling of peace.

☐ Aaron was celebrated as a man of peace: he "loved peace and pursued it" (*Avos* 1:16).

Thus, the members of this constellation — *succah* — Clouds of Glory — Aaron — peace — seem to be involved in an enriching interdependence ... But there is more to this relationship:

The *Zohar* (Emor, 103) points out that the letters of "Aaron"

(אהרן) are identical with those of "appear" (נראה), as in the passage, "Eye to eye did You, O G-d, *appear* to us, Your cloud standing above them" *(Bamidbar* 14:14). This is meant to imply that the Clouds of Glory were a medium for conveying to Jewry the clarity of knowledge of G-d that they had enjoyed in the Wilderness. This, too, was in Aaron's merit, and his role as Man of Peace was instrumental in bringing this about ... Let us see how.

The essential ingredient in the pursuit of peace and its attainment is *bitul hayesh* — a negation of the material aspects of life. For, in the final analysis, what prompts rivalry and arguments, envy and wars, among people? Only the illusion that material possessions have value. That *my* car, *my* home, *my* artifacts, *my* prestige bring me joy ... That increased happiness lies in winning away from others their precious attainments, which seem to give them special status. Materialism in its more extreme forms, then, would find in the gains of others a nagging source of discontent; at times, someone else's very existence can bring despair to the self-centered materialist ... Thus do arguments and wars break out.

By contrast, he who puts his sights on spiritual growth, ignoring the material attractions of life, can only find delight in the similar growth of others. In the realms of the spirit, there is no need for exclusivity, no place for rivalry, no pressure implicit in the gains of another. On the contrary, one person's gains can serve to elevate his entire community, bringing joy and spiritual riches to all who share his environment. Peace — the attribute for which Aaron is praised — is an outgrowth of spirituality, and at its peak it results in "eye-to-eye" contact with G-d (so to speak).

The *succah* — the temporary dwelling — offers a primary means for achieving *bitul hayesh*. Once one has fully absorbed the *succah's* message of negation of the material, he can come to perceive with an unrivaled clarity that the world is G-d's — His demands assume new dimensions of meaning, and throb with ever greater immediacy. The *succah,* then, can rightfully be described as *tzilusa demehimenusa* — the protective shade of faith. Beneath its sheltering roof, the blinding attractions of falsehood disappear ...* In its shelter the Jew becomes liberated

---

* This is also symbolized by the progressively diminishing numbers of daily sacrifices, which total "seventy oxen of the Succos Festival" offered during the holiday week. These represent the materialistic ideologies of the Seventy Nations of the world. As Succos advances, their number and the illusory significance of their beliefs dissipate.

from the shackles of conventional thought and dares aspire for more, reaching for greater spiritual growth. He becomes the "free man, committed to Torah" (Avos 6:3), governed by an inner peace, spreading light through all his actions.

◄§ Succah, Galus, and Unity

> "Why do we build a succah after Yom Kippur? ... Perhaps on Yom Kippur it will be decreed upon Israel to go into exile ... They will build succos and enter them, leaving behind their homes — and it will be considered before G-d as though they were exiled to Babylonia" (Yalkut, Emor 653).

To know G-d is to be aware of His all-pervasive unity. To be estranged from Him — to become enmeshed in idolatry** — is to splinter the various aspects of His presence, His numerous acts and deeds, into separate components and give them each a credence of its own. Doing so can bring a decree of galus on Jewry.

To love one's fellow is to identify with him and experience a sense of unity with him, to share his aspirations and to feel the pinch of his needs. Self-centeredness and the urge to enhance one's own material status give way to distance, cleavage, and rivalry. This estrangement between Jews and their fellows can also earn a punishment of galus.

Indeed, the Talmud records that the Jews suffered galus (exile) 1900 years ago because of unjustified hatred — sinas chinam. They had veered away from concern for others, and thought primarily of themselves. This urge to achieve material betterment and to add to one's possessions stems from the illusion that happiness is an outgrowth of having more — the same materialism that sees a personal threat in another's advancement.

The punishment they suffer — galus — also has the makings of the cure. For in man's incessant wandering, material gains are short-lived, and one who takes the galus experience to heart loses taste for further acquisition. Focus shifts to spiritual realms, and the galus lesson sinks in even deeper. — The result? The wandering Jew feels closer to his fellow.

The Jew in the succah who comprehends the message of his temporary dwelling, who internalizes its implications of bitul hayesh, can experience a flow of love toward his brother unbroken by the barriers of materialism that may have prevented

---

** Hebrew for idolatry is avodah zarah — which literally means "estranged service."

him from even being aware of others. Close to home as he is, he reaps the benefits of enduring a full-fledged *galus* ... even a *galus* in Babylonia, if need be.

◄§ Jews and Four Species — Bound Together

Another *mitzvah* associated with the *Succos* festival is the "four species" — the *lulav, esrog, myrtle, willow* — that the Jew is enjoined to bind together, hold in his hand, and wave. A well-known *Yalkut* associates each of these species with a different type of Jew, building on the characteristics of fragrance and flavor that each has or lacks in varying combinations. These, we are told, symbolize the nature and degree of observance and scholarship present among different types of Jews. Thus G-d says: "It is impossible to destroy them, so let them form one group and these will bring forgiveness on those." Through their concern and sense of association with others, those endowed with Torah (flavor) and good deeds (fragrance) will lend merit to those who are lacking in both. And the spiritually poor, in turn, will bring merit to the more virtuous by serving as a medium for their mentors' concern. As a result, they too are of vital importance to their more enriched brethren.

Thus, when Succos comes, and all segments of Jewry are bound together, like the four species, they will achieve a unity that overcomes all barriers of time, place, and self-centeredness, enhancing the entire community's standing before G-d. And the *succah's* message will have made its point.

Rabbi Yaakov Feitman

Succos:
The Triumphant Song
of Teshuvah

A free translation and adaptation
from Rabbi Yitzchok Hutner ל"צז's
Pachad Yitzchok

◄§ The Two-fold Yom Tov

SUCCOS is unique among the *yomim tovim*, simultaneously
closing the series of three pilgrimage festivals (the *Shalosh
Regalim)* and the *Yomim Noraim* — the Days of Awe. The dual
character of the *yom tov* becomes illuminated by a parable from
the *Midrash:*

> Two people who had appeared before a judge left the
> court, but we do not know which one was victorious. As
> soon as we see one flaunting his weapons, we know that it
> was he who was triumphant. In the same way, Israel and the
> Nations come before the L-rd in dispute on Rosh Hashanah
> and we do not know which is victorious. When Israel
> emerges from before G-d with lulav *and* esrog *in hand, all
> are convinced that Israel has triumphed.* (Midrash Rabbah
> Vayikra, 30:3).

This demonstrates that, while Pesach and Shavuos belong
only to the *Shalosh Regalim,* and Rosh Hashanah and Yom Kippur
belong only to the *Yomim Noraim,* Succos maintains a special

status in both realms. In fact, the *Midrash's* choice of metaphor highlights Succos's place in regard to the *Yomim Noraim:*

> ... *Israel and the Nations come before the L-rd in dispute on Rosh Hashanah and we do not know which is victorious.*

On the *Yomim Noraim*, a *havdalah* process begins, disassociating and isolating Israel from the Nations, pitting one against the other. On Succos, this process reaches its zenith and is completed.

Why is Succos designated as the *Yom Tov* of triumph over the nations and the attainment of the ultimate *havdalah?*

First we must examine the concept of *simchah* (joy) so deeply associated with the *Yom Tov* of Succos — especially the *simchah* experienced with *teshuvah*, a complete repentance from sin, which is accepted during any season, but is especially timely during the *Yomim Noraim*.

◆§ The Song of Teshuvah

The relationship between *simchah* and *teshuvah* was especially apparent at the *Simchas Bais HaSho'eivah* — "the rejoicing at the water-drawing" in the *Bais HaMikdash*, the joy that eclipsed all other experiences of human happiness. On this occasion, the *ba'alei teshuvah* — those who had repented for their sins — sang: *Happy is our old age which has atoned for our youth* (*Succah* 53a).

This *shirah* (song) for *ba'alei teshuvah* is indeed extraordinary. For what is *shirah* but the ecstasy of the soul overflowing, exploding from the joy of fullest involvement in performing the will of the Almighty, finally finding expression in the winged words and phrases of song! And this *simchah* of *Bais HaSho'eivah* is the one occasion that reserves a place for the song of the *ba'al teshuvah*. This, too, informs us of the special nature of Succos. First, however, a closer examination of *teshuvah* itself is required.

Central to the prayers of the Days of Repentance is "The Thirteen Attributes of Mercy" which G-d instructed Moshe to recite as a medium for gaining forgiveness for *Klal Yisrael* — first for worshiping the Golden Calf, and then as needed thereafter (*Shemos* 34:6-7). Our sages teach: "A covenant was made with (whoever recites) the Thirteen Attributes (that he) will not be turned away empty-handed" (*Rosh HaShanah* 17b).

This profound prayer, of paramount importance to everything related to repentance, opens with the Divine Name of

G-d "*Havayah*"appearing twice in succession. Our *Chazal* (Sages) explain that first the Name applies "before man sinned; the second time, the Name refers to after man has sinned and repented" (*Rosh HaShanah* 17b).

There is significance in the second "*Havayah*" as the source of Divine powers following *teshuvah*. For among all Thirteen Attributes, only "*Havayah*" cannot be translated nor transposed into human terms. That is, all of the *midos* (attributes) — "merciful, gracious, long-suffering, forgiving ..." can be transposed to other aspects of creation, and can be found or developed on the human level. We can understand them, extrapolate them into our own lives and situations, and conceivably emulate them.

Only the Divine Name "*Havayah*" applies exclusively to the Divine and cannot be translated or transmuted; only this Name can be the fountainhead for a life of repentance ... instructing us in a most important lesson regarding *teshuvah*.

◆§ The New World of Teshuvah

The power of *teshuvah* is not merely one of the forces that exist in the world; it is an entirely new world in and of itself. The most basic meaning of the Divine Name "*Havayah*" denotes creation and constant rejuvenation of the entire universe, from absolute nothingness to existence, containing as it does the letters of the word "existence." Since the Divine Name signifying creation applies to the attribute of *teshuvah*, it would be apparent that *teshuvah* itself involves a totally new creation.

Let us, then, re-examine our world: The cosmos that exists "before the sin" gains its power and vitality from the first Name "*Havayah*." After sin and repentance, an entirely new world is created, nourished and sustained by the creative force of the second name "*Havayah*." The fact that *teshuvah* alters the entire universe carries with it far-reaching consequences on all levels of existence. Most strikingly — because it is inherent in the literal meaning of the Torah's words — is the way this phenomenon relates to *tefillah* (prayer).

◆§ Praying in the World of Teshuvah

The Torah calls for man to pray in the passage: "And you shall serve the L-rd your G-d" — "service (*avodah*)" refers to prayer, as addressed to all of man's needs and aspirations, physical or spiritual (see *Taanis* 2a and *Rambam Hilchos Tefillin*

1:1). Yet, a new set of directives were given to *Moshe Rabbeinu* in regard to prayer related to repentance:

And the L-rd passed before him and proclaimed (the Thirteen Attributes) ... (*Shemos* 34:6). Rabbi Yochanan said, "Were it not written thus, it would be impossible for us to say such a thing. This teaches us that the Holy One, Blessed is He, wrapped himself in a *tallis (kaveyachol* — as if it were possible to say such!) like the *shliach tzibbur* (the leader of the prayers), and showed Moshe the order of prayer" (*Rosh HaShanah* 17b).

Why did G-d not teach Moshe this order of prayer before, when the concept of prayer was first introduced? Why was it necessary to do so only at this point? The new world of *teshuvah* is such that all things are rejuvenated and take on new aspects and character. The prayer of the old world of the first "*Havayah*" is inappropriate and, indeed, ineffectual in the world of the second. Thus, G-d instructed Moshe anew in the prayers to be used in the world of *teshuvah*. When we pray for assistance in the attainment of *teshuvah*, we can lose sight of the incredible wonder before us: A new world can be attained, a universe can be conquered — created — in but moments — through the act of repentance.

There are times and situations when conventional *tefillah* has no place: When the Jewish nation was backed against the Sea of Reeds and, in keeping with hallowed tradition, they prayed for salvation, G-d chastised Moshe: "Why do you cry unto me?" (*Shemos* 14:15). Our sages explain that the Splitting of the Sea was not a subject for prayer, for it had already been included in the plan of creation, and prayers only are addressed to events still to be determined within the framework of cause-and-effect of this world. In its own way, *teshuvah* is another example of the same phenomenon. Consider: how can one pray in the conventional manner for G-d's assistance and His acceptance of one's efforts for repentance, when *teshuvah* is so novel, so unique that its workings are almost as remarkable, as innovative as Creation itself? Conventional prayer has no relationship to anything that was preordained during the original act of creation, as was the Splitting of the Sea. Similarly, *teshuvah*, which demands a total re-creation of the universe and rejuvenates every particle of the cosmos, cannot be served by conventional mode of prayer. Thus the necessity for G-d's innovative action, as described by *Chazal*, when he instructed Moshe in the Thirteen Attributes of Mercy: "He wrapped himself in his *tallis (kaveyachol)* — and showed Moshe the order of the prayer." Simple verbal guidance — "Pray in this manner for *teshuvah*" — would not have been sufficient to instruct *Moshe Rabbeinu* in the *tefillah* for *teshuvah*. It was necessary for G-d to actually "demonstrate" for Moshe the method of prayer required for *teshuvah!*

◆§ Yom Kippur: The "Mattan Torah" of Teshuvah

Just as in the world of *teshuvah* prayer takes on a new meaning and necessitates a new order of *tefillah*, so does *teshuvah* require a new acceptance of the Torah. For this reason we find that the essence of Yom Kippur is expressed, not in terms of forgiveness or penitence, but in the fact that it is a *Mattan Torah* — a day akin to Shavuos, when the Torah was first given:

> Go forth, you daughters of Zion and gaze upon King Solomon, upon the crown with which his mother crowned him on the day of his espousals, and on the day of the gladness of his heart (Shir HaShirim 3:11).

> "On the day of espousals" refers to the giving of the Torah (Taanis 26b).

> This Giving of the Torah refers to Yom Kippur, when the second 'luchos' (Tablets of Law) were presented (Rashi).

The Nation of Israel received the Ten Commandments twice — once on the 6th of Sivan and again on the 10th of Tishrei, Yom Kippur (*Taanis* 30b). During the cataclysmic period in between, Israel sinned with the Golden Calf and then repented for its sin. It was at the last moment of its soul-searching penitential struggle, culminating in total *teshuvah*, that *Klal Yisrael* received the Torah the second time.

This was no coincidence. The world of *teshuvah* requires a total restructure and rededication, in keeping with the creation of an entirely new world. And what is a world without Torah? When Israel emerged purified into a *teshuvah* world, a *Mattan Torah* — presenting of the Torah — was inevitable. The universe of after-*teshuvah* is as unrelated to its previous state as is the proselyte to his previous uninitiated state. In the revivified universe of the after-*teshuvah*, the external world may look the same. The true inner nature of the *teshuvah* universe, however, is neoteric and fresh — unchanged to the eye, perhaps, but new to the soul — and so it demands that the very same Torah be given once again, and that prayer in the new dimension of the *ba'al teshuvah* be taught.

◂§ The Clouds of Forgiveness

Now that we have gained an insight into the world of *teshuvah,* we can once again examine the *yom tov* of Succos. On Succos, through the medium of the *s'chach* covering our *succah* huts, we are surrounded by the "clouds of the glory," which encompassed all of Israel when they left Egypt (*Succos* 11b). Surely, one would think, their commemoration should come in Nissan when the clouds first appeared, rather than in Tishrei, which seems unrelated to the event it commemorates.

In explanation, the Gaon of Vilna points out that our celebration of Succos does not only commemorate the Clouds of Glory, but also marks their return after their absence since the sin of the golden calf: At the moment of that fateful transgression, when Israel proved no longer worthy of extraordinary Divine revelation, the Clouds of Glory disappeared. The long *teshuvah* process began, culminating with the descent of *Moshe Rabbeinu* from Mt. Sinai on Yom Kippur, with the evidence of forgiveness in hand — the Second Tablets, for the new world of *teshuvah.*

The very next day, the eleventh of Tishrei, Moshe gathered together the nation ... ויקהל משה and the preparations for the *Mishkan* (the Tabernacle) began. During the three days that followed, the entire nation of Israel was profoundly occupied with gathering the materials for the sacred task of erecting a dwelling place for the holy *Shechinah.* On the fifteenth of Tishrei, these preparations were completed, actual work for construction began, and the Clouds of Glory returned. (See the *Gaon of Vilna's* Commentary on *Shir HaShirim* 2:17 and see also *Targum;* cf. for this chronology *Seder Olam Rabbah,* Chapter 6; and *Rashi* to *Shemos* 35:1.)

This offers us a new insight into Succos and its place in our past and present. The Clouds of Glory are not merely clouds of protection, but clouds of forgiveness. The salvation granted after the Sin of the Golden Calf restored *Klal Yisrael* once again to its position of being chosen from among the nations, with its special relationship of closeness to G-d. Indeed, just as *teshuvah* necessitated a new mode of prayer and a new granting of our eternal Torah, so was it imperative that the new nation of Israel — purified, purged, indeed re-created — be selected anew as the *Am HaNivchar* — the chosen of the L-rd.

The renewal of that Divine choice defines the essence of the *Yom Tov* of Succos. The "You have chosen us" of other holidays refers to the original selection of Israel — that is, belonging to the first "Havayah" — the gratitude and joy of having been chosen and rejuvenated after the Sin.

◄§ The Simchah of Teshuvah

A special relationship binds *simchah* and *teshuvah* together. It is clear from the *Rambam* that *simchah* is an important asset to the performance of any *mitzvah* (*Hilchos Lulav* 8:15). Yet, as elaborated upon by Rabbeinu Yonah (*Shaarei Teshuvah* 4:8), the *simchah* associated with having achieved repentance is a *special* joy that is not extrinsic to *teshuvah*, added on to embellish the *mitzvah*, but it is an integral part of its inner dynamics. Moreover, the anguish of having sinned can be assuaged *only* by the joy of having been forgiven, and thus *simchah* becomes a fundamental aspect of *teshuvah*.

Now the *Rambam's* directive to be especially joyful on Succos comes into sharper focus:

— "*Although it is a mitzvah to be joyous on all the holidays, on Succos there was an extraordinary joy in the Bais HaMikdash*" (*Hilchos Lulav* 8:12).

Succos is the *Yom Tov* of rebirth and rejuvenation through *teshuvah*, and *simchah* is an integral aspect of *teshuvah*. ... Just as *teshuvah* carries with it the special *simchah* that comes with the knowledge of forgiveness, so does Succos generate the special joy of a nation forgiven, reborn, and chosen anew.

Can there be, then, anything more natural than a song for *ba'alei teshuvah* on Succos?, At the lofty moment of *Simchas Bais HaSho'eivah* when the joy of Succos overflows and cascades into words of praise and notes of inspired poetry, a song for *ba'alei teshuvah* was inevitable.

Succos — the time when forgiveness was openly manifest, when the world of sin became replaced with a new world of forgiveness and purification, when an entire nation was reinstated as Chosen — there radiates a joy unparalleled on any other holiday.

◄§ The Danger of Havdalah

Just as the re-creation of Israel in the world of *teshuvah* is replete with unparalleled joy, so does it carry it with an inevitable danger as well. Every *havdalah* awakens a counteracting, antagonistic force, as well. Indeed, we know that the creation of Man involved his *havdalah* from the rest of the universe: "You singled out *(hivdalta)* man from the beginning and chose him to stand in Your Presence" *(Ne'ilah)*. Immediately, upon this act of *havdalah*, a company of ministering angels declared, "What is man that You are mindful of him, and the son of man that You think of him?" *(Tehillim* 8:5; *Sanhedrin* 38b).

Similarly, at the Splitting of the Sea, when the *havdalah* of Israel from Egypt was on the threshold of consummation, the opposing forces found a voice, "Why do You favor these over those? Have not both sinned?" (see *Midrash Rabba Shemos* 21: 7 and *Yalkut Reuvaini, Beshalach*).

The new *havdalah* of Israel after *teshuvah* awakens this same opposition to the selection of Israel. Thus we find that on Yom Kippur, when Israel is standing trial, it must once again struggle with the Prosecutor who is also representing the nations. In the thick of the battle, it is unclear who has won. Then, with the *Yom Tov* Succos, the dust settles and Israel emerges with its weapons intact — the *lulav* and *esrog*. We know who has been victorious.

↳§ The Inevitability of Teshuvah

We still do not know the polemic that the nations bring to the new trial. What fresh accusation have they contrived? What is the nature of the challenge that they fabricated to defeat Israel in the new *teshuvah* world?

The answer, perhaps, can be found in the ultimate confrontation between Israel and the nations in the End of Days. The nations will complain that in the world of *teshuvah*, justice has been inequitable. Partiality has been shown and *havdalah* is unwarranted, they will charge. And why? Because if justice and differentiation is to be decided on the basis of free will in the world, *teshuvah* for Israel seems to be an exception. For in the Last Days, *teshuvah* will be inevitable: " *... When all these things come upon you in the End of Days, you will return to the L-rd your G-d and hearken to His voice"* (Devarim 4:30). *"And it shall come to pass in that day ... a remnant of Israel shall return"* (Yeshayah 10:20-22).

The fact that *teshuvah* is ineluctable seems to work in favor of the nations' argument. How can Israel triumph in the great courtroom of *Acharis HaYomim* — the ultimate justice of the End of Days — when her return to G-d is irrevocable and inescapable?

To answer this protest, the Festival of Succos will be presented to the Nations.

◄§ Succos: The Final Test

The weapons of Succos — the *lulav* and *esrog* — are paraded after the war. They are no longer needed in the battle itself, but they are eloquent testimony to the identity of the triumphant victor.

How does this answer the apparent justice of the argument put forth by the nations? To understand, we must take advantage of the glimpse our sages have granted us into the world of *Acharis HaYomim:* "The nations will then plead, 'Offer us the Torah anew and we shall obey it.' But the Holy One, Blessed is He, will say to them, 'You foolish ones, he who took the trouble to prepare on the eve of *Shabbos* can eat on *Shabbos*, but he who has not troubled on the eve of *Shabbos*, what shall he eat on *Shabbos*? (It is now the Sabbath, too late to prepare with *mitzvah* observance). Nevertheless, I have an easy command known as *succah*. Go and carry it out' ... Immediately, every one of them will go and make a *succah* on top of his roof. But G-d will cause the sun to blaze forth ... and everyone of them will kick at his *succah* and go away" (*Avodah Zarah* 3a).

The *havdalah* of the future world will be crystallized by the *Yom Tov* of Succos. True, *teshuvah* for Israel may be inevitable. As a result, it is unavoidable that Israel be victorious. But the price for that future victory in a world without choice will have been paid in the temptation-laden world of today. The difficult, expensive, pain-filled world of "Fridays" is ample preparation and advance payment for the world of complete *Shabbos* to come.

On that grand *Shabbos* of the future, the once battle-weary weapons of yesteryear will take on an entirely new character: Armaments are *muktzah* on *Shabbos* — prohibited to handle, for their use is forbidden on the day of rest. But *these* weapons will have become ornaments to a nation finished with war. The weapons of battle become the laurels of peace and may be worn and admired in the *Shabbos* of post-war tranquility. " ... since Israel emerges from before G-d with *lulav* and *esrog* in hand, all are convinced that Israel has triumphed."

◄§ Succos: The Completion of the Mission

Succos, the last of the three Pilgrimage Festivals and the culmination of the Days of Awe, represents the completion of Israel's Divine mission. The Torah relates each of the three Festivals to a time of the agricultural year. Pesach is called the

Festival of the Spring, the season of planting; Shavuos the Festival of Reaping; and Succos, the Festival of the Harvest.

The *Maharal* elucidates this relationship between the festivals and the cycle of the land. There are three points of contact between an agent and his dispatcher: the moment he is appointed in his mission; the time his task is completed; and his return to the principal who has sent him, to inform him that he has performed his function satisfactorily.

Israel, too, was created as a Divine agent on Pesach, charged with the task of becoming the *Am Hashem* — worthy of being the chosen of the L-rd. On Shavuos, with the acceptance of the Torah, Israel became that chosen nation. Succos represents the ultimate return of the agent with his product to his sender — and, indeed, Creator. "I have accomplished my task," the *shliach* says on Succos, "and have returned the harvest to the Owner of the field."

The noble accouterments of the *lulav* and *esrog* declare an even more profound affirmation: "Although our task is complete, we still remain the agents of the L-rd. We did our work on '*Erev Shabbos*' — the era of preparation — so we may proudly display our weapons-cum-decorations on '*Shabbos.*'"

Thus is Succos unique in that it crowns both *Shalosh Regalim* and *Yomim Noraim*. Its particular joy extends from the depths of the overflowing heart of the *ba'al teshuvah* to the essence of the world of *Acharis HaYomim*, when the *lulav* and *esrog* will proclaim eloquently the victory of Israel.

Rabbi Joseph Elias

"And of Rejoicing: What Does it Do?"

King David's Tehillim
enjoins us to
"serve G-d with rejoicing"
but how can "rejoicing"
be commanded?

◄§ The Meaning of "Simchah"

To comprehend, we first have to understand what *simchah*, rejoicing, really is. Or, better, we might start by stressing what it is not. On the verse, "I said of hilarity that it is foolish, and of *simchah*, 'What does it do?' " *(Koheles* 2:2), *Shaarei Teshuvah* explains that hilarity is always foolish; but in connection with rejoicing, there is room to ask whether it is true rejoicing — for the sake of Heaven. As the *Rambam* put it, we are not commanded to indulge in foolishness but in such *simchah* as forms service to the Creator. Hence, even a *simchah shel mitzvah*, rejoicing on the occasion of a *mitzvah*, such as at a wedding, is not in itself enough, for its higher purpose and meaning could be lost sight of, and therefore it must be further reinforced by *Divrei Torah*. For this reason, too, we find that at the *Simchas Bais Hasho'eivah*, the rejoicing in the Temple on Succos, which was so extraordinary as to inspire the participants with *Ruach HaKodesh*, the central role was reserved for the elders and scholars who truly perceived the meaning of the celebration *(Shaarei Teshuvah, Orach Chayim, 697:3).*

What, then, is the special nature of *simchah*, rejoicing, that needs such safeguards? Perhaps we can say that, whereas hilarity is escapist and irresponsibly thoughtless, true rejoicing is the opposite: a state of mind that flows from the very deepest and truest understanding of reality.

Normally we struggle with life, and the multiplicity of problems that it poses; all too often we do not seem able to cope with them, or, indeed, to see any meaning in them. We are tempted to see ourselves buffeted by forces beyond our control, and we are sorely troubled and frustrated. But what if we suddenly are given the key to the meaning of events, and everything suddenly falls into place? Relief, happiness, *simchah*: "There is no *simchah* as great as that when our doubts are resolved"(*Remoh*).

And what is this key? A clear recognition of G-d as the guiding and ordering power in the world. "*Simchah* is the emergence of the certainty of a person's faith in and closeness to G-d," writes Rabbi Shlomo Wolbe, the *Mashgiach* of Beer Yaakov. Therefore, the true and proper observance of the *mitzvos*, as fulfillment of the Divine will, must be with *simchah*; and the Torah predicts *galus* for the Jewish people "because you did not serve G-d with rejoicing and a good heart" (*Devarim*, 28:47).

On the other hand, if a person is full of *simchah*, if it permeates his *mitzvos*, "this shows that his heart is loyal to his G-d, and demonstrates his faith and trust in Him" (Rabbi Nachman of Breslav). Hence, our Sages emphasize that the Divine Presence will not rest upon a person in a state of sadness or foolery or idle things, but only out of *simchah shel mitzvah*. And thus, too, the *halachah* stresses that "one should pray...only out of *simchah shel mitzvah*" (*Berachos* 31a).

◆§ The Glory of True "Simchah"

The level that can be attained in this way is indeed remarkable. Rabbi Yehuda Halevi, in the *Kuzari* (*II, 50*), points out: "Your humility on fastdays is no closer to G-d than your *simchah* on *Shabbos* or Holy Days, if this flows from pure intent and a perfect heart — and just as supplications require thought and intent, so also the rejoicing in His *mitzvos* requires thought and intent, so that you rejoice in the *mitzvah* itself, from your love for it, and recognize how He benefitted you by giving it to you..."

Our sages pointed out, in fact, that only those *mitzvos* that the Jews accepted joyfully remained strong with them (*Shabbos* 130a); and the *Ari HaKadosh* revealed to one close to him that all that he achieved in his service of G-d — where the gates of Divine wisdom and *Ruach HaKodesh* were opened to him — was due to the fact that every *mitzvah* was done by him with infinite *simchah*, born from his contemplation of the greatness of the Lawgiver and the generosity of His gift.

We could perhaps sum up what has been said so far, in the words of Rabbi Dessler:

> *Simchah is one's clinging to G-d through the recognition of the good that his soul perceives: "G-d is with me, I will not fear."*

The enormous *simchah* flowing from a direct recognition of this truth echoes every day in our prayers: "Blessed is our G-d Who created us for His glory, and separated us from those that err, and gave us the Torah of truth and implanted eternal life in us." The meaning of "life" here is multiple. It refers to the life after death, in which we all have a share; but it surely also refers to the fact that already in our this-wordly existence we are truly alive, as only somebody can be who understands what is going on around him and therefore can wisely and resolutely plot his actions. (This meaning of *life*, in contrast to mere *existence*, may have been alluded to by our forefather Yaakov when, in talking to Pharaoh, he distinguished between the years of his life and the years of his sojournings, *Bereishis* 47:9.)

This assurance of life, in its fullest sense — "You that cling to G-d, your G-d, are all alive today" — inspired King David to exclaim, "I will not die, for I will live to tell the deeds of G-d" (*Tehillim* 118:17), and it found expression in the words of that *Chassid* who observed: "How can one be sad if he believes that this-world is only an anteroom before the World-to-Come?" He surely did not mean that the meaninglessness of a this-worldly existence is compensated for by the reward to come, but rather that our this-worldly life itself receives meaning when it is in its true context, as a Divinely planned and guided preparation for the World-to-Come.

Thus, instead of being overwhelmed by the complexities and tribulations of daily existence, a person can perceive the blessing even in the bad that may, G-d forbid, befall him. "The one who trusts in G-d is enveloped in kindness" (*Tehillim* 32:10), for he senses G-d's hand in whatever happens.

The answer to our initial question seems therefore obvious:

we cannot, indeed, be commanded to rejoice, but we can — and are — enjoined to attain such an understanding of our life as children of G-d, that rejoicing flows inevitably from it.

⊸§ "Simchah" for the Sinner?

Yet, should not our recognition of G-d, in a way, lead to the opposite result? Should it not make us aware of our imperfections and trespasses, and make us so ashamed as to despair of our own worth and future? The Prophet, however, warns against such an easy capitulation: "After I returned I repented" (Yirmiyah 31:18). First must come the determination, born out of one's recognition of G-d, to turn to the path indicated by Him — only afterwards may he look back to regret past failures. The observation of our Sages that vayehi (it was) always introduces the account of some misfortune, whilst vehayah (it will be) introduces good tidings, has been explained by the fact that the past tense, pointing backward to what happened already, is the tense of sorrow — and the future tense is that of new promise, a new start, and regeneration. Teshuvah must start with the latter; that is why it can be allied with simchah, the true recognition of G-d.

⊸§ Rejoice With Trembling

There is, however, a difficulty pointed out by our Sages:

One verse says, "Serve G-d with rejoicing!" (Tehillim 100:2); another says, "Serve G-d with trembling!" (ibid. 2:11). How so? At the time that a person stands in prayer, he should rejoice that he serves G-d, like Whom there is nobody in the world; but do not act with lightheadedness toward Him but with awe (Yalkut Shimoni 623).

Apparently, then, simchah alone is not enough. As the sole moving force it may be dangerous because it can lead to unchecked exuberance and lightheadedness; hence it must be balanced by one's sense of awe and reverence for G-d.

At the giving of the Torah, Moshe Rabbeinu was enjoined: "Set bounds to the people, around them, saying: 'Take heed not to go up to the mountain...!' " (Shemos 19:12). Do not let them get carried away by enthusiasm. Such excessive enthusiasm, according to some commentators, was the failing of Nadav and Avihu and the Elders of Israel, when "they saw G-d, and they ate and drank" (Shemos 24:11). It may have been the "alien fire" that Nadav and Avihu offered amidst the rejoicing of the Dedication of the Sanctuary, and for which they were punished. It, again, was in evidence when the people of Bais Shemesh "lifted their eyes and saw the Ark and rejoiced to see it" (Shmuel I, 6:13) and were smitten for it. However, when we speak of the need for restraint in our rejoicing, it must be understood that this restraint — just as much as the simchah itself — flows from our recognition of G-d. Thus Ramban comments on Shemos (20:17) "In order to test you, has G-d come", to train you in His faith, for when He showed you the revelation of the Shechinah, the faith in Him entered your heart, to make you cling to Him; "and in order that His fear may be upon you, that you may not sin," when you saw that He alone is G-d, in Heaven and on earth … — The closeness to G-d as well as the fear of Him are the result of any encounter with G-d. Both forces are necessary: our joyful awareness of G-d inspires action, moves us to conquer new worlds, in our transcending desire to serve Him; while our awe of G-d inspires caution and avoidance of anything that may contradict His will and purpose. (It is noteworthy that the Ohr HaChayim, Devarim 28:47 identifies our failure to serve G-d joyfully with our failure to do His positive commandments.)

It is along these lines that Rabbi Shlomo Kluger interprets the passage from our prayers "They rejoice when they go out and jubilate when they come back; they do the will of their Creator in fear": "In approaching the doing of a mitzvah one should feel the greatest joy at the opportunity that offers itself. When completing the mitzvah, he should feel happiness at having achieved this goal. But while doing it he should feel the awe that should be experienced while standing before the King," when any wrong word or move would be a tragedy indeed (Yerios Shlomo).

◄§ The Incompleteness of Our "Simchah"

The primary and pre-eminent force, to be sure, must be simchah, however, for it alone can carry us to the greatest heights. The observation of the Ari HaKadosh that Purim is even greater than Yom Kippur (which is "Yom KePurim," a day like Purim) is well-known — and the explanation may be found in the outpouring of joy that marks Purim: "The understanding and recognition of the kindness of G-d, evidenced in G-d's retribution upon Haman (Amalek), brought about their rejoicing over the sanctification of G-d's name, evident here, and their dedication (by their free decision) to do His will, and the love that grows from this" (Michtav MeEliyahu) — leading all the way to a voluntary re-acceptance of the Torah, as our Sages emphasize.

Yet, when we talk of the enormous power of *simchah*, one word of caution is in place. If *simchah* is the result of the recognition of G-d, then it can never be complete and perfect — because our recognition of G-d is incomplete and imperfect. We live in a world marked by *hester panim* (the Hiding of the Divine countenance), by the loud and noisy self-assertion of evil in all its forms. Complete *simchah* must wait for the day when the rule of G-d over the world will stand revealed in all its splendor.

In fact, at the *simchah* of a wedding, we evoke the time, long past, when G-d gladdened man in *Gan Eden*, before the first triumph of evil; and we look forward to the time when there will again be heard the sound of rejoicing and gladness at the coming of *Moshiach*. Meanwhile, we experience some of this *simchah*, because every wedding represents a step toward the perfection of the world as well as the individual ("It is not good for man to be alone", "He who has no wife, lives without joy"); but the *simchah's* incompleteness is marked by the glass broken and the ashes on the forehead of the *chassan*.

But the incompleteness of our *simchah* in this world can and should serve as a spur. On the verse (*Divrei HaYomim,* 16:10) "Let the heart of those that seek G-d rejoice," a Hassidic explanation points out that usually *finders* rejoice, not *seekers;* but when it comes to seeking G-d, those who do so in sincerity can already find cause for rejoicing.

◄§ The Calendar of the Jew

The year of the Jew, with its sequence of *Yomim Tovim*, is meant to be one long quest for closeness to G-d. The awareness of our failings and the resultant punishment, which mark the months of Tammuz and Av, carry with them the lesson of our own nothingness and the need to search for the true meaning of our existence. Therein lie the roots of our consolation — expressed in the seven *haftaros* of consolation—and of our repentance and self-improvement — called for by the *Yomim Noraim.* And there results, in turn, the "time of our rejoicing," leading up to *Simchas Torah...* when hopefully, we can experience the true *simchah* longed for: "This is the day that G-d made — let us rejoice and jubilate with Him" (*Tehillim* 118:24).

Rabbi Avrohom Chaim Feuer

Simchas Bais HaSho'eivah:
The Art of Celebration

*A Succos message
for the entire year*

"He who failed to witness the celebration of Simchas
Bais HaSho'eivah never witnessed true joy in all his days"
(Succah 5:2).

THE FESTIVAL of *Succos* is generally described as "the time of
our rejoicing," and within the holiday a ceremony occurs that
expresses joy of the greatest intensity — *Simchas Bais
HaSho'eivah* — the ultimate celebration.

*Sparkling waters of the Shilo'ach Stream were drawn in
golden buckets and brought up to the altar of the Bais
HaMikdash, where they were poured into a silver basin.
Open at the bottom, the basin let the water spill into a cavity
within the altar walls, which led into the deep underground
foundations of the Temple. This ritual took place to the accompaniment of music and celebration of unprecedented
proportions.*

Why the poured-out water? Why the unbridled joy?

True joy is rarely experienced. Most people are involved in
the pursuit of happiness, yet happiness seems to elude them. For
happiness results from the realization of ambitions and aspirations, and O, how often do these remain woefully unfulfilled!
The sweet dreams men savor and the harsh reality they encounter
are locked in a terrible struggle, and the dreams usually lose out.

Man fancies himself a sculptor — carving for himself a self-image of personal success. Man attempts to be a designer — fashioning an elaborate blueprint for achievement and satisfaction.

But the drama of life seldom follows the man-made script. More often frustrations and grief are man's lot, simply because the divine fate ordained for every individual does not necessarily coincide with the destiny man has chosen for himself.

King David — dogged by tragedy, yet one of the happiest of men — provided a formula for maintaining a mood of unabated joy in spite of adversity. He taught that to *achieve* happiness, man must *abandon* its pursuit. Let man humbly submit himself to the hands of G-d and declare "My L-rd, You choose what is best for me. Please take my hand and lead me!"

G-d is my allotted portion and my share, You guided my destiny. Portions have fallen to me in pleasant places, indeed my estate was lovely to me. I will bless G-d who has advised me. (Tehillim 16:5-7)

David's master, the prophet Samuel, taught the Jewish nation the true meaning of submission. In an effort to inspire a spiritual renewal, Samuel gathered together all the people in Mizpah, and at his command:

They drew up water and poured it out before G-d (I Samuel 7:6).

They poured their hearts out like water in order to repent before G-d (Targum).

They humbly submitted themselves to G-d and proclaimed: "We stand in Your presence like uncontained water — spilled out!" (Rashi).

Water is the epitome of liquidity, for liquid is best described as "a substance with no form of its own, but which conforms to the shape of its container." Nothing fits this description quite like water.

Submission. Melt down your masterpiece. Dissolve your personal design. Pour out your heart in an amorphous, shapeless mass and plead with the Almighty: "Please, You give my existence a shape and a purpose! My identity is lost in Your presence ... then my true self may be found. I drown myself in Your being ... then my essence can emerge."

Pour out your heart like water in the presence of the L-rd (Eichah 2:19)

◄§ The Sweat of the Soul

Never underestimate the power of the tiny teardrop — it is one of the mightiest forces in the universe. What could be stronger than man's stubborn arrogance? — yet a tear can shatter human pride. In a moment of truth, man realizes the futility of his own designs, and the self-image of his own creation crumbles. He "breaks down" in tears and surrenders himself to a Higher Will. Rabbi Samson Raphael Hirsch calls tears "the sweat of the soul" — the product of a distressed spirit in the throes of upheaval.

Rabbeinu Yonah writes in the classic *Shaarei Avodah* (Section II): He who prays with tears is assured that his prayers will be heard. For, although all the heavenly gates are locked, the gate of tears is not sealed (*Bava Metzia* 59a).

How is the heart poured out like water? Through tears. Thus, one might well see in the waters poured onto the Temple altar at the *Simchas Bais HaSho'eivah* a symbolic outpouring of human tears.

The Midrash (*Bereishis Rabbah* 78) teaches: All the years that Jacob was in Bais-El he poured out water-libations before G-d. Rabbi Yochanan said, "He who can count all the water libations that our forefather Jacob poured can count the drops of water of the Sea of Tiberias." That is, just as the waters of the sea are beyond number, so too were the tears of Jacob too many to count. No one knew of these tears except the Holy One, Blessed is He, who *did* count them and cherish them and store them in His treasury (cf. *Shabbos* 105a).

> ...*From that well they watered the flocks, and the stone covering the well's mouth was very large ... and Jacob rolled the stone from the well's mouth* (Bereishis 29:2,10).

> *The word "be'er", well, is mentioned seven times in this episode — an allusion to the seven days of Succos when the well waters are poured on the altar (Baal HaTurim ibid).*

> *The Torah related this incident to teach that those who put all their trust in G-d are suffused with divine strength. Jacob arrived at the well utterly exhausted from his journey, but the holy spirit invigorated him with the strength of all the shepherds combined — and he lifted the huge rock single-handedly. This incident is a prophetic allusion to the time when flocks of Jewish pilgrims made their way to the Bais HaMikdash where they drew forth a new wave of*

strength and holy spirit at Simchas Bais HaSho'eivah (Ramban).

"And Jacob set up a pillar in the place where He (G-d) spoke to him, a monument of stone and he poured a libation thereon" (Bereishis 35:14).

He poured a libation of water before G-d just as his descendants would do in the Temple on the Festival of Succos (Targum Yonason).

Following the lead of their forefather, the seed of Jacob melt their hearts with tears on Yom Kippur. And on Succos, these tears were gathered in golden buckets and poured in His presence. Each and every Jew found himself enveloped by a power which embraced him, and reinforced every fatigued fibre of his being with unflagging strength.

Small wonder, then, that the entire nation displayed phenomenal stamina throughout the entire week of these festivites. Indeed, the Talmud (Succah 53a) relates that for the week's duration, no one slept! By day, all were totally absorbed with altar services, prayers, Torah study, and feasting; by night, in the spectacular celebrations. At best, a man could snatch a quick cat-nap on his neighbor's shoulder.

Men enraptured by the holy spirit have tapped the source of all strength. Infinite energy flows through their veins, their bones cannot grow weary.

Why was this ritual called Simchas Bais HaSho'eivah — "the celebration of the drawing"? Because it was from there that Israel drew forth a wave of Holy Spirit! (Yerushalmi: Succah 5).

⋖§ Abandon Your Self

In analyzing the word simchah—שִׂמְחָה, joy—one might find at its root machah—to erase (שָׂמְחָה, for he erased). If one truly wishes to rejoice, he must forget about himself.

An extremely pious man was asked, "What was the happiest moment in your life?"

He replied, "I was once traveling on a ship and because of my poverty I was assigned the worst quarters imaginable — in the lowest hold, together with the cargo. A group of rich and arrogant merchants were also on board. Once, as I lay in my berth, one of the merchants who had come down to the hold dumped some refuse on me. I appeared so despicable in his eyes that he simply pretended that I wasn't *there. I was shocked by this man's audacity; nevertheless, I assure you that I was not offended in the least. When I realized how indifferent I was to my own prestige, I was truly overcome with joy because I had achieved a level of genuine humility and self-effacement. (Rambam, Avos 4:4)*

As long as a person concerns himself with the figure he cuts as he dances, and thinks about the image he projects as he sings — he is worrying, not rejoicing. Erase your *self*. Only then will you relax — relieved of that terrible burden of self-concern that you drag around with yourself. Unshackled, released, your feet will dance lightly, your voice will soar free.

Rambam (Hilchos Lulav 8:14, 15) teaches that celebration is a fine art that demands no less talent and genius than other creative pursuits. Therefore, the unlearned people could not actively participate in *Simchas Bais HaSho'eivah* — they could only observe and marvel. The foremost scholars and saints — the Heads of the Sanhedrin and the *Roshei Yeshivah* — only they were permitted to perform — and how they performed!

Rabban Shimon ben Gamliel, the Prince of Israel, would juggle eight flaming torches simultaneously — and one torch never touched another. Then he would balance his body on his thumbs and lower his head and kiss the floor ... Levi juggled eight knives ... Shmuel juggled eight full cups of wine ... Abaye juggled eight eggs (Succa 53a).

Dancing, leaping, tumbling, twirling — normal decorum was forsaken, traditional dignity was cast to the winds. The sages put aside their status and positions and titles — the external trappings of society — and plunged themselves into sacred revelry.

Rambam explains:

The celebration of a mitzvah and the joy one expressed as a result of his love of G-d — such celebration is an extraordinary form of divine service! Whoever holds himself aloof from this festivity deserves to suffer punishment ... And, he who does participate but becomes filled with pride and seeks to attract attention and admiration — this man is indeed both a sinner and a fool. Concerning this, Solomon warned, "Do not make a spectacle of yourself in the presence of the King" (*Mishlei* 25:6).

But, whoever belittles himself on this occasion and takes himself lightly, it is he who is a truly great and dignified personage and it is he who demonstrates that he serves G-d out of a sense of deep adoration.

So said King David (as he danced with uninhibited abandon

in honor of the *Aron HaKodesh* — the holy ark), "I would be yet
more lightly esteemed than this, holding myself lowly in my eyes"
(*II Shmuel* 6:22).

True majesty and glory is to rejoice in the presence of G-d, as
it is written, "And King David was leaping and twirling in the
presence of G-d" (*ibid.* 6:16).

Children of Israel! Brothers! Dance! Battered, beaten,
bruised — we are nevertheless a work of art. Tossed about by the
raging storms of history, we still remain firm in our position as
G-d's masterpiece. What is a Jew? No more than clay in the hands of
the potter, stone in the grip of the sculptor. Every blow is artistry
— a step closer to assuming the divine form.

For this we sing. For this we pour our souls like waters of
joy.

≈§ Chanukah / *The Festival of Lights*

the ongoing historical Chanukah ...
the miscalculation of reigning priests ...
the opacity of reliance on clear thought ...
the family clustered 'round the
menorah ... the transcendental light ...
gratitude rising above self-interest ...
light of solitude in darkness ...
the battle to reject contemporary realism
... the fast day that follows

From the writings of
Rabbi Samson Raphael Hirsch צ"ל

In the Light
of Chanukah

*Insights on the
unresolved conflicts
behind the festival*

I.
The Ongoing Battle of Chanukah

ON THE EVE of the 25th of Kislev you kindle the first
Chanukah light in your home, and for eight days with a
greeting of the ever-increasing light, the memory of an old story
of ancient times crosses the threshold of your mind.

Is it still the same old story? Do, then, the Jewish dead never
die? Does the Jewish past never fade away?

No, the Jewish dead do not die. One who had died for Jewry,
nay, one who has lived for the cause of Jewry, can never die; in
eternal gratitude a people which knows how to value its past
heroes cherishes his memory and past history; Jewish history in
all its grandeur accosts every coming generation, ever fresh and
ever new, to remind, to warn, to comfort and to elevate.

And now just this story — oh, that it were indeed old, if with
its sorrow and its glory it would after 2,000 years be so old to us
that its sorrow might seem incomprehensible to us, and its glory
commonplace!

"But Joshua preferred to be called Jason, just as his younger brother (they succeeded one another as High Priest) preferred to be called Menelaus instead of Chonyah. Now, when Menelaus together with the sons of Tobias had (in the dispute with his brother over the office of the High Priest) to yield to this violence, they approached the King Antiochus, and offered to throw off immediately their Jewish laws and customs, and to conduct themselves in accordance with the statutes and customs of the king and the Greeks. They, therefore, asked permission to erect a Greek college in the city of Jerusalem, and when it was granted they let their foreskins grow, so that even when naked they might appear quite similar to the Greeks; and thus abandoning all the customs of their forefathers they adopted the habits of foreign people." (Josephus, Ant. Bk. 12, 5. 1)

Is this a story of the past?

⋖⋗ Look to the Future

If religious decadence in the Jewish sphere fills you with grief and sorrow, if you are nigh to despair of our future, if in fear you exclaim "Has there ever been so gruesome a situation in Israel?" — then consider this story; see how once before, 2,000 years ago, High Priests, men entrusted with what is most sacred in Jewry, with the highest religious office, were themselves the first to betray G-d and His Holy Law, to woo the favor of kings by religious treachery, seducing the Jewish nation and its youth. They vied with the well-to-do and the educated of their people in contempt of the Divine laws and of Jewish morals, in honoring and adopting un-Jewish ways and un-Jewish culture — see how already thousands of years ago, the alluring light of culture and political advantage, in the shape of civic rights, had been employed by Israel's seducers to tempt them to revolt against G-d and His holy word. Yet observe how this epoch of betrayal and revolt was left behind, and how it was succeeded by the centuries, millennia of faithfulness, of devotion and self-sacrifice for G-d and Judaism; and learn from this to look to the future with confidence.

For you must note that this revolt of which voices of the past have just given an account, this revolt was not one provoked from without, it was not the consequence of Antiochus's wild attack on Judaism; this revolt of the Jewish teachers of G-d's Law and of the upper classes of society in Judea was voluntary; it preceded the frenzy of the King; it was, strictly speaking, the actual cause, the real origin of the subsequent fanatical anti-Jewish outbreak. Not in his wildest dreams would it have occurred to Antiochus to convert Jews from Judaism to Greek culture, had not Jews and priests of Jewry disclosed to him that Judaism no longer held first place in their heart, that they were only waiting for the royal command to place Zeus on the altar of the Eternal, and that at the same time the common people, the lower classes, could be easily lured into the other camp — or made to suffer martyrdom if they refused. Similarly even in the darkest centuries of persecution, it has never entered the mind of any despot to "reform" Jews and Jewry.

◄§ One Little Crucible of Oil

Jewry was persecuted, but everyone believed that Judaism was everlasting. It required nineteenth-century priests and disciples to set the spectacle of disloyal Jews before the eyes of princes and people, before any statesman conceived the idea of reforming Jewry by means of decrees and legal measures. It is only natural; respect yourself, respect your past, respect your own sanctuary, and you will see that whatever opinion is held of you, whether you are regarded with favor or with disfavor — respect will not be denied you. But if you do not respect yourself, if you look contemptuously on the tombs of your ancestors, if you no longer consider your sanctuary worthy of respect — even of recognition — how can you demand that a stranger shall respect you, or respect your fathers? You may find many things in the world, but for respect you will beg in vain.

What was the mistake made by these *men of progress, men of culture, priests of reform*, the political traffickers in religion of the time of Antiochus in Judea? Listen to the illuminating tale of the Chanukah lights:

"The renegade sons of Judea had gone to such lengths that the Greeks themselves finally dishonored the divine sanctuary by using it as a temple for Zeus. They had profaned all oil intended for the sacred lamp of G-d. The victorious Hasmoneans found but one small crucible undesecrated; and it was enough for only one day. But in this one crucible was revealed the miraculous salvation of Divine power. For eight days the lamp was tended with it, until fresh pure oil could be prepared."

One single pure spark, loyally treasured in but one single

Jewish heart, is sufficient for G-d to set aflame once more the whole spirit of Judaism. And if all the oil, if all the forces that were to have preserved the light of G-d in Israel, were to be misused for the light of paganism — even then, one little crucible of oil, one heart, which in a forgotten hidden corner, imprinted with the High Priest's seal, has faithfully remained untouched and undefiled, this one crucible is sufficient to become the salvation of the entire sanctuary when the right time and hour has come. *"And even though all countries were bowed in obedience to Antiochus, if every man forsook the land of his fathers and assented to the king's command, even then, I and my sons and brothers will not forsake the laws of our fathers"* — thus spoke the loyal Hasmonean heart of one single hero advanced in years — and Israel's sanctuary was saved.

II.
Hellenism, Judaism and Rome

K ISLEV with its joyous Festival of Lights, of the reconsecration of the Temple which the spirit of the Hasmoneans and the courage of the Maccabees had won; Teves with its first day of remembrance, which marks the downfall of the Jewish Temple and state in all their glory; Kislev with its triumph over the Hellenic spirit, Teves with its defeat by Roman politics — this sequence of events is a challenge to serious reflection. It presents, for our consideration, the following thesis: It is not Hellas [Greece] that Judaism has to fear, but Rome. It is not the Hellenic spirit that caused the downfall of all that is sacred to Judah, but the Roman mind and Roman tendencies ...

And, indeed, Israel can rejoice wherever the Hellenic spirit of civilization extends its realm among mankind. For this civilization in its pure essence is nothing but the flower of the highest development of human nature left to itself. From it, Israel's mission to mankind has nothing to fear; on the contrary, it will thrive on it. The spirit of the religious Doctrine and the Law which mankind is destined to receive from the hands of Israel expects the mind and soul not to sink into a state of ignorance and dullness but to be enlightened and full of life. Only the enlightened mind is receptive to the light of the Jewish teaching; only the soul ennobled by freedom is receptive to the blissful life of the Law.

It is true, Israel also knows the trials and tribulations which the Hellenic spirit of civilization imposes on it, as it develops by its side. The times of Mattisyahu were not to remain the only ones in which that spirit — still developing, still immature, in its understandable overweening estimation of itself and pretentious vanity — believed in its own vocation to educate the house of Jacob which eluded its comprehension ...

All that is sacred to Israel has nothing to fear from the spirit of human culture which originated in Hellas. Israel has always welcomed the Hellenic spirit as a precursor and helpmeet of its own mission to enlighten and civilize mankind and likewise has wedded itself to the truth and humanity produced by that spirit. And although that spirit, with its immaturity and its excesses, occasionally, as in the days of Mattisyahu, has also caused confusion within Israel, the "Light of the Jewish Tents" has again and again triumphed anew and always led to a new Chanukah, to a new consecration of its old, undiminished, eternal Sanctuaries.

⋖§ Rome's Sword: Its Soil

Different is Rome's relationship to Israel and all that it holds sacred — Rome, whose overwhelming onslaught spelt for Jerusalem the beginning of the catastrophe which is commemorated on the tenth day of Teves.

It was not Roman valor that triumphed over Jewish valor. The Jew can be proud of the catastrophe which meant his political annihilation. The valiant heroism of the men of Judea — striving so little for martial glory — the inexhaustible resourcefulness of their strategy, their cold-blooded defiance of death, their bravery, nay, their invincibility perplexed the Roman emperors and their legions accustomed to conquest. It was not Rome's sword that triumphed over Judea.

It was the spirit of Roman politics which ever since Pompey had ensnared the all-too-willingly compliant heads of Judea's people; the Roman ideas and tendencies which had become more and more familiar especially among the political leadership of the Jewish state and had supplanted the Jewish spirit — it was all these that undermined the Jewish Sanctuary, that imposed Roman hirelings as kings on free Judea and that had made of Judea a "captive" of Rome long before the hand of the legionnaires threw the fatal firebrand into the Jewish capital.

It is this Roman spirit which Israel has got to know if it wants to realize who is its most redoubtable enemy.

Whereas the Hellenes had safely enjoyed, from an early date, their own soil, sufficient for their peaceful development, where they could flourish under a serene sky and bring to fruition all that is noble in man, Rome's cradle, to speak in the tradition of our forefathers, bears the inscription: "Your sword is your soil."

The origin from which Rome was to grow into a giant was so insignificant, such an insecure foundation, that only the sword could make something of it; the sword which, once successfully brandished, would never willingly return to its scabbard. What the sword had conquered, only the sword could preserve, only the sword could enlarge. Whereas Hellas took recourse to the sword only in its prime and for its own defense, Rome's prime, even its mere existence, was the product of armed power, of cunning, rapacious force. *Ovadiah*'s words (1:2,3), "Behold, I have made you small among the heathen: you are greatly despised. The pride of your heart has deceived you, you that dwell in the clefts of the rock whose habitation is high; that says in his heart, 'Who shall bring me down to the ground?'" were applied to Rome by the poignant perspicacity of the Jewish sages — Rome, which was devoid of national roots of its own (בלא כתב ובלא לשון; *Avodah Zarah* 10a), had climbed the rocky heights of such political eminence only by means of violent presumptuousness.

Thus Rome's essential character, in contrast to Hellas's idealistic outlook, bears the stamp of blatant materialism. Its aim was the aggrandizement of material possessions; and glory and might themselves were only a means towards it. Usefulness was the measure of things and actions. Rome had neither time nor inclination for anything that might elevate the mind and lead the soul to a noble, freer development, for anything that might render man more human, and only insofar as these nobler things of the spirit appeared necessary, or, at least, useful for the preservation and furtherance of the base, material things, did those higher and nobler things become significant factors in the calculations of Roman wisdom ...

⋖§ Princes of Judea, Roman Tools

It was at this time of greatest degradation that the state of Judah first came into conflict with the Roman autocrats. Two brothers of the House of the Hasmoneans who were disputing the throne, which moreover, had been usurped, called upon one of the Roman legates, advancing at the head of his legions, to act as arbitrator. A third claimant also appeared — the people accused both of them that they, or rather their House, by usurping royal honors alien to the Jewish institutions, had violated the people's most cherished rights and had endangered all that it held sacred.

At the very moment when Pompey's legate, Scaurus, saw Jewish envoys before him, some 130 years before the fall of Jerusalem, Jerusalem was lost. From that moment Rome did not take her eyes off Judea. While, through their governors and the hirelings raised by them to the rank of princes, they sucked the blood of Judea, they inoculated Judea's princes and grandees with the spirit of their system, plunged them all into the sink of sensual debauchery and taught them at the same time to misuse religion, temple, priesthood, the judiciary, fatherland and their status as princes, as mere tools and means of power and self-aggrandizement, and to degrade everything holy and pure, everything great and divine to the role of counters in egotistic petty jobbery.

The spirit of Rome had banished the soul from the Jewish temple, and because of this the Majesty of G-d delivered up the temple and priests, king and throne in anger to the Roman legions and, with the faithful people, went into exile.

Let, therefore, the days in the Jewish Calendar that commemorate the downfall be to us a warning against the Roman spirit.

Not Hellenic idealism, but Roman materialism, is what we have to fear. ...

Rabbi Avrohom Chaim Feuer

Chanukah: The Other Side of the Coin

The downfall of the Chashmonaim in the political arena

⋖§ Why Victorious Warriors Failed as Kings

THE CHASHMONAIM, as the heroes who made possible the rededication of the Bais HaMikdash, are responsible for having given us the Chanukah celebration. But their further history and its significance is not as widely known as their glorious victories, though it offers us an equally important insight into the special nature of the Jewish people. In essence, we celebrate the spiritual elevation of the Chashmonaim at the time of the *Chanukas HaMikdash,* and close our eyes to their anti-climatic downfall:

• The entire 103-year reign of the Hasmonean dynasty was scarred with bloodshed and turbulent internal strife.

• Finally, the last remnants of the family were assassinated in a most disgraceful manner by their servant Herod.

What was it that toppled the *Chashmonaim* from the height of glory to defeat and disgrace?

Our father Yaakov decreed: "The staff of monarchy shall not depart from Yehudah" (Genesis 49:10). For any other tribe to assume the monarchy was to defy the will of Yaakov, and to encroach upon the rightful domain of Yehudah. This was the sin of the Chashmonaim who assumed the monarchy in the period of the Second Bais HaMikdash. Though they were saints of the highest order — were it not for them, Torah and mitzvos would have been forgotten in Israel — they were punished most gravely (Ramban).

We can hardly believe that the Chashmonaim were unaware of the expressed desire of Yaakov, and the law of the Torah requiring that the monarchy must remain in the house of Yehudah. Perhaps we can re-construct their thinking along these lines:

Of course the monarchy must be held only by Yehudah — *in normal times;* but these are not normal times. *Klal Yisrael* is achieving political and religious independence for the first time since the destruction of the first *Bais HaMikdash.* Two hundred and eighty-four years of exile and domination by foreign powers are now coming to an end. We are witnessing the liberation and rebirth of our nation. At such a critical juncture in the history of our people, we cannot entrust leadership simply on the basis of a hereditary claim. There must be at the helm of our nation the most saintly priests *(Kohanim)* whose dedication and abilities have been proven on the field of battle and in the sanctity of the *Bais HaMikdash.* We have suffered the inroads of the Hellenist culture with its worldly philosophies, its atheism and hedonism, its antipathy to Torah. The masses have been weaned away from Torah, and the sovereignty of Torah in Jewish life must be restored. Surely we who have fought and bled for the *Derech Hashem,* for the Way of G-d, are most capable of leading our people through this critical period. "In a time when we must stand up for G-d, we may momentarily annul His Law" (Tehillim 119:126).

◆§ Lofty Thoughts

These were lofty thoughts, nobly motivated, but the grim fate of the Chashmonaim, the *Ramban* observes, proves that they sorely miscalculated.

Precisely because of the disbelieving spirit of the times, an era of philosophical questioning and searching, an age when all human thought was being held up to the probing light of logic, and that which man's limited mentality failed to comprehend was deemed false — precisely in such a period must Patriarchal traditions and Torah law be unswervingly guarded. It was in such a time, more than any other time, that the Jewish People dared not pit the human intellect against the immutable, eternal, unfathomable word of G-d.

The Jewish nation was fully aware of the superiority of the Chashmonaim in every way. Were they not the most faithful, fearless and unflinching servants of G-d, proven by their courage to take up battle aganst overwhelming odds? Had not the Almighty shown them a special sign of Providence and affection manifested by the miracle of the menorah? Were they not of the most aristocratic lineage, unparalleled for purity and nobility, renowned for their service to *Klal Yisrael* for generations? And most important and decisive, the reins of goverment were theirs — free to do as they wished — and worthy of the highest reward for their heroic efforts. Who could the house of Yehudah present to equal these uncontestable prerequisites in a bid for the throne?

◀§ The Sovereign is His to Choose

If at that moment the Chashmonaim would have stood up and boldly proclaimed: "It is G-d's will which crowns kings" (*Mishlei* 8:14) — the sovereign is His to choose, and no human calculations can dispute His choice. *The staff of monarchy shall not depart from Yehudah.* Yaakov Avinu expressed G-d's wish that Yehudah should reign, and no human reason could annul this divine stamp of approval. Who can tell how much disbelief in the sanctity of Torah would have been wiped out from amidst *Klal Yisrael* with such an awesome measure of faith? Who can tell how much *Kavod HaTorah* would have triumphed with an act of surrender to the divine will?

The Chashmonaim had just experienced a miracle which enabled them to use only the purest materials in serving G-d, and saved them from resorting to contaminated oils which may be used only in cases of emergency. An expression of the divine will was inherent in this miracle: At this crucial moment, Torah must be kept pure and whole — without compromise. Perhaps it was the glory of victory that blinded these *tzaddikim* ever so slightly and caused them to misunderstand the message of the Chanukah lights.

Our brothers in Israel have seen miraculous events in our time. The celebration of Chanukah should refresh our memories of the miracles which throughout the ages have kept us alive in violation of all the "laws" of history. May the Chanukah lights illuminate the pages of Jewish history that we may clearly read its message.

A. Scheinman

"And 'Darkness' —
That is Greece"

*Philosophy as
the hand-maiden of Torah
as opposed to
the Greek philosophy*

OUR SAGES, when explaining the deeper meanings of the
Torah's account of creation, have written that the nihilistic
forces of *tohu, vohu, choshech,* and *t'hom (void, formlessness,
darkness,* and *abyss)* are manifest in four nations that have risen
to rule the world: Babylonia, Persia, Greece and Rome ... Greece
is equated to darkness. This is puzzling, for although w
recognize the many faults and shortcomings that lie beneath t¹ ᵉ
civilized veneer of Greece, compared to the swamp of idolatry a: .d
ignorance that preceded it, it would seem that Greece was a spark
of light, rather than a shroud of darkness. Was it not Greek
thought that planted the seeds of reason that ultimately displaced
polytheism in modern society?

There was a long period in Jewish history — from Rabbeinu
Saadiah Gaon (10th Century) through the *Rishonim,* up until the
R'mak and the *Ari* (16th Century) — when the main thrust of
religious thought was based on philosophy. Although the conclu-
sions of the rabbis' reasoning were certainly different from those
of Greek philosophers, their terminology and approach were

definitely based on those of the Greeks. Did not the great *Rambam* state: "In all matters submetaphysical Aristotle is correct?" and "Aristotle almost reached the rank of *navi* (prophet)?" The justification for this approach lay in the interpretation the sages give to the verse, "The beauty of *Yefes* adorns the tents of *Shem*," *(Bereishis* 9:27), inferring that the beauty of *Yefes* (i.e. Greece) has a definite place in the tents of *Shem* (i.e. Israel) [See *Rashi*]. How, then, do we differentiate between philosophy as *chachmas Yevanis* (according to one interpretation), in which one is prohibited to engage under the penalty of loss of one's share in the World to Come, and the philosophy of "the beauty of *Yefes?*" (A complete answer would fill many tomes, encompassing scores of different interpretations. This article is focusing on just one of the many aspects of this question.)

⥁ Two Aspects of Philosophy

To understand this, we must differentiate between two different aspects of philosophy: a disciplined thought system, used to explain and categorize events; and a "way of life" and a parameter of existence.

The first aspect is that which is included in the "beauty of Yefes," which one may bring into the tents of Shem. It is one of the "seventy facets of Torah," and as such was employed by the *Rambam* and many more of the *Rishonim* as a method of expounding the Torah.

Yet, there is another aspect of philosophy — one that is normative rather than descriptive. It rests on the axiom, "Nothing exists that cannot be comprehended through reason, and anything that cannot be comprehended through reason does not exist." Here lies the unbridgeable schism between Israel and the philosophers of Greece. For, while Israel's is a theo-centric world, employing thought and logic to understand that which is accessible to logic, Greece's is a homo-centric world, using reason to define its boundaries. Even if the thinkers of Greece understand and accept G-d and Torah, it is because *they* perceive it thus, and *they* understand it so. While we believe that G-d created man, to their view it is man's understanding that created G-d.

It is in this aspect that Greek philosophy was a darkness infinitely worse than idolatry. For an idolator still understands the world to be theo-centered, and if he searches long enough, he will find the Initial Cause — like the conclusion in *Avraham Avinu's* debate with Nimrod, the fire worshiper: "Worship water for it is stronger than fire; worship clouds for they are stronger than water; worship winds, etc., etc." By following this chain of thought, one can someday arrive at the ultimate destination, the true Deity. By contrast, once a person is locked in the vicious cycle of self-belief, he has no hope of exiting. Even if someone convinces him of the truth of G-d and the Torah, *he* still is the god; he believes because *he* believes! His awareness-cum-belief encompasses the two "I's" of philosophy. The "I" of thought and the "I" of existence.

Various sages have been quoted as saying that all philosophy is worthless, save for Kant's. One feels that this refers to the elements in Kant's philosophy (i.e. critique of pure reasoning) that limits the scope of philosophy itself. By showing that philosophy is limited, and cannot be used as a parameter of existence, Kant took a courageous step in the right direction.

An Orthodox Jew who has occasion to mingle with people far removed from Torah, whether Jewish or not, may often find himself treated with respect or understanding regarding his way of life and practices. Yet one point always seems to bother others: "It is nice, but you don't really believe that a G-d came down and told you to do all these things, do you?"

In light of this, it is no accident that Greek idols all possessed human characteristics — super-people with human frailties on a divine scale. *For it was humankind as a whole that was being idolized* ... A western journalist visiting India ridiculed the animal worship so rampant there. The Indian countered, "But you too worship an animal."

The journalist inquired, "Which animal?"

"Man," answered the Indian.

⊰§ Monarchy or Kehunah

The leadership of *Klal Yisrael* is divided amongst the monarchy, the *Sanhedrin* and the *Kehunah Gedolah* (high priesthood). The first two were usually the leaders of *Klal Yisrael.* Yet, against Yavan the *Kohanim* were picked to lead the fight. For it was not the Torah *per se* that Yavan was trying to uproot; rather, it was Torah as stemming from the Divine source. Thus it was the task of the *Kohanim* as the agents of G-d on earth to combat Yavan.

When Alexander (who heralded the beginning of Hellenization) came to *Yerushalayim,* Shimon HaTzaddik the *Kohen Gadol* confronted him in the full regalia of his office. When Alexander bowed to him, the eventual victory of *Yisrael* over Yavan was assured for the generations to come.

Rabbi Avrohom Chaim Feuer

One Candle
for One Nation

*The unifying force
of the Jewish family
... and Chanukah*

THE SMALL CANDLE flickers madly, feebly trying to spread
and prolong its light. It counts its ebbing moments of life, as it
swiftly consumes itself in its sacred mission of fiery death.

All eyes are fixed upon these frail flames, searching for a
fresh vision; a new spark of deeper meaning. *"Mai Chanukah?"*
What are these days really all about? How different is this
festival! Other festivals are doubly blessed with pageantry:
bursting with historic backdrops to their timeless themes. Other
holidays are wonderfully packed with full-time holiness and
celebration.

Not so Chanukah. Eight days — a long stretch of oppor-
tunities for ceremony. Yet the chances are often squandered. Each
day seems to merit mere shreds, scraps of remembrance. A match
strikes a box, and a candle is quickly lit. The family hastily
gathers for blessings and rousing song. With more haste the
group abruptly disperses, each to his own pursuits. The lights
linger on — lonely — but not for long. So ends the daily ritual.

Strange — Chanukah: a morsel of inspiration snatched almost imperceptibly from the daily grind.

I stare, I search, I wonder. Where in these tiny candles shall I find a lesson for all time? My wandering eyes stray from the luminous menorah and focus upon the close-knit group which gathers around it. The family clusters together, attracted magnetically both by love and the Chanukah lights. *"Neir echad ish u'veiso"* — One candle for a man and his family. That is quite sufficient. All else is embellishment. Interestingly, this law — even this terminology — is not found elsewhere. Convenience, closeness, and camaraderie bring relatives together for Succos and Pesach. On Chanukah, however, the *law*, not *circumstance*, makes necessary the kindling together with kin. Why? There is a faint feeling here, a subtle sense of touching a truth. Let us try to unravel the winding thread of thought.

◦§ A Nation of Families

The people of Israel have long been chastised and condemned for their clannishness. Jewish family life confounds the evil and bitter hearts of our foes. So we take no insult from the charge: it is this closeness we exalt.

Family is the fabric of our People, a durable cloth woven by a tenacious and baffling nearness. *Mishpachah* is one of the warmest words in a vocabulary which overflows with warm phrases.

We are the Chosen, yet few know why. We bear a message, but only a handful know it. Read it for yourself: G-d promised *Avraham Avinu* that he alone would father prophetic people. Why? "For I have known him, to the end that he may command his children and his household after him, that they may keep the way of the L-rd ... " *(Bereishis* 18:19). No mention here of the myriad converts which Avraham brought under the wings of the *Shechinah.* No trace nor whisper of his piety. Avraham was, above all, *a father.* Sons, daughters, descendants: these are the fundamentals of the future, the bedrock of the universal mission. Only these will cement the chosen family.

A family resembles a mound of stones. When one is removed, the entire heap trembles. If one is added, the whole mound is strengthened, (Bereishes Rabbah 100:7).

Moderns have little use for cumbersome family ties in their life style. Relationships are perfectly casual and free of responsibility. The bounties of the fascinating future await only those who will courageously jump forward and free themselves of the past. The new world beckons only to those who have forsaken the old.

Such was the philosophy of the Greek who preached for a departure from tradition. Reality demands a fresh start, a breakaway. Only in the myths could parental prides still be tolerated and protected.

Perhaps this was a legacy from father Yefes, the sire of Yavan and of all Greeks. He was the first to call out, *"Every man for himself."*

The sons of Yefes were ... Yavan. ... Of these were the isles of the nations divided in their lands, every one after his tongue, after their families, in their nations (Bereishis 10:2-5).

Ramban observes that the progeny of Yefes differed from all other families in that others assembled within specific boundaries, whereas Yefes spread out and scattered. Each son of Yefes struck out for himself: alone, in far off lands and on far flung islands.

Noach hinted at this in his blessings to his sons. "May G-d spread out Yefes and dwell in the tents of Shem." Shem personifies communal solidarity (tents) and a tight social structure. He displayed this by his efforts to protect the honor of his father and family. Yefes lacked that binding force. His offspring crumbled into a piecemeal collection of warring factions and countless, autonomous city-states. Indeed, this fragmentation was abundantly evident in ancient Greece, the land of miniature monarchies.

As her mighty armies spread the world-over, Greece's iconoclastic ideas followed the camp. The havoc, which conquering hordes failed to bring upon the Jewish fold, threatened to be wrought by the soft and persuasive tones of the divisive foreign culture. The schism was inevitable. The new arts, the fresh forms and shapes — all these could not conform to the archaic ancestral design. The gap between the generations grew wider. Jewish children were lured from their fathers with slogans: "The individual loses his identity within the family." "Everyone who wants to be someone must make his own life style." The age-old family harmony was no more. Once proud homes stood desolate and forlorn. Tradition heaved a lonely sigh.

Yet at the core there remained a precious seedling which struggled to survive. The *Kohanim*, sons of Aharon, dug in; they

Chanukah

would not budge. They zealously guarded their genealogy and strong family ties.

> *An incident occurred concerning Miriam the daughter of Bilgah (the priest) who turned apostate and wed an officer in the service of the Greek monarchy. When the Greeks entered the Bais HaMikdash, she banged on the holy altar with her shoe and shouted, "Wolf, wolf, how long will you devour the money of Israel and yet fail to help in the time of their duress?" When the Sages heard of this they fined her entire family unit ... (Succah 56b).*

The Gemara goes on to explain that a child is the product of his environment. The youth reflects the flaws of his elders. No parents carry so great a responsibility to protect their children as do the *Kohanim*, thereby justifying the severity of the punishment. Sons of Aharon are the chosen within the Chosen — older brothers to all the family of Israel.

And so it was fitting that Mattisyahu and his sons took the offensive. Only a priestly family, steeled by a patriarch, could counter the invader. Here the spiritual menace was met measure for measure, matched blow for blow. These brothers risked their lives and lost them, in fighting for the nation as a whole. It is here that yet another neglected theme of Chanukah presents itself with passionate impact.

◆§ Martyrdom for the Mishpachah

No sacrifice less than *mesiras nefesh* could save Israel's soul. Only martyrdom could keep the great *mishpachah* intact. Remember — do not forget! — Chanah's seven sons, who as one, sanctified G-d's name. They died embraced as seven bodies sharing one brotherly soul. Fortunate is the family which unites in such glory!

"And I will be sanctified in the midst of the Children of Israel." Martyrdom, death for the glory of G-d, is the only *mitzvah* which the Torah insists be carried out before a *minyan*. All other requirements for a *minyan* were enacted by the Rabbis. The Torah teaches that self-sacrifice, self-destruction, is a futile effort unless it contributes to the collective sanctity of the community. G-d does not ask us to die for His sake alone. He has no need for our sacramental flesh and blood. G-d only asks a Jew to lay down his life so that the family of Israel will derive an awesome and staggering inspiration from his death.

"This is my G-d and I will glorify Him ... " *(Exodus 15:2).*

When does this glorification have full meaning? When does sacrifice have true content? — When it is (as the passage concludes) ... "My father's G-d, and I will exalt Him."

It is from this verse that we derive the precept of *hiddur mitzvah*, enhancing a *mitzvah* for G-d's glory. Chanukah is unique in its emphasis on elaborating and embellishing the lighting of the candles so as to be classed among the *mehadrin min hamehadrin* — a term found nowhere else, perhaps because Chanukah is the holiday most concerned with exalting the G-d of our fathers, their traditions, and the Jewish family.

'Blessed are You, Hashem our G-d, who has sanctified us with His mitzvos, and has commanded us to kindle the light of Chanukah.' — And where do we find that the Torah has thus commanded? From the verse, ' ... Ask thy father and he shall tell you; your elders, and they shall say it to you' (*Shabbos* 23a).

Again and again we find Chanukah closely tied to family. This is the festival of fathers and sons. This is the holiday of the re-established home.

He who is careful with the lighting of the (Chanukah) candles will merit sons who will be talmidei chachamim (*Shabbos* 23b).

The house in which the Chanukah flames are kept is guaranteed to be a home. The father who painstakingly preserves their lesson is assured the proper development of his sons.

◆§ Cluster Round the Candle

And so we begin to understand why the family clusters around "one candle for one house." Chanukah commemorates not only the miracle of the oil, but also the marvel of the family which lights it. Chanukah is the family of Israel reborn.

Four times, the Sages tell us, Jews were in exile: Babylon, Persia, Greece and Rome. The first three have come and gone. Now we patiently endure the fourth — our nation dispersed the world over. By definition, exile means a loss of one's land; and being uprooted from heritage and home. This was true of the exiles of Babylon, Persia, and Rome. Yet, under the iron fist of Greece, we never suffered uprooting. How then were we in exile?

The home of the Jew is not his land. We are at home wherever we are at peace with our Father, our G-d. True, our land — the Land of Israel — is as close to His abode as we can be; yet there are times when even on the holy ground we remain estranged from our Maker. By alienating us from our G-d, the Greeks succeeded in driving us into the bitterest of all exiles. By depriving us of our Father, we were left with the emptiness of a broken home. By sowing the seeds of dissension among Jews, the Hellenes "dispersed" us into deep spiritual and social diaspora. For what is the darkest pain of exile if not estrangement from G-d and man?

Mesiras nefesh was the price that had to be paid in those terrible days in order to bring back the flock and gather in the fold. Only this brings the family back together. History is repeating itself in our trying times.

The modern State of Israel is a phenomenon which defies definition. Jews feel at home and yet we are well aware that the exile has by far not ended. At any moment we might, Heaven forbid, be driven from our land. Daily deaths and the constant fear of all-out war are stark reminders that *Moshiach* has not yet come. The churches and mosques that occupy our holiest places repudiate our false sense of rest. We live within our biblical boundaries as a sovereign commonwealth, and yet we are not fully free: in exile in our own Land.

We call modern Israel "the ingathering of exiles," yet the nation is far from unity. Party strife, dissension, militarism — all these fragment the nation. What sort of home breeds animosity among brothers? Pitiful are the wretched orphans without a Father ... .

Would that we could unite in a coalition for life, with spiritual meaning ... Would that we could cluster around the one candle of Chanukah — not simply of Yahrzeit and remembrance. For we are all brothers, sons of One Father. "*Neir echad ish u'veiso.*" One candle for G-d and all of His children.

Adapted from Bais Yisroel
by Rabbi Nosson Scherman

Chanukah Gems

Selections from the writings
of the Gerrer Rebbe,
Rabbi Yisroel Alter ל״צז

⋖§ Chanukah Rededication, and the Mark of Abraham

WHEN THEY DROVE the Syrian-Greeks out of Jerusalem, the Chashmonaim converged on the Temple to kindle the Menorah anew. But the enemy had contaminated all the jugs of pure oil. "They (the Chashmonaim) searched but they could find only one jug of oil which still lay with the seal of the *Kohen Gadol* — the High Priest" *(Shabbos* 21b).

It seemed clear that no pure oil was to be had. Nevertheless, they searched and found! That, too, was one of the eternal lessons of the miracle of Chanukah: There is no room for despair in Jewish life. One must search; and if one seeks, he will find. When effort is expended, results are achieved.

The *Sfas Emes* (Gerrer Rebbe at the turn of the century) said in the name of his grandfather, the *Chiddushei HaRim*, that in a deeper sense, the "seal of the High Priest" has many more implications beyond the particular priest of the Temple service in the era of the Chanukah miracle. It can also refer to our father Abraham. Abraham is described in Scriptures as "the eternal priest" *(Tehillim* 110:4), and, of course, Abraham towered high among spiritual giants. We can therefore interpret in the eternal spiritual sense that Abraham was a *Kohen Gadol* (High Priest) whose seal safeguarded the precious little jug of oil — his offspring, *Klal Yisrael*. The qualities of Abraham became indelibly sealed into not only the flesh of his progeny (a reference to circumcision of which it is said that Abraham sealed his offspring with the sign of the eternal covenant), but also in their personality and character. The determination of Abraham in his youth to seek out the identity of Him who created heaven and earth was transmitted to all future generations. Thus it was that his descendents could muster the zeal to continue searching for a means to rekindle the extinguished flames of the Menorah long after it was "conclusively proven" that no purity could have survived the long ravages of Antiochus's hordes.

King Solomon taught in Proverbs: "Train a youth according to his way, even when he is old, he will not withdraw from it" (*Mishlei* 22:6). In addition to the simple meaning, that proper training in youth will leave its mark through adulthood and into old age, the verse has a further message. The word *chanoch* "train" in this verse refers to education, but it is also related to Chanukah — dedication of the new, and rededication and renewal of the old. Training and renewal go hand in hand, for it is an essential characterisitic of greatness that one never grows stale and static. One must always retain the vigor and intellectual suppleness of youth. Train a youth, and renew your own youthfulness — for the "youth" you are responsible to train need not only be your neighbor's or your own progeny; the youth should be *yourself*. Your own training and renewal, too, dare not be neglected.

This lesson, also, is foreshadowed by Abraham. When he surmounted the final supreme challenge, the *akeidah*, the Torah tells us, "and Abraham returned to his youths" (i.e. his servants). Homiletically, we are taught that even in his old age, at the zenith of his career, Abraham returned to his *own* youthfulness. He had triumphed over all adversity, but satisfaction with his lot did not enter into his makeup. Instead, he returned to the youthful quest of new challenges and greater heights.

It was the same quest for greatness that had characterized his ascent of the mountain with Isaac. Then, he had mustered all his strength to rise to the occasion. Now, too, he returned with the freshness of which newer triumphs are made. Symbolically, when Abraham announced to his servants that he would climb the mountain escorted only by Isaac, he said that he and the lad would go עַד כֹּה, until there. The word כֹּה has the numerical value of twenty-five, an allusion to Chanukah which begins on 25 Kislev. He was declaring that he and Isaac were embarking on a journey to attain the conceptual heights symbolized by Chanukah. Indeed, Chanukah — training and renewal — is a call to youthful vigor and determination. It is Abraham's legacy.

◦§ Chanukah, Aharon, and the Public Celebration

Chanukah is a time when all Jews can draw close to the service of G-d. As *Chiddushei HaRim* said, the merit of the Chashmonaim was that by risking their lives to sanctify His Name, they effected a change ... an enhancement of the Jewish people's composite character, enabling all Jews to be worthy of G-d's miraculous salvation. The Chashmonaim acted on behalf of the entire nation and because they did, they imbued all Israel with the capacity to serve G-d better throughout all generations. That generation of *Kohanim* contributed its bravery and dedication — and the historic result they brought about — to the rest of the nation through all future generations.

This helps us understand the significance of the priestly seal which attested to the purity of the lone useable jug of oil that was found in the otherwise totally defiled Temple. This process had been set in motion by the first and quintessential High Priest, Aharon, who is described as one who loved and pursued peace, who loved people and drew them close to Torah. Aharon was concerned with the needs of others and sought ways to benefit them. Chanukah, too, is a time that calls upon us to seek to help others, as we find that an integral part of the commandment to kindle the menorah is *pirsumei nisa*, to make a public display of the remembrance of the miracle. That a private observance is insufficient implies that we are required to bring about in others as well as within ourselves a heightened awareness of G-d's greatness and mercy. This is indeed the attribute of Aharon, who labored to bring people closer to Torah.

This quality of Aharon is a major feature of his particular role — and the role of the priestly family in general — among Israel. For at the time when the *Mishkan* (tabernacle) was dedicated in the Wilderness, each tribal leader had his own day when, as the *nassi* of his tribe, he brought gifts and offerings to the newly built *Mishkan*. Aharon, however, was given no such privilege, although he was the *nasi* of the tribe of Levi. He grieved at his exclusion and assumed that it was because of his role in the erection of the Golden Calf. G-d comforted him by commanding him to kindle the Menorah, telling him that his role was greater than theirs "for you are to stand and prepare the lights" (see *Rashi* at the beginning of *B'haalos'cha*).

King Solomon in *Mishlei* refers to the human soul as *neir*, a light of G-d. Aharon's calling was to kindle — to kindle flames of a Menorah and flames of human souls. As *Ramban* comments, the other tribal leaders would have their day of spiritual glory, bring their offerings, and then retire to the sidelines. Aharon's task, however, would endure forever, for not only the *Mishkan* and Temple service would begin with the preparation and kindling of the Menorah, but his descendants at the time of the Chanukah miracle would rekindle the eternal light of Torah which had nearly been extinguished and which, but for them, would have been snuffed out.

Aharon's other task, the responsibility to kindle human beings and ignite them to greater efforts for G-d and for Torah — that, too, would continue forever. As prophesied, his descendants proved it dramatically by being the instruments of the Chanukah miracle and its resultant elevation of the entire nation with the zeal to sacrifice for Torah and the ability to bring about miracles. The outcome of the rebellion against the Syrian-Greeks was due to the valor of the Chashmonaim; but, true to the tradition of their priestly ancestor, they did not keep the fruits of victory for themselves. They shared the flame, the lights, the brilliance with others. They proclaimed a festival, an integral part of which is promotion of the public awareness that the flame of Torah is the central motif of the nation, the magnet that draws every Jew closer to his Maker.

◆§ The Left in Service of the Right

In "*HaNeiros Halalu*" we say, *These flames are holy, we have no right to use them.* The term *Kodesh*, holy, has a particular connotation, for the Sages teach that it is incumbent upon a Jew to sanctify himself particularly in areas that are permitted to him (see *Ramban* in *Vayikra* 19:1). There is a particular moral danger in indulgence in the permitted pleasures of life. It is much more difficult to avoid kosher gluttony than to avoid bacon. Indeed, the moral triumph over the undue desire for the permissible is the major factor in producing the *holy* person, as opposed to the person who merely avoids transgression.

To attain this degree of holiness, a person must resolve that he go beyond avoidance of over-indulgence in physical pleasures lest he become a pleasure-oriented person; he must even learn to utilize the permissible for holy ends.

Sifsei Tzaddik quotes *Chiddushei HaRim* on the custom of giving *Chanukah Gelt*, gifts of money to children in honor of Chanukah. Scripture states, "בשמאלה עושר וכבוד" — *in the left hand is wealth and honor" (Mishlei 3:16)*. The implication is — as real life bears out — that wealth brings honor in its wake. Who does not know that the rich receive tributes undreamt of by the poor? But the same verse begins by saying, "Long life is in the right hand." "Long life" refers to the values that are eternal, that live on forever — dedication to the study of Torah and acceptance of the yoke of G-d's kingdom. Once those priorities are firmly grasped in the strong right hand of a person's value system, he need not fear the tempting distractions of prosperity and honor. These moral marauders all too often lead a person away from a life of spiritual values and holiness, but not the person whose first priority is Torah and reverence of G-d. With that sense of what he aspires to be, he will know how to utilize the most tempting temporal successes for their proper roles. He will turn them to the service of his overriding aspiration to hold Torah and fear of G-d uppermost. Thereby, his use of the mundane for high purpose will raise his level of holiness.

Alluding to this concept is the *halachah* that when the Chanukah flames are kindled in a doorway, the *mezuzah* adorns the right-hand doorpost while the menorah is placed next to the left-hand doorpost. "Right" represents the lofty, spiritual aspects of life, while "left" represents the mundane and material. The chapters inside the *mezuzah* express man's acceptance of G-d as King. With that done, the Jew's primary world, his spiritual values, is set aright. Now his material world, represented by the left side, can be enjoyed. But even then, these passions and possessions must also be sanctified by *mitzvos*, for the Jew dare not relegate this service of G-d merely to the obviously "religious" functions of Torah study, prayer and charity giving. Thus, even the left-hand side — symbolic of the totally secular areas of life — is used for the placement of the menorah.

Further expressive of this concept is the Talmudic statement that it is forbidden to count money by the light of the Chanukah flames. The Sages were careful in their choice of illustration for the law prohibiting use of the menorah's illumination for mundane purposes: "counting money" is the best example of temporal goods dedicated to amassing further wealth and luxury. The left side of life becomes hallowed by the *mitzvah* of menorah — it should not be soiled and debased by thoughts of possessing money for the sake of simply accumulating more money. If money *per se* is important to someone, it can be destructive. But if money does not matter, then it becomes truly significant because it has been relegated to a means of doing good.

In this sense, "*HaNeiros Halalu*" declares that the flames are holy. True, their sanctity is not equivalent to that of a sacrificial offering or a pair of *tefillin*. Nonetheless they are holy, for they are meant to represent and bring about the attitude that renders holy all aspects of life.

Indeed, the expression *neir*, flame, alludes to people as well as to fire, because the soul of man is referred to by Scripture as a flame. Man's own soul, no less than his possessions, must be sanctified. Such an achievement need not — in most circumstances *can* not — come about suddenly and completely. With commitment comes a gradual elevation. Often, only a single area of a man's existence will be sanctified, but that single small step can be enough to transform a person entirely, because holiness has a way of expanding and overcoming opposing forces within man. The Talmud teaches that the Chanukah menorah may be kindled until the last *footsteps of pedestrians* disappear from the nighttime marketplace. Following our line of interpretation, we may read into this *halachah* the idea that the person kindling the menorah must strive to remove his *own* feet from the corrosive influence of the wordly marketplace.

Is that a small achievement? The "foot" is no longer present — but what of the rest of his body, his mind, and his desires? The Talmud teaches in a different context that if an owner proclaims "May the foot of my animal receive the holiness of a burnt-offering," the entire animal becomes a burnt-offering, because the holiness of the foot spreads and encompasses the entire animal. Such is the power of sanctity. And such is the intent of the Sages in cryptically using the disappearance of a "foot from the marketplace" as the controlling factor in the time of kindling. Aside from the chronological implications, Chanukah's very purpose is to inspire Jews with the resolve to take the first step in attaining holiness. Let that step be taken, and the entire person has been placed on the road to sanctity.

Interestingly enough, the Sages derive that the binding nature of the Rabbinic decrees, like the requirement to kindle the menorah, are from the Scriptural injunction that Israel is not to deviate from the words of the Rabbis "to the right or to the left." Upon this verse the Sages expound that even as they tell you that your left hand is truly your right hand, you must believe them. The Sages cite this exegesis in connection with Chanukah because the commandment of Chanukah is precisely that: take your left — your earthly physical desires — and transform them into your right. Make *everything* in your life a vehicle for holiness by obeying those who teach you to do so. Therefore, the *halachah* teaches us further that even if one must borrow or sell his belongings in order to raise funds to buy Chanukah lights, one must do so. Through his willingness to sacrifice what little property he has for the sake of Chanukah, he will be given a blessing commensurate with his deed. By putting the *mitzvah* ahead of the material dictates, he removes his "left hand" from the domination of material concern; his reward will be that the left hand will be filled with wealth and honor — because it made itself a willing and eager servant of the holiness represented by the right hand.

◂§ Chanukah, the Termination of the Bikkurim Season

Chanukah is climaxed on the eighth night — we find other *mitzvos* that involve the number eight: *Shemini Atzeres;* the eighth dedication day of the *Mishkan;* circumcision on the child's eighth day of life; and the eighth day of Solomon's joyful dedication of the *Bais HaMikdash.* Always, the eighth represents completion of a holy task, the attainment of a level exalted above the mundane earth, which was created in only seven days. Everything is evaluated according to its completion. If a noble effort ends in failure, then the steps leading up to it lose their significance, even though one is rewarded for having made the attempt. But if it ends in success, then every effort contributing to that success shares in the greatness of the achievement: The number of flames increases in importance as it leads to the successful conclusion of the holy series of days.

The *Mishnah* teaches us that if someone neglected to bring in his *Bikkurim* (first fruits offering) before Succos, as the Torah commands — he may bring them to the *Bais HaMikdash* until Chanukah — but he may *not* read the required chapter that is meant to be recited when the first fruits are presented to the *Kohen.* If the fruits were not brought by Chanukah, then last year's fruits may no longer be brought, for with the advent of Chanukah, a new season begins.

This law, apparently unrelated to Chanukah, is actually a lesson in the deeper significance of Chanukah. With the coming of the holiday of dedication and renewal, a new period begins. The past is gone and the Jew looks ahead to the new year and a new resolve that the first fruit he produced from a new set of labors is to belong to G-d and His most loyal servants, the *Kohanim.*

Thus does Chanukah teach a lesson of freshness and rededication. Never be satisfied with the past. Continue to advance. Whether the past brought success or frustration, Chanukah marks the time to move on to new service and new sacrifice, to look forward to the time when one can say, "I have transcended my earthly desires, G-d. The first fruits of my labors are a source of pride to me, and therefore I present them to You!"

Rabbi Zev Hoberman

Chanukah
and Hoda'ah

*The festival of gratitude
and the
"magi'a li" syndrome*

IN RESPONSE to the question, "What is Chanukah?", the Talmud gives a brief account of the Chanukah miracle, and concludes that these eight days were established as a festival to be celebrated with *Hallel VeHoda'ah* — praise and gratitude. As the basis for Chanukah, they are certainly both worthy of study. The following discussion focuses on the thread of *hoda'ah*, which interwoven with *Hallel* forms the cloth from which Chanukah is cut. To appreciate the role of *hoda'ah* in Chanukah, one must gain a broader understanding of *hoda'ah* in general.

◆§ Four Who Say Praise

The *Rambam* instructs us: "Four are required to give thanks: a person who has recovered from illness, a released prisoner, a sea voyager safely ashore, and a journeyer through wilderness who has safely reached a settlement. Gratitude must be proclaimed in the presence of ten, including two wise men, as it says: 'Exalt Him in public, praise Him in a session of the Elders' (*Tehillim* 107:32). How does one offer thanks and how does one honestly express the *brachah*? He stands among them and recites the *brachah: Hagomel lechayavim ...*" (*Hilchos Brachos* 10:8).

While in the main the *Rambam* seems to have recorded only what appears in the *Gemara*, a subtle difference is present: "How does one offer thanks? ... He stands among them." In the *Gemara* no mention is made of standing "among them" — rather than "before them." The *Rambam* had codified existing laws and would not have introduced such a requirement on his own. We shall endeavor to uncover the source of this requirement and to examine its profound implications.

The Midrash tells us that although a day will arrive when all *tefillos* and *korbanos* (prayers and sacrifices) will become extinct, *hoda'ah* and the *korban todah* will remain: two expressions of gratitude will prevail in the House of G-d, those of *tefillah* (prayer) and *korban* (sacrifice). Two questions arise: Why are the *hoda'ah* of *tefillah* and the *korban todah* fated for eternity, in contrast to all other *tefillos* and *korbanos*, which are not? What is the distinction between the two expressions of *hoda'ah (tefillah* and *korban)?* — for the Midrash does classify them as two separate entities.

One can better understand the ramifications of gratitude by examining the contrasting nature of ingratitude. There are many causes of ingratitude, but most pernicious is the *magi'a li* syndrome — when a person tends to consider whatever benefits he has been granted as his due, not the result of another's generosity. Thus, the recipient is without reason to be grateful for what he feels he justly deserves.

◄§ The Total Dependence of Man

In dealings between man and his peer, the *magi'a li* attitude is the classical attitude of *"sheloch sheli"* — the ill conceived notion that another's possessions are for one's own use. When the same proposition is applied to affairs between man and his Maker, it thoroughly undermines man's subservience to Divine dominion.

This point is brought into sharp focus by the *Maharal's* interpretation of the Talmudic discussion regarding the Thirteen Attributes of Mercy, which begins with the repetition of the Name signifying mercy: *Hashem, Hashem ...* [meaning] ... *I am merciful to man.* This expression of mercy is repeated because G-d is *twice* merciful to man: once before he has sinned and again after he has sinned *(Rosh HaShanah* 17).

The unavoidable question is: *Why must man avail himself of Divine mercy even before he has sinned? As long as his earthly* record presents only credits, has he not earned his keep? Is he not entitled to sustenance without the benefit of mercy and grace? The *Maharal* responds to this question. There are no Divine debts. Man's Maker owes him nothing. In the best of circumstances, man has nothing to bank on but Divine grace and mercy.

This premise is further substantiated by the *Ramban's* commentary in *Chumash:* Reward for *mitzvos* is *tzeddakah* — a Divine act of charity; for man's position is like that of a servant who is his master's property and as such is obligated to serve him with no claim to recompense. Whatever reward his master grants him is but *tzeddakah!* — the benefaction of His kindness. Thus, whoever seeks requital from his Maker is not a true servant of G-d, and has cast off the yoke of Divine dominion.

◆§ The Person-Factor in Hoda'ah

Man's resistance to fullest *hoda'ah* becomes clear from what appears to be an inconsistency among the verses in *Tehillim* that deal with the four aforementioned who bear the obligation of *hoda'ah*. Each of the four is reminded of his duty: "Pay homage to G-d for His grace and the wonders performed for the benefit of man" (*Tehillim* 107). However, only in reference to one who has recovered from an illness does the Psalmist also command *"Bring forth a korban todah."* Yet the *halachah* requires the sea-farer, the desert traveler, and the released prisoner to bring this *korban* as well as the recovered invalid.

Perhaps this inconsistency can be understood through a study of Job's reaction to his agonizing tribulations. He had been completely wiped out, left totally bereft of family and possessions. Nevertheless he was able to say "G-d gave and G-d took." This would seem to be the supreme *hoda'ah* — man saying to his Maker: *You owe me nothing. You are entitled to the return of all that You have entrusted with me.* But this still is not *hoda'ah* to perfection.

When Job was subsequently smitten with physical disease, he retained the superb fortitude to proclaim, "The good we accept from G-d, would we not accept the evil?" The verse then testifies: "And Job did not sin with his lips," to which *Chazal* add, "but in his heart he did sin." Despite Job's impeccable conduct in the face of the severest of tribulations — indeed, his lips had honored the most stringent demands of *hoda'ah* — in his heart a silent protest had stirred against the injustice of losing his physical well-being. He had felt entitled to this one miniscule claim from G-d, although he would not bring it to his lips. Thus he had fallen short of perfection, the unconditional confession that ... man has no claim on his Creator ... not even his own person.

A *korban* is meant to be a surrogate sacrifice of its owner. When bringing a *korban todah*, the owner sings: "King David's Song of Gratitude. ... He has fashioned us, and we are His" — even our very person is His. He proclaims before his Maker: You spared my life, but were not beholden to me to do so, for my life is not mine but Yours, as is borne out through the sacrifice of my *korban todah*.

The Psalmist's singling out of the recovered invalid to offer the sacrifice of a *korban todah* now becomes clear. True, the lives of the sea-farer, the desert traveler and the released prisoner have also been spared, but only from extraneous threats; none was attacked from within as was the man whose body was racked by illness, surviving a threat to his very person. All four who survived a mortal threat should bring a *korban todah*, but none so much as he whose ordeal was akin to Job's.

Thus we have the division of *hoda'ah* into categories: *todas hatefillah* — the gratitude expressed through prayer for the security of one's life and one's possessions, and *todas hakorban*, which deals specifically with the *hoda'ah* for the sparing of one's flesh and bones. The heart of the "*ba'al korban todah*" must succeed where the heart of Job was found wanting.

◄§ The Eternity of Gratitude

There is an element in *hoda'ah* and *korban todah* that invests them with eternity which other *tefillos* and *korbanos* lack. Again we refer to the *Maharal*, who addressed himself directly to this principle: *tefillah* is essentially a request for the fulfillment of human needs. When the Messianic era of fulfillment arrives, *tefillah* will be without purpose. *Korbanos* are meant to correct man's deficiency in one area or another: again, in an era where perfection will be the norm and deficiencies a thing of the past, *korbanos* will be obsolete.

Hoda'ah and *korban todah*, however, are neither requests for the fulfillment of needs, nor means for correcting deficiencies, but expressions of recognition of Divine sovereignty and grace which are all the more appropriate when Heavenly benefaction is at its zenith. The obligation to be thankful never ceases; it grows in proportion to the magnitude of the favor for which it is expressed. Gratitude is eternal and defies obsolescence.

The Individual and the Congregation in Hoda'ah

"Sacred matters require a quorum of ten."

"The *brachah* of *hoda'ah* is recited in the presence of ten."

These two rulings appear to be a statement of *halachah* and its applications, two aspects of the same principle. It is our contention that they are parallel — similar in course, but never intersecting. The quorum for the performance of sacred acts is referred to as an *"eidah,"* while the *minyan* required for *Bircas Hoda'ah* is referred to as a *"kahal,"* ("Exalt him in a congregation of the people.") The term *"eidah"* is understood in the sense of *eidus* — testimony — for it is the mission of *Klal Yisrael* to bear witness to the omnipresence and omnipotence of the *Shechinah.* *"Kahal"* implies a gathering of individuals, forming them into a single composite unit, of one mind and one heart; a blending of souls into one entity, akin to an individual man.

In the context of *kahal,* the individual trades his personal identity for a share in the composite identity of the *tzibbur.* Just as "There is no *eidah* numbering less than ten," so too, "There is no *kahal* numbering less than ten" (see *Rashi, Kesubos* 7b). *Eidah* and *kahal* indeed do seem similar. There is a difference, however. All that an *eidah* within *Klal Yisrael* demands is the minimum participation of ten of its souls. A *kahal* is different, as is implicit in the *Rambam's* requirement that *hoda'ah* be proclaimed not "before" a *kahal* of ten, but "amidst" the ten. As long as one retains his individuality, he is apt to fall prey to the *magi'a li* syndrome, tending to believe that whatever has been granted to him by the benevolence of his Creator is owed to him. Let him stand *among* them — let him blend with the *kahal* and share in their collective identity, so that his *hoda'ah* will flow from that realization that: "Man has no claim on his Creator." A sacred act conducted in the presence of an *eidah* can be performed "before" them. *Hoda'ah,* however, when recited in the presence of a *kahal,* is enhanced if it is expressed from "among" them.

The Hoda'ah of Chanuka

Hoda'ah has a very special relationship with Chanukah. The nature of the Greco-Syrian *galus* can be traced to the fountainhead of Greek imperial domination, Alexander the Great. A revealing insight into his nature emerges from an incident related in the Talmud *(Tamid* 32). On one of his explorations, Alexander chanced upon a spring of water that exuded an extraordinary fragrance. He followed the spring toward its source, to the gate of *Gan Eden*, whereupon he asked permission to enter. He was refused with the verse: "This is G-d's gate, the righteous may enter through it" *(Tehillim* 118:20).

He challenged this, exclaiming, "I am a king worthy of honor! You must grant me my demands!" In spite of his protests, Alexander the Great was refused entry into the Garden of Eden because its gate, as described in *Tehillim,* is reserved for the righteous.

The verse in *Tehillim* immediately preceding "This is G-d's gate," proclaims: "Open for me the Gates of Righteousness, I shall enter them and I shall express my gratitude *(hoda'ah)* to G-d." The implication is that these gates of Eden, reserved for the righteous, are opened to those who come forth with *hoda'ah*. And consequently, Alexander the Great was denied entry through these portals because he failed to express the required *hoda'ah*. Indeed, Alexander the Great was the antithesis of *hoda'ah* — far from standing among the *kahal,* permitting his identity to blend with others until it no longer bears the mark of his individuality. On the contrary, he stood at the very threshold of *hoda'ah* insisting: "I am King! You must grant me my demands!" The unspoken protests of Job in circumstances of severe provocation were fully articulated without restraint by Alexander the Great: "It is only just that you pay me my due, in accordance with my worth as a deserving individual."

As the fountainhead, so flows the stream. According to Hellenistic philosophy, man is a royal creature worthy of making his own way. Human qualities and endeavors are glorified to a point where they seem to justify demands for personal recognition and continuing sustenance.

It is this frame of mind which commits us to the imprisonment of *Galus Yavan*. Our redemption can only be signalled by a true-felt *hoda'ah,* imbued with the fundamental truth that "Man has no claims on his Creator." Chanukah is the final link in the chain of festivals. It must ultimately lead us along the path of *tzaddikim* to the portals of *Gan Eden*. Alexander the Great and Hellenism have come and gone, but *Klal Yisrael* illuminates herself and all the world with the glow of eternity — the eternal light of gratitude.

Rabbi Avrohom Chaim Feuer

The Age
of Illumination

*Some thoughts on introspection
and the nature of
the Chanukah lights*

OUR PROGRESSIVE AGE, by virtue of its countless advances
and discoveries, has been endowed with a great variety of
names: the Space Age, the Atomic Age, the Jet Age — to name but
a few. May we suggest yet another descriptive label: the Age of Illumination.

For many, many centuries man was actually half-blinded.
Daylight allowed his curious eyes the liberty of roaming at will,
but come night, man's free vision was limited by a blinding
darkness. Candles, oil, and wood fires were among the only
means of dispersing the enveloping gloom. These were either
costly, hazardous, unsteady, malodorous, dim, short-lived, or all
of these. In those, days, wax meant wealth, and adequate light
was a luxury reserved for the privileged. Many a mastermind
developed, and many a masterpiece was painstakingly created, by
the meager light of pale moonbeams.

Only recently — barely a hundred years have elapsed since
the invention of the lightbulb — did the genius of man transform
this bleak situation. Today, mankind's blindness is banished by
billions of powerful and enduring bulbs. Artificial light has

become so economically feasible that even the poorest can afford to squander it. Everything glows in the Age of Illumination.

One tends to take this abundance of light for granted, for even if one were to seriously evaluate the impact of light in its bountiful supply on the lifestyle of modern man, it would probably be measured in terms of convenience. In truth, universal illumination is far more than a pleasant fringe benefit of modern technology. It is a phenomenon that has had a profound effect on the mentality of today's man. The genie of the lamp has indeed performed a wondrous magical feat in which it has altered the nature of man decisively.

Modern man is under constant distraction. Endless illumination has given him the opportunity to become intensely aware of his surroundings. A result of this is an absorbing fascination with the world around him, accompanied by an oblivion to the complex cosmos *within* him. Modern man is pitifully neglected, for while he has scrutinized, analyzed and categorized every fragment of his environment, he has ignored himself. Modern man suffers a self-imposed loneliness.

Early man, the man in the dark, was sheltered from a great many distractions. The absence of technological sophistication was a handicap, but it brought rewards in other ways. Deprived of the ability to view the world without, man in the dark was afforded the opportunity and incentive to focus his undivided attention on the world within. In the unlit hours he had nothing else to do but think, and so he thought for himself and developed his own unique identity and opinion. He was not condemned to endure the pains of loneliness, but rather was blessed with the rich pleasures of solitude.

◄§ Finding the Light of Man's Soul

If one would look deeply enough into the dark one *will* see a light. It is the inner light, the soul of man.

"The candle of the L-rd is the soul of man, exploring all of the inner chambers" (Mishlei 20:27).

This is not meant as fanciful poetry or empty words. Those who have experienced the inner glow know that its radiance is very real, very meaningful ... It comes in flashes of truth and self-knowledge. And it is, indeed, a very splendid thing.

Our codifiers also recognize the validity of flashes in the dark. The *Rambam* teaches (*Hilchos Talmud Torah*) that although one is obligated to study the Torah at all times, the major portion of a person's wisdom is acquired in the still of the night. Torah study is, among other things, an exercise in self-discovery and improvement, and it should be studied in undisturbed nocturnal atmosphere. This inner light is very sensitive and must be carefully preserved: "A hasty step reduces the light of a person's eyes ... This light may be regained at the *Kiddush*" (*Shabbos* 113a).

The man who is engrossed in the frantic pursuit of all that he sees around him is doomed to lose sight of the candle that burns within him. Only the serene sanctity of the *Shabbos*, its tranquil cessation of activity and hot pursuit, can restore to man his awareness of the precious inner light of his vision and his soul.

There is yet another period in the Sabbath day that is especially suited for regaining the awareness of the inner light.

"One hour of repentance and good deeds in this world is more precious than all of the World to Come" (*Avos* 4:22). The *Rebbe* of Kotzk explained: "This refers to the very last hour of the *Shabbos* when all of the feeble candles have long died out. In the grip of the inescapable darkness one is finally confronted with the grim reality of one's self. The man who know himself cannot fail to repent."

Anyone who has partaken of a *shalosh seudos* meal without artificial lighting — in a twilight fading into an enveloping blackness — has also experienced the pinpointing stab of inner light that the Kotzker Rebbe describes.

✺§ The Light of Thirty-Six

No Jewish holiday so lends itself to the challenges of the Age of Illumination as does the holiday of Chanukah, the festival of lights. If in doubt as to which lights are being celebrated, the outer or the inner — one need only to consult our sacred literature and find that these eight days are dedicated specifically to these latter lights, the internal illumination that brightens the soul.

The *Rokeach*, Rabbi Eliezer of Worms, a noted medieval scholar and authority, pointed out that a total of thirty-six candles are lit on the eight days of Chanukah. This corresponds to the first thirty-six hours of creation when a special unearthly radiance lit the universe. This spiritual light was quite different from any light we know now. But its potency was too intense to serve man's everyday, earthly needs and G-d hid it from view. Yet that light still exists — in the Torah — and it is for this reason that the Aramaic term for Torah is *Oraisa* — source of light.

One may wonder — if it was destined for concealment why did G-d ever create this advanced form of light? The answer to this is classically Jewish — better a hidden light than no light at all. For even though it was hidden, the light does exist and can be revealed to anyone who sincerely strives to find it. Those few who have succeeded in perceiving this light are the legendary *lamed-vav'niks*, the thirty-six righteous men concealed from recognition in every generation.

Actually, one need not be a *lamed-vavnik* to uncover at least a portion of this hidden light, for anyone who studies Torah with sincerity may discover its splendor.

The *Chasam Sofer* made the following observation: "The two *brachos* that precede the recital of the morning *Shema* seem to be totally unrelated. First, in the blessing of "*Yotzer HaMeoros*" we praise G-d as the creator of the Heavenly lights. Then we proceed to an entirely different theme and in the blessing of "*Ahavah Rabbah*" we thank G-d for giving us the Torah. There is significance in the juxtaposition, for nothing illustrates a point as vividly as comparison. Torah is a source of light, and so are the heavenly bodies. In the *brachah* of "*Yotzer HaMeoros*" we observe the limited external lights. It is then that we can truly appreciate the penetrating and revealing inner light of the Torah, which lights up our eyes and instills within us a deeper awareness of the concealed dimensions of reality. 'Light up our eyes with Your Torah,' we plead. External light and secular analysis at best can only illuminate the object being studied. Torah, by contrast, lights up one's very eyes."

◆§ Eye Appeal

All of this, of course, is related to the Chanukah theme. But in dealing with Chanukah, we must begin with the threat that brought about the entire Chanukah chapter in our history — the Greeks and their mighty civilization. Yavan, the prototype Greek, was the son of Yefes (Japheth), whose province was *yofi* — aesthetics and eye-appealing beauty (*Bereishis* 9:27). G-d endowed Yefes with an extraordinary genius for visual arts and skillfully executed forms. However, the passage concludes, "*but He will dwell in the tents of Shem.*" Graceful shapes are only superficial, so G-d has selected the inner chambers of the humble tents of Shem for his place of dwelling.

The contours and shapes of things fascinated the early Greeks. The exquisite curves and smoothly sculpted flesh of the human form were especially dear to their appreciative sense of beauty. They were exhilarated by the contemplation of precise geometric forms and angles, and symmetrical architectural colossi left them breathless. They also relished verbal beauty. Flowing rhetoric and impressive sophistry enjoyed great popularity. In short, appearance and form counted far more than inner content. The package prevailed over the product. And when Socrates started to search for substance he was treated to a cup of deadly hemlock.

The Greeks followed their eyes. The Jews followed their soul. The Torah warns: " ... And you shall not stray after your hearts and after your eyes" (Bamidbar 15:39). Rashi comments: "The eyes see and the heart desires ... ." Man's heart is caught up in an eternal tug-of-war. The eyes against the soul, the outer light against the inner light. The eyes breed desire while the soul fosters content. Each element seeks to overwhelm the other. And this is the Kulturkampf of Yefes versus Shem, Greek versus Jew.

◌§ The Inward Focus

There was a time when it seemed as if the Greek conquerors of Judea were going to be victorious in this fierce ideological struggle. Suddenly, the Chashmonaim, the priestly guardians of the inner sanctum, entered the struggle and overcame the Greeks. The Festival of Chanukah commemorates their renovation and rededication of the Bais HaMikdash. But in truth, their main objective was to renovate and rededicate the Jewish heart. They had to rip the Jew's attention away from the outer lights and focus it once again on the inner glow. They fashioned a new menorah, not out of the customary metal, gold, but rather out of plain iron rods (Rosh HaShanah 24b). Aesthetics have a very prominent place in Torah philosophy, but only as long as the external ornament serves to enhance the inner spirit. The Greeks had taught the Jews to appreciate adornment purely for its own sake, to accept beauty as an independent value. The Chashmonaim sought to refute that doctrine by practicing a rigid simplicity.

But why did they select the menorah for emphasis? Actually the Talmud (Shabbos 22b) questions the very necessity of a menorah in the Temple: "Did they then need it for light? (They had ample light from natural sources.) Rather, the light of the menorah was a testimony to all the peoples of the world that G-d's presence dwelt inside the sanctuary."

Centuries ago, prior to the Age of Illumination, people did

not waste light. A fire with no function was promptly extinguished, and the fuel was carefully hoarded. If the flames of the menorah burned constantly without any apparent function, it must have been that this was not a light made to shed external illumination, but rather to symbolize the inner glory associated with G-dliness.

For this reason, it is prohibited to use the Chanukah candles as illumination for any ordinary activities. Such utility would strip the candles of their essential message — that there is more than one kind of light, that of the soul besides that of the eyes.

"The time for lighting the Chanukah candles is from sunset until the time that all traffic ceases in the marketplace" (*Shabbos* 21b).

As long as men are involved in the affairs of the market place, as long as they are engaged in the pursuit and purchase of all that their eyes see and their hearts desire — then they are still in need of the lesson of the Chanukah menorah.

No doubt, our era is the age of the eye and the age of the market. This is so self-evident it does not require much elaboration. When before in history has the consumer been flooded with so staggering an array of tempting products wrapped in billions of dollars worth of "eye-catching" advertisement? When before has the human eye been so constantly exposed to the distracting sights of the stage, screen, and street? In the Age of Illumination, the outer lights have all but successfully blotted out the inner lights.

It is time to gather around the thirty-six candles of the menorah and give the inner lights the opportunity to convey their soft, subtle, penetrating message.

Rabbi Moshe Sherer

Golah or Ge'ulah

Reflections on
Chanukah

IN THE HAFTARAH of Shabbos Chanukah, the Prophet
describes his vision: *And behold there was a golden Menorah*
with a bowl (gulah) *on its top (Zechariah* 4:2). Our Sages
declare in the Midrash that this Menorah is symbolic of *Klal*
Yisrael; and then, in a beautiful word-play, point out that the
work gulah (גֻּלָּה), the golden bowl topping the Menorah, implies
Golah (גָּלָה) — dispersion, and *Geulah* (גְּאוּלָה) — redemption.

The Menorah symbol bears within it these two paradoxical
aspects: how one interprets this symbol in his approach to life
determines whether he takes the road to *Golah*, to disaster, or to
Ge'ulah, to victory and eternity. The events of Chanukah help us
better understand how this one symbol can branch off into two
such diverse ends.

☐ The Jewish camp in the days of Antiochus was split. The
Hellenists *(Misyavnim)* stressed the outer forms of Judaism, the
ceremonial. All they saw in the Menorah was the pure glittering
gold which pleased their aesthetic sense. The Chashmonaim, on
the other hand, looked deeper and saw the pure oil, the inner
warmth emanating from a light kindled in holiness. A concern
with the externals of religion leads ultimately to *Golah*, to a loss of
Jewish cohesiveness. The road to *Ge'ulah* demands penetration to
the substance, commitment to the core — to content.

□ The miracle of the one day supply of oil that burned for eight days is central in the Chanukah theme. Many commentators have given differing explanations as to why Chanukah celebrates an *eight*-day miracle, which the *Bais Yosef* points out was actually only a *seven*-day miracle, since there was sufficient oil to burn the first day. One sage wisely observed that the miracle of the first day was manifest in the courage of the Chashmonaim to initiate the lighting of the Menorah, when logic dictated that their effort to maintain the *Neir Tamid* would quickly be dissipated. To achieve *Geulah* one must have the capacity to reach out for the unattainable. Were the Jew to have been deterred by his inadequacies and inhibited by his limitations, he would long ago have been swallowed up by the *Golah*.

□ The events of Chanukah yield another significant insight. The Greeks contaminated the oils in the *Bais HaMikdash*. The question arises: If the Greeks aimed to black out the Menorah forever, would it not have better suited their purpose to *completely* destroy the oils instead of only contaminating them?

However, their method exposes their sinister intentions. The Greeks reasoned: Let the Menorah lights burn brightly — but let the flames arise from contaminated oils; let them shed a false light. The Greeks understood that their devilish design to subvert Torah would be better achieved if they could cause the Jewish people to illuminate the world with impure oils. The purity of Judaism is the determinant of *Golah* or *Ge'ulah*.

◆§ The Light That Penetrates

In recent years, Madison Avenue has developed a booming Chanukah industry in an effort to exploit the Menorah, as they did *(lehavdil)* with the Xmas tree. During this season, newspaper advertisements offer varieties of Chanukah Menorahs (all styles and shapes — even musical Menorahs that play *Hava Nagilah)*, Chanukah greeting cards, Chanukah candies, Chanukah wrapping paper. With all this hoopla, the meaning of Chanukah has had little impact on the uneducated Jew. Contrast this with the experience of our grandparents: many of them lit their *neiros* in crude utensils, but the light they kindled penetrated every nook of their homes.

Like the Hellenists, our generation has enthroned the externals of the Menorah, and extended this philosophy into all aspects of their Jewish living. We have taken a leaf from the lessons of a super-salesman, Elmer Wheeler, who instructed restauranteurs: *"Don't sell the steak, sell the sizzle!"* By selling the "sizzle" of *mitzvos*, instead of the life-giving substance of Yiddishkeit, the spiritual hucksters have projected our generation on the *Golah* road instead of the road to *Ge'ulah.*

Furthermore, our generation has lost its belief in miracles, and has placed its faith in studies, surveys and resolutions. They have exchanged the spiritual daring of our fathers for a cold, pragmatic approach to Judaism. Proper goals for genuine Judaism are often diluted because they do not seem practical. The lesson of the one-day supply of oil of the Chashmonaim era seems to have passed by our generation, as we plod along with our chilling 'realism.'

What is most remarkable in this analogy is that the strategy of the modern-day Hellenist forces is strikingly similar to the tactics of the Greeks of old. Only the scenery has changed. There are very many movements in Jewry that have kindled lights which they hold proudly aloft, but the flame in their Menorah comes from the defiled oil, which they themselves have contaminated by trampling on basic Jewish concepts. All of these Menorahs that have been lit by the forces that work from within to overthrow Torah authority and classical Judaism, have contributed to the chaos and confusion which characterize Jewish life today.

In Israel, for example, a Jewish flame has been lit which casts its light into every corner of the globe. Indeed the Menorah has become the official national symbol of the State of Israel. As each year goes by, it becomes increasingly obvious that the light that goes forth from Zion is hardly *distinctively Jewish.* Indeed, it is difficult to distinguish it from all the other national lights that emanate from the nations of the world. Is building a Jewish State without the Jewish soul a step toward *Ge'ulah,* or is it creating yet another spiritual *Golah?*

In the United States, Jewish life can best be characterized as glittering and dazzling on the outside, but eroded and cold on the inside. Here too, the modern day Hellenists are building a Judaism based on slogans instead of sincerity, on theatrics instead of theology. The endless-varieties of Judaism competing for the attention of the American Jew are making a pretense of saving our youth with cliches and ceremonials. Today they are the sad witnesses of the appalling results of this policy of serving our youth adulterated spiritual lollipops, instead of inspiring them with the broad majestic sweep of our Torah.

ᐰᔥ ᐰᔥ ᐰᔥ

In contrast to all other *Yomim Tovim*, where there is a specific *mitzvah* of *simchah*, a command to rejoice, we find no such *mitzvah* regarding Chanukah. Why? Should not the victories and miracles of Chanukah also be marked with the same degree of joy as all other holidays?

A great rabbi once gave this explanation: The battle of Chanukah, although blessed with temporary victory in the days of the Chashmonaim, *never really ended* — it continues to this very day. It was essentially a struggle against the forces that had set as their goal להשכיחם תורתך ולהעבירם מחוקי רצונך — to make the Torah a museum-piece and to assimilate the Jewish masses by subterfuge and internal subversion. This battle to confuse and betray true Judaism still rages in our times, and while engulfed in the smoke of battle, one does not pause to rejoice. In such a continuing crisis, one must concentrate with greater vigor towards the *Ge'ulah* goal: total Torah commitment must replace tokenism; complete consecration must replace crippling compromise.

Rabbi Avrohom Chaim Feuer

Three Dark Days
In Teves

The inter-relationship
between
three consecutive days
of calamity

THE OCCURRENCE of a single calamity in isolation might be attributed to chance. Even two tragedies coming together might be interpreted as merely a spate of hard luck. But when *three days* of misfortunes occur in a row, one attempts to discern a definite pattern to the events. Such is the case with the month of Teves, wherein we encounter three consecutive days of mourning. In truth, the events of these three fateful days occurred in different generations, and no apparent relationship exists between them. Moreover, this calendar of grief must be read backwards — ten ... nine ... eight ... — for that is their order of occurrence. Yet three tragedies in series can be no coincidence, so we must search for a thread that can bind these separate events with one tragic theme.

◆§ Estrangement from Homeland and Heritage

The month of Teves marks the estrangement of the Jew from his homeland and his heritage. On the tenth, Asarah b'Teves, in the year 3338, Nebuchadnezar, King of Babylon, began his successful siege of Jerusalem which ultimately brought about the destruction of the Temple and the dispersion of Israel into far-flung exile. Toward the end of the seven decades of exile that followed the destruction, the Jews appeared to be on the verge of being swallowed up by these foreign lands, when Ezra the Scribe appeared on the scene. This leader worked incessantly to rebuild the land to fortify the faith, until he died on the ninth of Teves in 3448 (see *Orach Chaim* 580, *Magen Avraham* 6).

At this point, the destiny of the Jewish people seemed uncertain, and to the onlooker, events could have turned either way — fast fidelity to tradition, or experimental innovation. With the absence of Ezra, the fate of Israel and its Torah seemed to hang in balance.

On the eighth of Teves the die was cast. This day marks the completion of the first translation of the Torah into a foreign language — Greek. The monumental work is known as the *Targum HaShivim*, the translation of the seventy, or the Septuagint.

The year was 3515 after the Creation, and the *Kohen Gadol*, Elazar, brother of the renowned Shimon HaTzaddik, dispatched seventy-two brilliant scholars to Alexandria to translate the Torah for Emperor Ptolemy Philadelphus of Egypt. Ptolemy, the tolerant and enlightened bibliophile, was motivated by his ardent love of books and manuscripts. Some reports tell us that his vast bibliotecha contained 300,000 volumes; others put the figure at a staggering 700,000 *(Seder HaDoros)*. Without a translation of the famed Jewish Torah, his library was not complete.

The events surrounding this episode seem to suggest that Elazar, the High Priest and spirtual leader of world Jewry, may have had more than the wishes of Ptolemy in mind when he consented to this epoch-making undertaking. His actions may have been spurred by holier motives, for he was witness to a painful decline in Jewish literacy and general awareness. In some of the more remote Jewish communities, the identity of Israel was slowly becoming assimilated into the reigning culture of Greece. The large and influential Jewish community of Alexandria, capital of the Greco-Egyptian empire, was especially alienated from its Jewish heritage, estranged by the foreign culture which saturated the very air they breathed. To make the word of G-d accessible to the vast Greek-speaking and thinking community may have been Elazar's purpose in cooperating with the monumental enterprise known as the *Targum HaShivim,* the Septuagint version of the Bible. This would serve to convince the straying youth that the Jews did indeed possess a glorious literature rivaling that of the Greeks. This was the first recorded propaganda action geared to inform the world of the worth of Torah.

◆§ Earth Rejoiced, Heaven Mourned

Even the heavens seemed to sanction and encourage the project. The work of the translators was blessed by an auspicious miracle. Ptolemy isolated each of the seventy-two scholars in private quarters on the isle of Pharos to insure that each would present an independent piece of work. As they grappled with their tasks, each one of the scholars came to realize that the Torah in its authentic, unamended form would be subject to misinterpretation in the translation. Changes would have to be made. Wondrously, all of them were divinely inspired to make the exact same alterations — fourteen in all.

For these reasons, the Jews of Alexandria and Egypt celebrated the eighth of Teves as a holiday for many years. Philo reported that the Jewish populace would go out to the Isle of Pharos on that day to commemorate the event with feasting and song.

As we find so often in our study of Jewish history, the earth rejoiced, but the heavens mourned. The Torah had been defiled.

"When the Torah was translated into the Greek the world was shrouded in darkness for three days" (Megillas Taanis).

"This event was as disasterous as the creation of the Golden Calf, for it is impossible to translate the Torah faithfully" (Maseches Sofrim 1:8).

Those who had designed the Golden Calf were spurred by the finest intentions. "G-d is too awesome and remote," they said. "We need a substantial intermediary to bridge the gap between heaven and earth."

This may sound impressive, but it is heresy. For although G-d is lofty, He is near. He is awesome, yet loving. He is beyond human comprehension, yet His truth is most simple. If an intermediary is introduced between G-d and man, one is left with nothing but a pagan perversion.

Those who sponsored the *Targum HaShivim* were also spurred by holy zeal. "The Torah is too esoteric," they said. "Its language is too removed from our daily life. Let us make a translation to fill the chasm between the Torah and man."

This may sound appealing, yet it is heresy. For although the Torah is lofty, it is very near. The Torah is vast, yet painstakingly specific. The Torah envisions Utopia, yet it is so practical in meeting the demands of ordinary life.

The Torah is a book of life — as amazing and frightening and powerful and awesome as life itself. Translate the Torah, and it becomes merely another volume *about* life, a text *discussing* life, a lifeless piece of literature.

◆§ Ezra's Solution

The full impact of the debacle which befell us on the eighth can only be appreciated when compared to the achievements of Ezra the Scribe, the hero who departed on the ninth.

This great leader had also lived in troubled and tragic times. He lived in an age when confusion was supreme. The lines of communication between the Torah and the people had been all but obliterated by decades of foreign exile.

The *Rambam* describes the acute situation of illiteracy, and the Scribe's solution for it (*Hilchos Tefillah*, Chapter 1:4):

"*From the time that the Jews had been exiled by Nebuchadnezzar the wicked, they mixed with the Persians and Greeks and other nations. They bore children in these foreign lands and the language of their offspring became confused and garbled, and the speech of each was a mixture of many tongues ... as it is written (Nechemiah 13:24): 'And the children spoke half in the tongue of Ashdod, and could not speak in the Jew's language, but rather according to the language of each people.' Consequently, when any of them wished to pray, or to recount the praises of G-d, he was unable to do so in the Holy Tongue without mixing in other languages. So when Ezra and his Bais Din became aware of this, they arose and composed for the people Eighteen Benedictions in an orderly fashion ... so that the prayer would be set and organized, and so that the people would learn to pray in a pure and flawless speech.*"

This was only the beginning of Ezra's educational plans. The basics, the very *Aleph-Bais* of the Torah itself, had been forgotten by many. Elementary principles of Judaism were slipping into disuse. So Ezra instituted the public reading of the Law thrice weekly, and had the text orally translated and fully explained by competent scholars who educated the ignorant and alienated populace. "And they read in the Book, in the Law of G-d, distinctly;

and they gave the sense (the translation) and caused them (the populace) to understand the reading" *(Nechemiah* 8:8).

This system represented an unprecedented and as yet unparalleled feat of nationwide adult education, which other nations have not come close to duplicating (see Josephus, *Contra Apion).*

◆§ To Change the Torah, or to Change the People?

Ezra and Elazar — both *Kohanim,* both leaders, both teachers. Both were confronted with the prodigious problem of nationwide Torah illiteracy. Each one tackled the problem differently. One changed the Torah to fit the needs of the people. One changed the people to fit the demands of the Torah.

Ezra realized that the Torah cannot be preserved if the entire community receives it second-hand, via translations which dismally fail to capture the deep meanings and subtle nuances of the Holy Tongue. The very spirit of the Law is inseparably woven into the fabric of this language, sanctified by the Law-giver. Each Hebrew word is pregnant with countless meanings which are the sources of innumerable derivations and interpretations of the sacred text. The original language is no mere linguistic happenstance. It is an indispensable vehicle with which to convey the very lifeblood of the Law. If the bulk of the community is knowledgeable of the original Hebrew, perhaps one may provide translations for illiterate individuals, for the integrity of the tradition still remains intact. But formally rewriting the Torah and then basing the fundamental knowledge of the majority of the people on such a source is a risk with our heritage that must never be taken.

Indeed, that very first translation testified to its own potential danger. As mentioned previously, a miracle had occurred and identical alterations had been made. This was essential to prevent misunderstanding, but at the same time, it demonstrated undeniably that once a translation is attempted, changes and misconceptions must creep into the hallowed pages. Should an entire nation be educated in such a manner, the authentic version is eventually grotesquely distorted. The parchment reeks of the spirit of Greece, and Torah becomes reduced to merely another piece of Greco-Judaic mythology (G-d forbid).

Ptolemy prided himself as being "Philadelphus," the tolerant man of brotherly love. It is possible that he would have respected Elazar's refusal to translate the Torah on the grounds that it was contrary to his religion. The ultimate blame for the dangerous translation must lie with Elazar himself.

By contrast, Ezra's ordinance is still honored by Jews the world over, and the text that he used is still read thrice weekly in the original Hebrew, just as in days of yore. As for the Septuagint — I have never seen one nor has my neighbor. Nothing remains of those Greek Jews of Alexandria. Had Ezra lived in those times, the translation would never have happened.

◂§ Reversed Sequence

Three black days in Teves. Three major setbacks in the progress of Israel's historic Torah mission. And for this reason is the sequence of these days backwards. The darkness began on the tenth — the day the siege of Jerusalem began ... *One day* ... Ezra struggled to dispel this darkness, but his efforts were cut short on the ninth ... *Two days* ... Had Elazar the High Priest guarded the Torah carefully, he might have succeeded in turning the darkness of both previous days back to light. But he failed, and so the darkness was destined to stay ... *The third day* ...

"*When the Torah was translated into the Greek the world was shrouded in darkness for three days.*"

"*The three-fold cord is not quickly broken (Koheles 24:12).*"

◈§ Purim / *Miracle in Disguise*

recognizing the "Hidden Face" of the Almighty ... threat, response and observance ... the defeat of impulsiveness the elusive king

Rabbi Elkanah Schwartz

Why Purim?

Some answers focusing on the Purim miracle and other "natural events."

FUNDAMENTAL to Jewish belief is recognition of Divine control of the universe. There are no accidents. Everything — literally everything — is so because the Almighty makes it so. The concept of *hashgachah peratis* (specific supervision) refers to the control of the Divine Being over everything that is and everything that occurs. In fact, this belief is the first of *Rambam's* Thirteen Principles of Faith: *"I firmly believe that the Creator, Blessed is His name, is the Creator and Ruler of all created beings, and that He alone has made, does make, and ever will make all things."*

Divine control, however, functions in two patterns, *teva* — nature, and *neis* — miracle. "Nature" means that the Almighty moves everything within an identifiable and predictable order; we describe as "natural" those events that occur by Divine control within this order. Miracle means "unnatural" — something which, while occurring through Divine control, does not fall within any identifiable or predictable order. Miracles, too, function in two patterns: in one, the *neis niglah*, Divine control is revealed, and the miracle is recognized as such; in the other, the *neis nistar*, Divine control is hidden, and the miracle is made to appear as a natural occurrence. The miracle of Chanukah was through the first pattern; the miracle of Purim, through the second. While the miracle of Chanukah was obvious — a one-day supply of oil burned for eight days — the miracle of Purim was not obvious. The entire Book of Esther reveals nothing miraculous: a pleasant story, of almost fairy-tale outline, telling of a wicked man's downfall, and the triumph of the hero and heroine.

The Rabbis of the Talmud discuss this, reporting that the Book of Esther, which does not mention even once the name of the Almighty, is a case of a miracle camouflaged to appear as a natural occurrence.

◆§ Nature of Hiddenness

One might wonder whether any natural-appearing event is really a camouflaged miracle. If so, is one required to make a holiday for every joyful event, since one cannot always know whether, like Purim, it is a miracle in disguise?

Perhaps so — were it not for our Rabbis who revealed the miraculous nature of the Purim events, thereby teaching faith in the Almighty, to recognize that He is truly directing the circumstances surrounding individual and collective lives along patterns destined for their benefit, though one may not at the time be aware of it — just as Mordechai, Esther, and the other Jews of the time were initially not aware of the miraculous nature of the "natural-appearing" events of their time. Now that Purim has been identified as a miracle, it is to be treated as such. Many a disguised miracle may be taking place at any time, but we do not treat them as such since they have not been identified.

The unique standing of Purim as a hidden miracle later revealed, is identified in the Talmud (Chullin 139b): "Where is Esther indicated in the Torah? In the verse, For I will surely hide (astir) my face (Devarim 31:18)."

Rather than merely developing a play on words (Esther/astir) the Rabbis of the Talmud were teaching "Where is it indicated in the Torah that there can be a miracle in disguise? — in the verse wherein the Almighty tells Moses that He will always guide the Jews through all the tribulations that may befall them except that His hand may not be revealed in the process; that He will never forsake His children, though they may not always be conscious of His presence; that 'Hester Panim,' literally 'Hidden Face,' is also a process of Divine Guidance."

In fact, Sforno comments on that verse: "Wherever the Jews

may be, My Divine Presence will be hidden within them." Truly, how can the continued existence of the Jewish people throughout these milliennia of *galus* and persecution be explained, other than to recognize the Divine Presence within Jewry, even if it be hidden from them?

◄§ Universal Significance

As is well known the miracle of Purim took place outside *Eretz Yisrael*, in contrast to the miracle of Chanukah, which occurred in Jerusalem. Purim is the reassurance to the Jewish People that they will never succumb, even amid the worst offensives by the nations of the world — on their own terrain.

And while Purim was not the only time that the Almighty helped His children through difficulties by natural-appearing methods, Purim is the only such event whose identity was revealed to give Jews an annual reassurance of the Divine Presence behind the *Hester Panim* (the "Hidden Face").

That is why the Purim celebration goes beyond celebrating the miracle of Mordechai and Esther, just as Mordechai and Esther willed to the Jewish People that it go beyond that. It must enter the realm of year-round service to the Almighty, to seek greater grasp and deeper understanding of faith in the Almighty.

Purim occurs exactly one month before Pesach. The miracles of Pesach are recounted for us: in the Torah, in the Haggadah, and every day in our prayers when we speak of rememberance of the Exodus from Egypt. The miracles of Pesach occurred not only before the eyes of the Jews but before the eyes of all the world, who recognized the miracles as such: *"The peoples have heard, they tremble: pangs have taken hold on the inhabitants of Philistia. Then were the chiefs of Edom frightened; the Mighty men of Moab, trembling takes hold upon them; all the inhabitants of Canaan are melted away. Terror and dread falls upon them; by the greatness of Your arm they are as still as a stone"(Shemos* 15:14-16). The miracle of Purim might have slipped by as another of many events where good triumphed over evil, had not the secret been revealed. The reason — to remind us of that important aspect of our faith: the "Hidden Face" of the Almighty, which functions not only on Purim, but eternally.

◄§ Unique, Yet Ordinary

Small wonder, then, that the fulfillment of Purim is through acts which appear ordinary, but when understood within the above context become extraordinary. Consider, first, the reading of the *Megillah:*

Every *Shabbos* and *Yom Tov* morning, and every fast day following the reading of the Torah at *Minchah,* a selection from the Prophets is read with blessings. Every *Tishah B'Av* evening, the entire Book of *Eichah* is read without the preface of a blessing. Thus, the essential practice of reading Scripture publicly is not unique to Purim, but Purim is the only time one *must* both read Scripture (other than the Pentateuch) from a parchment scroll and recite blessings over the reading.

Then, comes a second *mitzvah* of Purim, *mishlo'ach manos,* sending food packages to a friend; and a third *mitzvah, matanos la'evyonim,* gifts to the poor; and a fourth *mitzvah, seudas Purim,* the festive meal. None of these is unique as are blowing the shofar on Rosh Hashanah, handling the *lulav* and *esrog* on Succos, or eating *marror* and *charoses* on Pesach. There are other times during the year when we read from the Scriptures; when we send gifts to friends and to the poor; and when we enjoy a hearty meal.

But then, if Purim is a celebration of a miracle disguised as a natural event, then the fulfillment of Purim should also appear as something natural, although in reality it is not. One must be aware, while listening to the reading of the *Megillah,* sending food packages to friends, giving gifts to the poor, or enjoying a festive meal, that all may appear "natural" — but in reality are not. Instead, one must be mindful of loftier meanings. It is simpler to be reminded of faith when doing something exotic; it is more difficult to be so reminded when we are doing something ordinary. But then, once reminded, the ordinary becomes extraordinary.

In a very special way then, Purim is an annual reminder of the very special way the Almighty takes care of His children: He is always there, even when they do not realize it.

Rabbi Nachman Bulman

Anti-Semitism and the Jewish Response

*Reflections on Purim
and its implications
to contemporary problems*

PURIM is a holiday with a mask.

Behind the mask, however, there lurks adult thought-fulness and penetrating insight. And there are three things of importance to be learned from Purim: the causes of anti-Semitism; the proper methods of defense against it, and how we ought to celebrate deliverance from its effects.

⮫ The Causes of Anti-Semitism

> *And Haman said to King Achashveirosh:*
> □ *"There is a certain people scattered and (yet) separated among the peoples in all provinces of thy kingdom;*
> □ *and their religious laws differ from those of all the other peoples;*
> □ *neither do they keep the religious laws of the king;*
> □ *nor would it profit the king to let them remain!"*

A Step By Step Evaluation

□ *scattered and (yet) separated*

These words are a concise and pungent statement of the dilemma which is at the heart of anti-Semitic sentiment. The anti-Semite sees Jews everywhere "scattered;" nowhere do they strive very hard to retain a cohesive and distinctive pattern of Jewish identity. He sees at the same time, however, that as a group, Jews are characterized by a quality of "stubborn indissolubility."

He may mistakenly attribute the paradox to a dark and ignoble hypocrisy on the part of the Jew. He may mistakenly attribute the paradox to the Jew's insufficiently strong desire for complete self-effacement and assimilation. He may never begin to fathom the matter as testimony, that *collectively*, the Jews *cannot* escape their historic destiny. He may never begin to sense that the seemingly interminable capacity of the Jewish people to renew its life from ashes of destruction, with creative powers unimpaired, is perhaps the most eloquent testimony that there is Divine meaning in the historic process.

He certainly fails to see himself as a "rod of Divine anger," whose purpose sometimes is to prevent the people of G-d from breaking down the Divinely established boundary "between Israel and the nations," to recall the Jew to an awareness of his Divinely ordained character and task, of his specific dependence for life and well being on Divine Providence, of his utter inability to find security through reliance on the good will of the nations.

All the same, he senses powerfully — often more so than individually "unconscious" Jews — the grip of the riddle of Jewish survival on his own psyche and that of his world. And without understanding, he rages frenziedly at the Jew because of the existence of the riddle.

□ *their religious laws differ from those of all the other peoples*

Here again, the eyes of hate sometimes penetrate, despite their distorted line of vision, to a depth of insight that cold and objective analysis does not reach. Haman perceived rightly, together with anti-Semites of every age, that Judaism is different, not only from *any* other religion, but also, from *all* other religions. He noted correctly that in human society religious denominational differences are usually harmonized under a broader common denominator of *fundamental substrata* of beliefs and values giving inner character and impulse to society; that usually the economic, political, social, and recreational phases of life, and even the inner state of the religious phase, are motivated by those "root" values, rather than by the doctrinal particularities debated in the official religious institutions.

But, he noted also, with sharp perceptiveness, that there are elements in Judaism that make impossible for its adherents genuine absorption in the total configuration of life's activities, with the peoples among whom they live.

An elusive and indefinable *otherness* remains. Some Jews seek to talk it out of existence by refusing to recognize the chosenness of Israel as a *historic* fact and referring to it as a "mere dogma" — which they can then contemptuously dismiss, as a vestige of "chauvinistic tribal thinking," and which therefore can hardly have meaning for people who live in the 20th century, and have made the spirit of its culture and science their own.

But Israel's chosenness is *not* a "mere dogma." It is a fundamental principle of Judaism to whose truth all history bears witness. Jews may sometimes not find that fact a personally pleasant one to perceive, but anti-Semites often *do* perceive it, as did Haman, when he railed at our being inseparably bound to a religion generically different from *all* other religions.

□ *neither do they keep the king's religious laws*

There have been times when the pressure exerted upon the Jew to conform to the dominant religious pattern, at least *in addition* to his own, has been direct and open. But even in democratic countries, where freedom of religion is legally guaranteed to the Jew, *the same pressure exists, though concealed.*

Social exclusions, occasional political and economic disabilities, discriminatory practices even in education, act upon the Jew's consciousness as a very real pressure to melt and reduce his own spiritual stature towards conformity with that of his surroundings.

In such a setting, blatant religious persecution may be replaced by friendly calls for Jewish self-effacement as a means of finding favor in the eyes of the Gentile world; the Jew finds himself dependent upon Gentile goodwill even in democratic countries. The net result is the same. There, destruction inflicted by outside hate; here, spiritual suicide, indirectly stimulated from without. (Let it be noted that these indirect pressures *need not* be decisive. In democratic societies they are not imposed through the total assent of the general community. In America, for instance, there are powerful currents which strive for the final removal of all inequity from American life; and for untrammeled liberty of body and soul for all Americans. Our point is that uncritical surrender by us to pressures for conformity to the mores and standards of our environment is by no means an indication of loyalty to America. Such surrender destroys the American dream. Our insistence on the right to remain what we are through Jewish history, experience and destiny, is precisely in line with the aspiration of the best of America. What is criticized here is the widely held fallacious notion, that in order to be good Americans, we must make common cause with those elements in American society that strive to mold America in a monolithic cast in every area of life other than the political.)

□ *nor would it profit the king to let them remain!*

This is the final hammer blow.

Substitute the idiom of the twentieth century for these words, and you will hear in them a most familiar note.

"Do you, little Jew, perchance live under the illusion that your genius and your efforts have contributed something of abiding value to our country? Are you fool enough to imagine yourself indispensable to us, on the basis of your record of achievement? How pitifully mistaken you are. Our future welfare is not dependent on whether you stay or go. Your Einsteins and Frankfurters we hate. Your Rickovers we know how to snub. In some places you are dirty communists, and in others, dirty capitalists. Some of you are too grasping in business. Others preach too loudly and too passionately against social injustice. Your children fill our academies of higher learning out of all proportion to your numbers, and many of them are much too brilliant. Too many of you are physicians and attorneys. You are almost a controlling force in our entertainment industry. And of late you have even invaded engineering in force."

As of today, these sentiments are shared consciously by, probably, only a small minority of the American people. Let us hope and pray that the numbers of that minority may change only by diminution. On too many occasions in our past history, however, such minorities have become majorities. It would hardly be the best part of wisdom, therefore, for us to seek *security* in the knowledge of our great contributions to the well-being of our land. Too often have we learned that the anti-Semitic cry "nor would it profit the king to let them remain, " is not stilled by reference to charts of Jewish achievement. (This article was written in 1964. In the light of recent history, the above point seems to have been prophetic. Editor)

⋖§ A Proper Jewish Response Pattern to the Threat of Anti-Semitism

Let us re-read the elements of the response pattern of the Persian Jewish community to the menace of Hamanism. Those elements were:

☐ *the ingathering of the Jewish community for common effort;*
☐ *fasting and repentance;*
☐ *Esther's intercession with the king.*

☐ *the ingathering of the Jewish community*

The first step in planning a Jewish defense effort against anti-Semitism must be the cultivation of a sense of common Jewish destiny. It may often be true that "where there are nine Jews there are ten opinions," and that, in the formulation of our own views and opinions on Judaism and the problems of Jewish life, we have often been a very fragmented people. It is equally true, however, that the threat of physical injury or annihilation from without has always served us as a unifying agent of uncommon effectiveness. We often may ardently and zealously differ in defining the *character of Judaism.* We have always known instinctively, however, that anti-Semitic blows aimed at the body of any single Jew, are aimed equally at the collective body of all Jews — whether of low or high station, whether materially poor or wealthy, whether religiously devout or not. An alarm of physical danger, therefore, has always transformed our inner divisiveness and our jealous insistence on unregimented individualism, into unity of purpose and self-regimented collective discipline.

If in our time and place the cry of Jews, let us say, behind the Iron Curtain, faced by a threat to their very existence, fails to elicit from us a sense of spontaneous solidarity with their cause, we ought to know that we have lost an irreplaceable element of Jewish strength for life.

☐ *fasting and repentance*

A sense of Jewish solidarity alone, however, for all its importance, will not suffice. Vitally necessary is a collective effort to retrieve the lost sense of Jewish spiritual unity, and to bring about a reunion between the people of Israel and its G-d and Torah. A central pillar in the structure of Jewish resistance against anti-Semitism has always been the unclouded awareness *that our own mental and emotional alienation from Torah is one of the most potent unseen allies of our enemies.* Through weakening our Jewish pride, such alienation makes us receptive to the unspeakable suspicion that perhaps our enemies are at least a little right. Sometimes it even reduces us to the degradation of "embracing the soul of our enemies," through blind aping of their way of life, at the very moment that they physically seek to destroy us.

On the other hand, rootedness in the knowledge and the love of Torah gives us an inner strength and dignity that physical persecution can never take from us. It spares us the humiliation that is the cruelest torture our enemies can inflict upon us. It safeguards us against the emotional collapse that is the lot of victims of physical persecution who are made to feel that their own existence is senseless. In one of the Jewish schools of Nazi-occupied Vilna, a Jewish child was asked: "If you could go to a non-Jewish school outside the ghetto, in which you could enjoy the warmth of sunshine and the pleasures of going to parks and playing with toys, wouldn't you rather go there, even if you had to become a Nazi to do so?" The child answered : "No, I would not. I would rather stay here." The choice of that child is the secret of Jewish eternity. In a lightning flash, anguished as we are by the *hester panim* (hiding of the Divine countenance) which attends Jewish suffering at anti-Semitic hands, we learn once again, that unless the soul takes precedence over the body, humanity must return to the jungle. We also learn, from the child's answer, that the only hope for a humanized humanity lies in the assertion of that supremacy.

☐ *Esther's intercession with the king*

In our day, the utilization of the services of our brethren in high station, who have free access to powerful persons or agencies, might be one of the most popular aspects of Jewish defense activities. Indeed, the method could be a proper one, given certain conditions, and has often been of great value in the alleviation of Jewish suffering.

Its limitations, however, ought also to be known. They are:

1. The Achashveiroshes of history are often erratic, vain, and stupid individuals. They are not always reliable. If their moods

and caprices happen to be fortunate ones for us, then "the evil decree" will be averted. But should our "Achashverosh" happen not to take favorable notice of our "Esther," then woe to us and woe to her. Sustained and *exclusive* reliance on the Achashveroshes of history has availed us little in time of need.

2. In approaching our "Esthers" and pleading with them to come to the assistance of their people, we would do will not to be fawning and excessively flattering. There are wellsprings of Jewish loyalty in the hearts of "Jews who live in palaces" too, but the wisest way to awaken that loyalty is to speak to them in the accents of Mordechai's admonition, "Think not to yourself that you will escape in the king's house, more than all the Jews. For if you altogether hold your peace at this time, then relief and deliverance will arise for the Jews from another place, but you and your father's house will perish."

To set up our "Esthers" as arbiters of Jewish destiny by making them authoritative Jewish communal figures in payment for their assistance towards the alleviation of Jewish suffering, is to commit a grievous error. It will not inspire them with greater dedication in the discharge of their task, *than can* the claim of unavoidable Jewish obligation. But it may, and often does, infect *us* with their alienation from Judaism, when we allow our "Esthers" a decisive voice in our religious and educational affairs, on the basis of their "defense" activities.

⋞ The Adopted Form of Purim Observance

In the traditional observance of Purim, the following aspects are included:

☐ *historic recollection;*
☐ *clever pedagogy;*
☐ *Jewish brotherhood;*
☐ *concern for the poor and needy; and*
☐ *merriment that is not escapist.*

☐ *sober historic recollection*

There is a striking introduction to the "carnival" spirit of Purim. Each year, on the day before Purim, the Fast of Esther is observed. A spirit of gaiety will soon be felt, but not one of senseless abandon, for we may not forget that travail and a terrible fear of impending doom precede the experience of Divine Providence and joy that accompany deliverance. Both must be re-experienced, else the true meaning of joy would soon be forgotten. The festival would soon cease to be a source of strength and *Jewish* renewal for us, and would therefore cease to be a *Jewish* festival. When night falls we read the *Megillah* containing the story of Purim. And the *halachic* obligation to listen attentively to every word of the *Megillah* underscores the primary importance of "sober" historic recollection in the whole pattern of Purim gaiety.

☐ *clever pedagogy*

Modern Jews are often much concerned with the problem of how to steel their children against the effects of some cruel anti-Semitic remark or incident. In other times and places, the wider prevalence of anti-Semitism may have been ground for much greater preoccupation with this matter on the part of Jewish parents. But even in our time and place, we are occasionally made aware that unless our children are mentally and emotionally strengthened against the after-effects of exposure to anti-Semitism then resultant feelings of insecurity, inferiority, and fear can greatly damage their proper Jewish and human development. What rare pedagogical cleverness there is, therefore, in giving our children a weapon of such devastating ridicule as the repeated sounding of the *gregger* upon mention of Haman's name.

And as the jeering of the *gregger* gives voice, with triumphant derision to our deep-seated conviction that the end of our enemies can never be different than Haman's, do we not find ourselves in possession of a subtle pedagogic device of rare effectiveness for imparting to our children an abiding faith in the eternity of Israel; a faith whose strength will make them immune to the psychological hurt of anti-Semitism? (Let it be noted, however, that the *gregger* element of Purim when exaggerated — as we often allow it to be — will lose its effectiveness. As in all things, a sense of proper balance is vital.)

☐ *Jewish brotherhood*

In our contemporary frame of Jewish reference, the emphasis on the importance of brotherhood activities is often "restricted" to the inter-religious or inter-denominational brotherhood. We somehow forget that the cultivation of human love in a universal sense needs for its native soil a sense of love for one's own. Where love of one's own is absent, the seeds of universal love can find no place in which to take root and grow. The area, in which the soul of a person is formed and molded, is first and foremost the limited orbit of childhood relations; a person must learn the meaning of love within his family before he can learn to love his community. Chronologically, too, love of people is preceded by love of community. One can never learn to love the whole wide world without first having learned to love his own people. How terribly twisted is the logic that inverts the natural order of these various radii by cultivating the capacity of the individual Jewish human soul to love others before itself. Often the impression is inescapable that some of our brotherhood programs are a "cover-up" for the lack of these same qualities among our own.

How much more is this true in times like ours, when the non-Jewish world is not only unaffected in the least by our "protestations of brotherhood," but has evinced for us only hate or, at best, cold disregard for our suffering? And it is as if the beautiful Purim custom of *mishlo'ach manos* — gifts to friends — were to say to us: "When the hatred of Hamanism surrounds you, doubly reinforce among yourselves, the love and concern of one Jew for another."

□ concern for the poor and needy

On Purim, with even greater emphasis than on other Jewish holidays, we are enjoined to make certain that no Jew or Jewess be deprived of the joy of the festival because of material poverty. And this we are bidden to do personally, not organizationally. Our own Purim feast, would be incomplete were we not to enable other Jews as well to have a Purim feast. And this direct, personal mode in Jewish charity is the one most distinguishing and necessary feature of Jewish giving for the alleviation of need. Where Jewish charity ceases to be personal, it ceases after a while to be Jewish.

□ restrained gaiety

The usual accompaniments of a carnival — such as masquerading, drinking intoxicating beverages — are foreign to the Jewish mood of life on all other days of the year. Purim, however, is an exception. Normally, it would be considered a strange thing for the Rabbis to approve or condone, much less foster forms of enjoyment and relaxation that seek to give pleasure through a strong enough stimulation of the senses and the imagination to temporarily "block" out the sense of reality and of rational and moral experience that has its roots in reason and conscience. Of Purim, by contrast, the Rabbis say: "A person is enjoined to drink on Purim till he no longer knows the difference between the words 'cursed be Haman' and 'blessed be Mordechai'." Masquerading has also been proverbially popular on Purim. Frivolous impersonations of even the most respected leaders and members of the community, rabbinic as well as lay, has always been encouraged on Purim.

Even at this point, however, there is a distinctively Jewish note to be discerned. For one thing, even devout and pious Jews, to whom the fulfillment of a *mitzvah* is a felt necessity whatever the cost and whatever the inconvenience, somehow never manage to fulfill "the *mitzvah*" of inebriation on Purim quite completely. They become a little high perhaps, but hardly ever manage to lose sufficient clarity of consciousness and conscience to be properly classified as drunks. In fact it is precisely when they have imbibed — when the elements of subconscious motivation often break the bonds of their normally clever ability to conceal them — that the true nobility of the *Torah-formed personality* shines through. For in those moments, there becomes apparent how deeply the study and life of Torah affects the substructure of personality.

There is still another "inversion" of a deeply rooted Jewish attitude, which reflects rich symbolism — the recitation of *grammen* (rhymes). *B'nei Torah* fortify themselves sufficiently, but not excessively, with spirits to cast away their deeply ingrained reverence for each work and phrase of the Torah and the writings of the Rabbis, and utilize Torah and Rabbinic texts torn out of context, for rhymed perorations that frivolously satirize the failings both of the community and of its outstanding personalities. Aside from serving as a valve for the release of popular grievances, and imposing upon the community's leadership the awareness that their behavior is periodically subject to critical review, the recitation of *grammen* is perhaps an indirect expression of an abiding Jewish conviction: the understanding that the hand of Providence allows anti-Semitism to do us harm only after we become *Jewishly weakened* by our own failings and shortcomings. And it is as if we were saying through the mask of merriment: "We have not forgotten that our own striving for Jewish self-improvement is the strongest and truest safeguard against the menace of anti-Semitism — for, has not King Solomon taught us that 'the heart of a king is in the hand of *Hashem*'? And, therefore, can any enemy prevail against us unless our own shortcomings have made us vulnerable by taking from us the shield of Divine Protection?"

Rabbi Avrohom Chaim Feuer

Holding Back the Wind
— the Renaissance
of Restraint

Purim thoughts
for our times

TIMES ARE CHANGING. The heavy hand of the energy crisis
is slowing down our mobile society, forcing it to drag its once
unfettered feet. The world pauses to catch its breath and to
seriously re-examine some of its previously unchallenged values.
Whereas yesterday the super-swift were acclaimed, today
speeders are denounced. Caution, conservation and control are
becoming household terms.

To the Torah mind, this new climate of discipline and de-
escalation is most welcome. Our teachings have always condemned excessive haste. Indeed, our sages observed that the pas-
sion to achieve results with utmost speed is a form of greed. Lust
demands instant gratification.

Observing the current situation from this vantage point, we
detect a ray of hope in the gloom. We may yet reap a rewarding
moral harvest from the fuel famine. Perhaps we shall witness a
new mood with the renaissance of restraint.

◆§ Leaping to the Top

It will not be easy to change the values of a "souped up,"
over-charged generation. The world still admires ambitious go-

getters who unhesitatingly take plunges. By contrast, *Chazal* detected this as the impulsive, greedy ambition in our arch-enemy, Haman.

The *Megillah* introduces Haman, under the pseudonym Memuchan, as the least significant of Achashveirosh's advisors *(Esther* 1:14). The King was embroiled in a domestic predicament — how to react to the insubordination of his wife, Vashti. While the assembled cabinet of ministers judiciously weighed this delicate problem, Haman spoke. Court protocol dictates that only the wisest speaks first, the inexperienced last. But rules and etiquette do not exist for a man in a hurry to get ahead:

> *"And Memuchan replied before the King and the Ministers ... Vashti will never again appear before the King, and let the King confer her royal estate upon another who is better than she."*

Overnight Haman was catapulted to the pinnacle of power and prominence. His blitzkrieg tactics succeeded. All were spellbound and paid homage to this brilliant new star of the Persian court. Only *Chazal* failed to be impressed.

> *"Chutzpah — audacity — is sovereignty without a crown" (Sanhedrin 105a).*

> *"The brazen-faced wield great power; the only thing they lack is a legitimate royal crown" (Rashi ibid.).*

This lack of legitimate royalty makes all the difference. Aristocratic pretensions and imperial titles are not the mark of majesty. Thus, to Rav Kahana, Haman's meteoric rise to power proves only one thing:

> *"From Memuchan we learn that it is the* hedyot *— the coarse, common boor — who leaps to the top" (Megillah* 12b).

Chazal also point out (ibid.) that the name Memuchan is most appropriate for an opportunist, for *muchan* literally means alerted, prepared. — Prepared for what? for *success*, thought Haman. *Chazal* say, "Prepared for his ultimate downfall." Even as Haman rose, he was paving the way to his own decline.

The *Rambam* points out that the name Memuchan contains the word *"mum"* — blemish, *for the greatest blemish is a character flaw. Rambam* sums up his analysis of Haman's personality with the words of King Solomon in Proverbs:

> *"The fool lets out all of his wind, whereas the wise man is praised for his restraint" (Mishlei 29:11).*

The fleeting impulse overwhelms the *hedyot* and drives him into rash action. Impatient, he summons up all his resources in one all-out thrust, and his wind is thus swiftly spent. His blazing star of fortune, so suddenly erupted, fast fades into oblivion.

Not only did Haman end with a noose around his neck, but his ten sons were similarly executed — all ten at the same moment. We commemorate this by reciting their names in one breath. Perhaps the significance of this custom is to display that their downfall came because they 'let out all of their wind' at once, whereas Jews are admonished to hold back their breath.

✺§ The Majesty of Self-Mastery

The essential ingredient of a Torah monarchy is patience. Thus, the kings of the Davidic line were anointed in a symbolic location, along the meandering stream Shiloach. Commoners often fail to appreciate this subdued, low-keyed style, which fails to live up to the fabled image of the dashing, whimsical autocrat. They preferred the magnificent style of Pekach ben Remalyahu to the humble austerity and Torah-directed caution of Chizkiyahu (Hezekiah), and for this foolishness, the prophet Isaiah lashed out:

"This nation despised the waters of Shiloach which flow slowly ... Therefore I will raise upon them the waters of a river, abundant and powerful, the king of Ashur and his host; it will rise from every spring and overflow all the banks" (Yesayah 8:6-7).

In the roots of Jewish history, Reuvain, the firstborn, lost his claim to monarchy only because of his impetuosity. On his deathbed, *Yaakov Avinu* told him:

"Reuvain, you are my first-born, my might, the first fruit of my strength, the excellency of dignity, the excellency of power. But rash as rushing water rapids — you shall not have the excellency!" (Bereishis 49:3-4).

This trait of restraint also figured prominently in a debate among our Sages as to King Achashveirosh's true nature. Was he a clever king, or a fool? One of the Rabbis says in his favor:

"This man acted favorably on four counts:

1) After ascending to the monarchy, he patiently waited three years before taking a throne and a crown (to better establish the royal power before assuming the regal trappings).

2) He waited four years before marrying, to find the most suitable wife.

3) He never acted without consulting his counselors.

4) He did not forget a favor and would carefully record anyone who did him a service."(Esther Rabbah 1:15)

Esther, his choice as queen, was also highly disciplined. The Gaon of Vilna points out the sharp contrast between Esther and the other contestants for the royal appointment.

"And when the turn of each maiden and maiden arrived to come before the King Achashveirosh" (Esther 2:12).

The melodic note, the *"trop"* above the words *"maiden and maiden"* is *kadma v'azla* — which literally means *"they went forth early."* Every other girl competed to be first to appear before the king. But by pushing to the forefront they betrayed themselves and revealed the commonality that disqualified them from the throne.

"And upon the arrival of the turn of Esther bas Avichayil ... "

Here the musical notes are four straight *"munach"* signs — implying: rest, rest, rest, rest. Not only did Esther not push forward, she restrained herself and went with reluctance and calm.... She needed no royal tiara. Her nobility of character had already crowned her as queen.

◆§ Hot Water and the Fly

Haman's impetuosity was an old tradition in the line of Amalek.

"Amalek is the first of nations, but he will end in oblivion" (Bamidbar 24:20).

When the Israelites triumphantly marched out of Egypt, Amalek seized the opportunity to be their first attacker — no matter how heavy the price.

"Remember what Amalek did to you on the road as you went forth from Egypt. How he suddenly surprised you on the way and struck all who straggled behind you, when you were faint and weary and he feared not the L-rd" (Devarim 25; 7-18).

"He had to be the first nation to display to others that Israel could be attacked. A parable: a boiling hot bath into which no one dared enter until a rash youth jumped into it. Although he himself was scalded, he cooled the bath for others" (Rashi ibid).

Fools rush in to be first, not caring if it kills them. Amalek inherited his rashness from his progenitor, Eisav. From birth, Eisav pushed ahead. Rashi tells us that although Yaakov was conceived earlier, Eisav emerged first with Yaakov grasping his heel. Later Eisav sold his birthright because he was overcome by a yen for some beans; and he was so anxious for the pleasure that he could not eat the delicacy with a spoon. Instead he begged Yaakov to empty the pot into his throat.

More, Edom-Eisav and his line are likened to a z'vuv — a fly, which never sits, but swiftly pounces on any surface that attracts its fancy, neglecting any danger.

"Amalek is like a z'vuv — and in *Melachim II*, 1:2, we find *Ba'al Z'vuv* the god of Ekron (Caesarea of Edom)" (*Ba'al HaTurim, Shemos* 17:14).

"Why is Amalek like a fly? — because he rushes to lick a festering wound" (*Tanchuma Ki-Seitzei*).

"The yeitzer hara — evil inclination — is like a fly dancing about upon the gates of the heart (Berachos 61).

❧ The Grabber

"He who attains even one of the following is considered blessed with the most desirable of earthly treasures: wisdom ... strength ... riches. When is this so? Only when these gifts are bestowed by heaven and are deserved by merit of Torah. When not obtained from the hand of G-d, they are destined to be lost ... Two extremely wealthy men arose in the world: Korach from Israel, and Haman from the nations. Both vanished from the face of the earth, because their gifts were not from G-d — rather they grabbed them on their own" (Midrash Rabbah Devarim 22:6).

G-d decrees exactly how much every man will receive from the riches and pleasures of this world. It is impossible for anyone to use what has not been pre-ordained as his portion. The only option is the timing. If one has patience, then his rightful portion will eventually be his — permissibly and with minimum effort. If one grabs and insists on immediate gratification, however, he will pluck his portion prematurely — while it is yet forbidden fruit. The fruit of haste is regret.

Adam and Eve could not wait. Late in the sixth day, *Erev Shabbos*, they bit into the forbidden fruit. The *Ari HaKadosh* relates that had they only waited until *Shabbos*, the ban would have been lifted and they could have eaten all they wanted.

"Where in the Torah do we find an allusion to Haman?
From the verse (Bereishis 3:11): HaMin Ho'etz — "Have you
eaten from the tree (Chullin 139b).

The root of Haman's grasping nature lies in man's very first
error of haste.

"He who impatiently anticipates the moment of oppor-
tunity will be repelled by the moment. But he who holds
back and awaits the moment — for him the opportunity will
wait" (Berachos 64a).

The Ultimate Restraint

The Kotzker Rebbe once asked his disciples, "Why do we
read the Torah portion dealing with Amalek on the *Shabbos*
preceding Purim? Wouldn't it be more appropriate on Purim
proper?" The first Gerrer Rebbe, Reb Yitzchok Meir, replied:
"The very first words of the Torah provide the answer, for it
states, 'And when G-d will let you rest from the enemies around
you — (then) shall you eradicate Amalek!' We can only conquer
Amalek from a position of rest — Sabbath rest."

"Better a handful of quiet nachas, than two fistful of
labor and striving after the wind" (Koheles 4:6).

"Better a small handful of Shabbos rest than both fists
full of the six days of toil" (Vayikra Rabbah 3).

Amalek's very name alludes to its philosophy of denying
G-d's presence and total reliance on human endeavor. The root of
the name "Amalek" is *amal* — labor. He who feels that he alone
controls his fortune, must labor incessantly, with no time for rest.
Understandably, Haman the Amalekite harbored a special
repugnance for the *Shabbos* and expressed this animosity when
he slandered the Jews before the king:

"They do not follow the statutes of the King. All year
they exempt themselves from the King's service with some
kind of excuse — It is Shabbos today ... It is Pesach today
..." (Megillah 13b).

"Yeshno am echad — There is one nation, says Haman,
that is always sleeping (yashno). They eat and drink and
declare, 'this is for Shabbos pleasure, this is for Yom Tov
pleasure' — refraining from work; they are an unproductive,
parasitic waste" (Midrash Esther 7:14).

The echoes of Haman's lie have reverberated through the
ages in condemnation of the Jews. Perhaps the present situation
will demonstrate to the world that not by physical action and

speed alone does the world progress. Much can be accomplished by restraint. When man will learn to hold back the wind, then the gentle breezes of peace and contentment will begin to blow.

◀§ Pesach / *The Season of Redemption*

*the spirituality of preparation and
performance ... the historical anomaly of
Yetzias Mitzrayim ... the living
perpetuation of ancient experience ...
from millions of slaves to a single people
... redemption within the camps of
despair*

Yehuda Leib Gersht

Jewry:
A Nation Unique

*The unusual circumstances
of the Exile in Egypt
and the subsequent Exodus*

◆§ How Israel Became A People

W HOEVER DEEPLY REFLECTS on the course of Jewish
history can discern through all its stages and developments
how the Divine Will is operative in history.

The very emergence of the Jewish People represents a
wondrous event without peer in the history of other peoples. A
lone family arrives — as a group of immigrants — in a mighty
country possessing an old, developed civilization. The results
should definitely have been one of total assimilation within the
Egyptian people. Such a lot would have befallen not only a small
group, but even a large people, who, for whatever reason, would
have migrated to so mighty a society. But this Hebrew family
itself walked round sphinxlike among the physical Egyptian
sphinxes. This family increased numerically, and utterly refused
to be swallowed up in the melting pot of the ruling society.

No people in the world was ever born under such conditions; neither till then, nor in subsequent times. It is therefore to

be understood that so unique a people necessarily elicited for itself not only amazement but also resentment and hate.

The ruling people mobilized all its government resources to liquidate part of this strange people, and to enslave the others in behalf of the country's development, which was based on the exploitation of tens of thousands of slave laborers. Under such conditions, no people could survive with a separate national identity.

The terrible persecutions transformed the grandchildren of the immigrant-family from Canaan into broken and tortured fragments. The slave-system was so well organized that it made impossible any consolidation of the slaves. Nevertheless, the slaves did not cease to exist as a unique people with an abiding hope for miraculous liberation.

◆§ The Exodus Could Only Come About Miraculously

When *Moshe Rabbeinu* appeared in Egypt on G-d's command to redeem his enslaved brothers, he struck two serious obstacles which there was no possibility to overcome naturally. A great power, such as Egypt, was certainly not ready to oblige the demands of some visionary not backed by any strength other than the authority invested in him by G-d — whom the Egyptians did not acknowledge. Aside from this, Pharaoh could not afford to free the masses of slaves whom he needed for the development of his country. Hundreds of thousands of slave laborers were engaged in the erection of treasure-houses and fortresses around which entire industries must have functioned, and which must have been guarded by entire legions of supervisors. The freeing of masses of forced laborers was bound to shake to its foundations the entire structure and the state of the economy of the country. That, Pharaoh and his advisors could certainly not permit.

The only way to free the Jews was through supernatural, miraculous intervention because under natural circumstance the Egyptians themselves would never have freed their Jewish slaves. As our Sages have said: "Why was G-d revealed from the Heavens above, and spoke with Moshe from the thornbush? — Just as the thornbush is more 'difficult' than all the trees in the world and any bird which enters cannot emerge uninjured, but is severed limb after limb, similarly was Egyptian bondage more difficult before G-d than any bondage in the world. Never did a slave or maidservant leave Egypt free ... " *(Mechilta D'Rashbi).* Indeed, no other instance is known in which a group of slaves proved capable of breaking the chains of enslavement imposed by a ruling people, after the fashion of the People of Israel in Egypt.

◆§ In The Wilderness And At Sinai

Not only the deliverance of the Jews from Egypt was effected by supernatural means. Their endurance and consolidation after their liberation were similarly not possible through circumstance. All the borders of Egypt were sealed. In the eastern and western parts of Canaan there lived entrenched peoples who were under no circumstances willing to grant entry to the wave of liberated slaves planning to erect a state of their own. The Philistines concentrated in the west on the shores of the Mediterranean; the Emorim in the central and eastern parts of the land; the Edomim, Moabim and Amonim in the south, all stood as an iron wall before the emigres from Egypt. What purpose did the entire liberation have in humanly understood, naturalistic terms?

The historical facts are that previous efforts to pierce those boundaries by force ended in failure (as was the case with the B'nei Ephraim at Gas and the battle at Charmah). Only one way remained: supernatural help from above. All other political or military plans to achieve the goal of conquering the promised land were hopeless.

The life-condition — especially the struggle for survival — of those who left Egypt was thus radically different from that of all other neighboring peoples. And the high point of this uniqueness and wondrous differentness was certainly Ma'amad Har Sinai (the stand at Mt. Sinai); and no less the implanting of the Torah given at Sinai.

The entire Torah stands in total contradiction to the Egyptian way of life, in the midst of which the Jews had lived till now. Egyptian culture was based on a fetish idolatry. The worship of animals with its attendant abominations was the foundation of the religious views of the Egyptians.

And suddenly the recently liberated slaves received a Torah which — in total contradiction to Egyptian religion — emphasized the exalted concept of a "G-d, Most High, Possessor of Heaven and Earth," who could not be grasped by the senses, and who prohibited the make or use of any physical representation in His worship. The Torah proclaimed the idolatrous symbols of the Egyptians and of other peoples as the most terrible of abominations to be fought without compromise. Even more — not only did the Torah prohibit and hold in abhorrence idolatry itself, but also every aspect of the way of life of idolatrous societies which were rooted in idolatry. "Do not turn to the idols ... like the practices of the land of Egypt where you dwelt you shall not do ... and like the deeds of the land of Canaan that I bring you there, you shall not do and in their statutes you shall not go."

Likewise was the institution of slavery — the separation of the people into masters and slaves, the exploitation of foreigners and recent settlers — an integral part of Egyptian civilization. The Torah forbade such practices: "And if a stranger will sojourn in your land you shall not oppress him ... and you shall love him like yourself because you were sojourners in the land of Egypt, I am *HASHEM* your G-d." Still more — it is in nature of liberated slaves to carry bitter enmity to their erstwhile oppressors. The Torah, however, taught an opposite and original principle: "You shall not hold an Egyptian in abhorrence, because you were a sojourner in his land."

We see here that the Torah given to the Jews was a total revolution against the entire way of life which the Jews witnessed in Egypt. And though some of the traditions which Jacob and his children brought to Egypt still survived in the memory of their grandchildren, nevertheless, life for so long a time in the surroundings of Egyptian defilement certainly failed to exert good influences for safeguarding the purity of those traditions of the Fathers.

It is therefore easy to understand how difficult a transformation it was to implant, in those who had left Egypt, the concepts and the way of life of the Torah from Sinai. It was therefore not possible to implant in them the world of the Torah through a natural process of cultural development. It required the supernatural act of the giving of the Torah — the commandment of G-d, which gave the Jews the strength to lift themselves out of the hedonistic Egyptian swamp, and to transform them into a unique people without any similarity to the spiritual conditions of contemporary peoples.

From this it is also possible to understand why the Torah itself relates the act of the giving of the Torah with the Exodus from Egypt. "You have seen what I have done to Egypt, and how I lifted you upon the wings of eagles, and I brought you to Me ... and you shall be to Me a treasure from amongst all the peoples, for Mine is all the land." The uniqueness and the supernatural character of Jewish destiny was revealed at the giving of the

Torah exactly as at the exodus from Egypt. Therefore, for example, Rabbi Yehuda HaLevi, too, underscores this relation and says: "Thus did G-d begin his words to the masses of Israel: 'I am HASHEM your G-d who brought you out from the land of Egypt ... ,' that stand was clear to them from what they had seen with their eyes, and afterwards there came the continuation of tradition, which is therefore also like direct vision" (*Kuzari* 1:25).

◦§ Egyptian Decline And Jewish Eternity

After the event of the Exodus, the Egyptian kingdom gradually recovered from the blows it received while its slaves were being liberated. The Egyptian kingdom still existed for approximately a thousand years till the invasion of the Greeks. But with the loss of its political independence, there followed a destruction and decline of the national culture, till Egypt ceased to play any significant role in world history.

All that remains of the mighty Egyptian kingdom are the ruins of the pyramids, and the mummies. Egyptian civilization believed that it could make its power eternal with the help of mighty material achievements, but from all that nothing more remains than blocks of stone monuments and hills of sand.

The liberated slaves, however, came to a humble mountain in the wilderness of Sinai. There they received — as the foundation of their existence as a people — the two stone tablets, on which there were engraved the Ten Commandments, the essence of its Torah, which was to stand in sharpest contradiction to Egyptian culture. And it was precisely the content of *these* two *stone* tablets which sufficed to breathe a spirit of eternal life into the people of the freed slaves who can today proudly lift up their eyes in the direction of the pyramids and proclaim — on the basis of their experience — where the secret of eternal existence for peoples and states lies hidden.

Rabbi Fabian Schonfeld

In the Light
of Pesach

*Selected adaptations
from "Sfas Emes"*

T HERE ARE many reasons offered to explain why the *Shabbos* immediately preceding the Feast of Pesach is traditionally known by the name *Shabbos HaGadol* — The Great *Shabbos*. Most of these are quite well known and need no repetition. The deep philosophical and religious implications, however, need to be brought to the fore and the thinking of the *Sfas Emes* on this subject and on the entire range of Pesach, are a source of stimulation to a deeper and more significant understanding of Torah in its broadest sense.

◄§ Shabbos HaGadol and the Power of Good Intentions

We know that the very first Pesach celebrated by our ancestors in Egypt — known as *Pesach Mitzrayim* — fell on a Wednesday. Thus the divine commandment of ... *they shall take to them every man a lamb* ... which referred to the selection of the *Korban Pesach* on the tenth of Nissan instructed them to do so on *Shabbos*. This being so, why was that day perpetuated in our calendar to coincide with *Shabbos* rather than with the tenth day of Nissan? All our festivals are observed on the calendar date and not on the day of the week on which the events they commemorate took place. Thus we should normally observe the tenth of Nissan, without regard to the day of the week on which it might fall.

Nothing in history is a coincidence or accident. The Almighty guides and controls the destiny of mankind and no historical event just "happens." The commandment of the selection of the *Korban Pesach*, was the very first *mitzvah* that the Jewish community was bidden to fulfill. It was the first *mitzvah* given to *Klal Yisrael*, the total community of Israel, and our forefathers accepted it with unlimited love and willing obedience. It was this ready acceptance of the *mitzvah* which, in the eyes of G-d, is more precious than its actual performance. There always exists a gap between *intention* and *performance*, for there is no limit to one's desire to fulfill a *mitzvah*. In the world of desire and will it is possible to attain the maximum of one's ability. Desire and will cannot be contained within a specific area. They travel in spiritual space and know not the boundaries of time. It is therefore possible to achieve perfection in the area of intention and preparation. Such perfection is utterly impossible when we reach the point of the actual performance of a given *mitzvah*. The spiritual effects of preparation for and concentration on a *mitzvah* are everlasting, or can at least be so. The performance of the *mitzvah* lasts only for as long as it takes to fulfill it. Furthermore, it is beyond human ability to fulfill a *mitzvah* to the final degree and to the utmost perfection. In the actual performance there must be some defect, some blemish, since the doer is human and nothing done by human beings can be perfect. The value of the act is judged by the degree of *intention* and the strength and sincerity of the *desire*.

According to the *Tur Orach Chaim*, the days between Yom Kippur and Succos are meaningful because we are occupied with the task of readying ourselves for the advent of Succos. This statement is based on a Midrashic source which tells us that the Almighty forgives us our sins on Yom Kippur and does not begin to count our iniquities until the first day of Succos. Does this, then, imply that the days spent in preparing for Succos are more significant than Succos itself? This question is raised by the *Taz*. The answer is in the affirmative. Preparation, *intention* and desire — these are the elements of the *mitzvah* to which G-d pays heed. Mere performance is defective.

This concept is demonstrated in its highest sense by the institution of the *Shabbos*. There is, basically, very little positive performance of physical *mitzvos* on *Shabbos*. It is observed more by abstinence from work than by some positive effort. The proper understanding of the deep meaning of *Shabbos* is within the realm of the desire to accept the *Shabbos* — קבלת שבת. The entire range of *Shabbos* laws is based on the idea of negative observance and performance and positive will and desire. The term *shmiras Shabbos* means not only to observe but rather to *watch* over the *Shabbos* — to wish to preserve it. Similarly *shmiras hamitzvos* means *desire* to fulfill, to *will* the preservation of the *mitzvos*.

Thus the performance of the first national *mitzvah* was brought about by divine design to fall on the *Shabbos* because both *mitzvos* represent the concept of *desire* as an indispensable preliminary to *performance*.

It is for this reason that we commemorate the *Shabbos* preceding *Pesach* rather than the tenth of Nissan. For what took place then in Egypt was not so much a historic event as a spiritual lesson for all generations that have the task of the fulfillment of divine instruction. It is for this reason that this day was named The Great *Shabbos*.

◂§ The Wise Son's Statutes

The various laws of the Torah are divided into several categories. One of these groups, the *chukim*, are defined as commandments for which no specific reason is stated. We accept these statutes without comprehending them. While we are at liberty to seek a logical explanation, we have accepted the premise that even if such search does not yield the desired solution, these *mitzvos* must, nevertheless, be observed.

In view of this fact, it is rather difficult to understand the question of the *Chacham*, the Wise Son, who asks in the pages of the *Haggadah*: "What is the meaning of the testimonies and the statutes ... ?" This problem is even intensified by the verse in *Tehillim* 147: "He states his words to Yaakov, his *statutes* and ordinances to Yisrael."

The truth is that the reasons for such statutes *are* revealed to us. However, this revelation is only granted when the *mitzvah* is fulfilled and observed without knowing or even wanting to know the reason. The reward for obedience is the ultimate comprehension and the insight that results from the performance of the *mitzvah*.

The Hebrew word for reason *(taam)* is the same for the word "taste". Surely, there is a different kind of taste or flavor that one feels with regard to the performance of any given task the purpose of which one understands. The impetus and stimulus is so much more obvious when one knows and understands the reason, when one can feel the "taste." Yet such sense of taste can only be developed in time. This concept is illustrated by the matzah itself. It is basically a food with little or no *perceivable* taste. In its physical aspect it compares with the spiritual *chok*, the law without an apparent reason. It is this idea that the *Chacham* wishes to bring forth by his rhetorical question regarding the meaning of the *chok*. To his question the Haggadah provides the meaningful answer: "Do not partake of any other food after the eating of the last piece of *afikoman.*" Cling to the *chok* as you cling to the matzah. Then, and then only, will you find the reason and feel the flavor.

◄§ The Point of Matzah: Humility

The Rav Ba'al HaTanya in his *Siddur* states that matzah represents humility and *chometz* represents pride and conceit. The rising of the dough which causes unleavened bread to become *chometz* is very much like the inflation of one's ego and self-esteem. It was through the nearness of the *Shechinah*, the Divine Presence, that our forefathers were saved from the pitfalls of egotism and conceit. This is the meaning of the statement in the Haggadah: "This matzah we eat because the dough of our fathers did not rise through the Revelation to them of the Holy One, Blessed is He."

We find the same idea in the *Zohar to Pinchas*, where we are told that the difference between the word *chometz* and the word matzah in Hebrew script is the tiny point that elongates the line of the letter ה *(Hai)* and results in the letter ח *(Ches)*. The מ *(Mem)* and the צ *(Tzaddik)* remain unaltered.

What the *Zohar* endeavors to tell us is that the little point or line in the letter *Hai* is to teach us that all we possess in knowledge and virtue is but the little line or point. The longer we make of that line and the more prominently we insert that point, the closer we come to writing the letter *Ches*. Thus we turn the word matzah into the word *chometz*; thus we change from the noble state of humility and humbleness to the state of false pride and egotism.

Man is not wary of this danger at all times. The celebration of Pesach; the eating of the matzah and the destruction of *chometz* are designed to drive home this lesson during specific time of the year.

Dr. Isaac Breuer

The Pesach Night

*The Seder as a
means of reliving
the Exodus experience*

EVERY YEAR there returns a night in the life of the Jews that is set aside for the Jewish father to explain to his children the meaning of being a Jew. This night is pervaded by the spirit of a living nation of indestructible vitality. There resounds in it the sad plaint of a nation tried by suffering, surrounded by enemies; the proud triumphal song of a nation never defeated, outlasting all peoples and empires; and the hymn of praise of a nation close to its G-d, happy in misfortune, certain of its future. *He* knows the nature of Judaism who has grasped the meaning of this night: the Pesach night, the national night of Judaism.

The father gathers his children around the table on which is found the unleavened bread which our ancestors ate when they left Egypt, because the Egyptians had not given them time to let it sour; the bitter herbs, as bitter as the bondage in which Pharaoh had held our ancestors; all the family silver, some of which the Jews never lacked since they took that of the Egyptians into the desert. The questioning glance of the children passes over the table, bathed in candle-light, and appeals to the father: "What means all this?" And the father begins to tell them, according to the words of the *Haggadah*, the ancient document of national freedom: "Slaves were we unto Pharaoh in Egypt, and G-d, our G-d, brought us forth from there with a mighty hand and an outstretched arm: and if the Holy One, Blessed is He, had not brought forth our ancestors from Egypt, we, and our children and children's children, would have still continued in bondage to the Pharaoh in Egypt. Therefore, even if we all were wise, all of us men of understanding and experience, all of us knowing the Law, it, nevertheless, is incumbent upon us to discourse of the departure from Egypt, and he who discourses at length is praiseworthy ... "

The exodus from Egypt is not, to the Jewish nation, a legendary tale from ages long passed by, but historical certainty born from our own experience. It is as a witness to its truth that the father stands before his children this night ... he who heard it from the mouth of his father, closing the chain which across thousands of years links the slaves of the Egyptians to their youngest descendants.

"In every generation the Jew has to look upon himself as if he himself had gone forth from Egypt; as is said: 'And thou shalt declare unto thy son, on that day, saying that for the sake of this (Pesach service) G-d did this for *me* when I departed from Egypt.' For it was not only our ancestors whom the Holy One, Blessed is He, redeemed from Egypt but us, too, He redeemed with them; as is said: 'And He brought *us* from there, that He might bring *us* to the land which He swore unto our fathers'."

It is from his own experiences that the father tells his children. He does not speak to them as an individual, weak and mortal, but as representative of the nation, bearer of its national history, demanding from them the loyalty to be expected, not by him, indeed, but by the nation looking to its members. Woe unto the child who turns away in this night of national reflection, in a spirit of superiority objecting to the unleavened bread and the bitter herbs: "What does this service, which may have made sense for your ancestors, mean to you?" — To *you* and not to *him*? As he withdraws himself from the nation, you, too, should exclude him, as is said: 'For the sake of this (Pesach service) G-d did this for *me* when I departed from Egypt' — for *me* but not for *him:* had he been in Egypt he, in his disloyalty, would not have been redeemed...."

We were redeemed by G-d from Egypt, and turned by Him from slaves into a nation because we were willing to shoulder the Law. "Blessed is G-d, who has given the Law unto His people

Israel; Blessed is He." Those who deny the Law make themselves in retrospect unworthy of redemption.

Remember, children, we are not a nation like others. Who knows how they arose? They are borne by the natural conditions of survival. They revere the soil which nourishes them, the sun which gives them light, the strength which protects them. We, however, look at Terach the father of Avraham and Nachor. He dwelt across the river; there he stayed, sharing with Nachor the fate of the nations. Avraham your father, however, was led by G-d from across the river into the land of Canaan. Of his descendants, Eisav was given the mountain of Seir, and Yaakov and his sons came to Egypt. Whilst Eisav's descendants were already kings of Seir, hatred and envy enslaved us in Egypt, turning us into a horde of people without rest and rights. "And the Egyptians ill-treated us, afflicted us, and laid heavy bondage upon us." We did not know how to help ourselves for theirs was the power and strength. According to the laws of history we were lost. There was nothing left to us but the G-d of our fathers. "Then we cried unto G-d, the G-d of our fathers; and G-d heard our voice, and observed our affliction, our labor, and our oppression. And G-d brought us forth from Egypt, with a strong hand and with an outstretched arm, with terror, and with signs and wonders." Favor after favor G-d has heaped upon us ever since: "He brought us forth from Egypt, inflicted justice upon the Egyptians and their idols and firstborn, gave us their wealth, divided the sea for us, brought us to Mount Sinai, gave us the Law, ... brought us into the land of Israel, and built the *Bais HaMikdash* for us, to make atonement for our sins ..."

In Egypt, by our readiness to accept the Divine Law, we became a nation, G-d's nation, even though we had neither land nor state. Our transgressions have robbed us of Temple, state, and land. Ever since then, like in Egypt, "have enemies arisen against us to destroy us, generation after generation; but the Holy One, Blessed is He, delivered us out of their hand ... ": for we still remain G-d's nation, as long as we guard His Law. G-d keeps His pledge to our father Avraham; "It was this which always stood by our ancestors and us" and which will lead us back into the land that G-d swore unto our forefathers.

Halleluyah! Join in the Jewish national anthem, sung by King David in his hymn to the Divine government of history! History belongs to us, and so does the future. In Egypt we vanquished the death that befalls nations. At Sinai we received the light which, wherever we are, turns "bondage into freedom, sorrow into joy, mourning into holidays, darkness into great light — Halleluyah!"

He who has ever lived through this Pesach night, and has entered into its spirit, cannot doubt that the Jews are a nation. This night is dedicated to the children — that they, physically born in Russia, England, or anywhere else, complete their spiritual birth upon Israel's holy ground. There is no mention, this night, of *dogmas*, nor of the mystery of a *founder of a religion* living in communion with G-d. We speak of *history* this night, of the history of a nation.

Avraham, Yitzchak, and Yaakov, whom dry theology would turn into myths, arise before the eyes of the child as vividly as if it had only been yesterday that they blessed their children and lay down to rest in the cave of Machpelah. While scholars quarrel whether the Jews were, indeed, enslaved by Pharaoh, the Jewish child eats the bread of Egyptian affliction together with his ancestors, tastes the bitterness of their bondage, and joins with them in the national hymn of praise that Moshe intoned at the shore of the sea. A fine distinction between the ancient and the modern Jew is drawn by profound scholars; what does it mean in the face of the unity of consciousness which links the youngest Jew of today with Moshe and the prophets, with Dovid and Shlomo's *Bais HaMikdash*. There is no Jewish "religion" at all, in the ordinary sense of the word, but only a *national history*. To be a conscious Jew means to have experienced Jewish history, and to dedicate one's entire self to it, to become its bearer, and creator of its future.

Judaism does not — in the manner of religions — aim to gain acceptance by "convincing" the individual, but by giving him as the member of a nation, historical self-consciousness: "You are my witnesses!" exclaims the prophet Isaiah. The mere fact of your existence, here and now, is meaningless if you do not accept your past. Only one choice is left to you: if you affirm your history, it will give you a sense of being at home even abroad, the pride of a historic mission, and the triumphant confidence in ultimate redemption which you yourself will help to bring about; if, however, you withdraw from the historic sphere into which you were born, you will fall amidst the multitude of nations, without past or future, hammered and beaten, trodden down and crushed, until you cover the ground — dust of culture.

Rabbi Paysach Krohn

The Birth of a People,
The Emergence
of a Nation

*Fulfillment of
two Divine Commands
was essential to
the creation of a nation
from a band of
several million slaves*

A S THE JEWS in Egypt were preparing for their first *korban
  pesach* (the Passover sacrifice) they were commanded: *"If one
is not circumcised, he may not partake of it."* Unless each man
bore the attestation of *Avraham Avinu,* the Midrash says, he
could not taste from the *korban.* The reason for this prerequisite
is supplied by a parable in the Midrash: A king made a festive
gathering for all his friends, but made one stipulation — anyone
wishing to join the party must bear the official insignia. So, too,
in Egypt. A feast was held for G-d's people. To share in it, each
man had to wear the emblem that attested to his loyalty to the
king.

The Jews immediately gathered together and *Moshe Rabbeinu* (or according to some, Yehoshua) circumcised them. G-d
blessed each one, and upon seeing the fulfillment of these

mitzvos, pesach and *milah,* concluded that the Jews truly merited redemption. Later that night they left Egypt.

The Midrash seems simple enough, combining a satisfying rationale with an uncomplicated parable. One would tend to leave it at that. But probing the concepts of *pesach* and *milah,* developing the relationship of one to the other, a fascinating picture emerges as to what occurred in Egypt and how, on the night of Pesach, a nation came into existence.

◄§ Reach for Perfection as an Identity

Every nation, like the individuals it comprises, has particular characteristics and traits that make it singularly recognizable and discernible from others. The traits begin to form as the individual or nation grows, maturing and developing with time and experience. But a new nation, like a new child, must be given direction ... . In Egypt the Jewish nation was born and, as with a Jewish child, the matter of first importance was that of *milah* — the *bris kodesh* — the holy covenant of circumcision.

A philosopher once asked Rabbi Hoshea, "If *milah* is so favorable in G-d's eyes, why isn't man born circumcised?"

Rabbi Hoshea replied: "Everything that was created requires some modifying action. The lupines must be sweetened. Wheat must be ground, and man himself also requires amendment."

Man's purpose is to take things as he finds them, and then develop, improve and refine them until he has raised them to the level of perfection. This responsibility pertains to both man and his environment, both the internal and external spheres of his life and is manifest in the act of *milah.* At the outset of a Jew's life, shortly after his birth, the *tikun* — the emending process — begins. Indeed, the *bris* is primarily the responsibility of the father, for it is he who is responsible for the development of his son. The emending of a newborn infant, though he is physically complete, is the beginning of his spiritual development.

In commanding Avraham regarding *milah,* G-d said, "You have performed everything I have asked of you. Now 'go before Me and become perfect' — circumcise yourself." Thus for Avraham the act of *milah* was the attainment of perfection. To later generations, it was an *os bris* — a sign of the covenant that G-d made with Avraham — that reminds us to strive towards the perfection that Avraham reached.

The Midrash says: Once the Jews in Egypt circumcised themselves, G-d knew that they would comply with the covenant

He had made with Avraham. They too would strive to improve. They too would attempt to reach those levels of perfection that Avraham had reached. Hence, *milah* was a prerequisite to the Exodus, for without it they would not have merited redemption.

Milah, then, has always been a mark of Jewish identity — not only a physically identifying feature, but also serving as a symbol of the Jew's eternal struggle for perfection.

⋖§ The Blood of Unity

Until the Exodus, the Jews in Egypt were a scattered and divided people. Some had attained a level of authority. Some had become wealthy and some had even become honored citizens. These felt that they should not leave Egypt altogether. Others, such as the Tribe of Ephraim, miscalculated the timing of the redemption and left Egypt thirty years earlier, only to be killed by the Philistines.

The *korban pesach* was an initial expression of community, uniting all Jews with a common cause, indicating their willingness to become G-d's people and to follow His directives.

The Hebrew word for sacrifice — *korban* — has its root in the word *karov*, meaning to approach or come near. By responding to the command to make the *korban pesach*, even at the risk of their lives — for the lamb that was slaughtered was an Egyptian deity — the Jews, as a group, did come closer to G-d. The laws governing the preparation of the *korban pesach* bespoke unity .... It was to be eaten in groups. Every member had to be accounted for, and no individual could leave the assemblage. Members joined with their families, and families banded together to form larger units, on the basis of their common dedication. Thus, from dedication and sacrifice were forged the links of the unbreakable bond of Jewish unity.

This essential ingredient of unity was expressed by *Yaakov Avinu* almost two hundred years earlier, when he gave his final blessing to his sons and assigned them their individual roles in the future of Israel. The Torah relates that he called to them saying: *"Gather together and listen, sons of Yaakov, and hearken to Yisrael, your father."* The roles they would play in "Yisrael" could only succeed if they performed them as brothers of one father, Yaakov. If there would be a cohesiveness, if their works would complement each other, then Yaakov's sons could function as Sons of Israel.

This unifying factor was again present when the nation

emerged, when the Jews were instructed to select a lamb for each patriarchal unit as their *pesach* sacrifice.

Identification through *milah*; unification through the *korban pesach*; these were the basic components in the make-up of the new nation.

◄§ The Bonds of Closeness

Milah and *pesach* are the only two instances of positive commands where failure to comply results in the divine punishment of *koreis* — a severing of bond with the Jewish community by loss of life in both this world and the next. *Koreis* is usually earned by the active performance of an act that violates a basic tenet of Judaism. With regard to these two *mitzvos*, however, passive abstention is the equivalent of an active withdrawal from the commitments of Judaism. When an act of unity or identification is the order of the day, doing nothing is the greatest severing of bonds.

The first Gerrer Rebbe (author of the *Chiddushei HaRim*) notes that the converse must also be true. If the non-deed results in *koreis* — a separation of finality — then the deed must bring *kiruv*, an overwhelming closeness to G-d. This nearness is unattainable through any other *mitzvos*, for both *milah* and *pesach* are distinguished as expressions in the extreme of giving of oneself. In fact Rabbi Yitzchak Avohab, in his *Menoras HaMaor*, describes the *bris milah* as man's personal *korban* to G-d .... Giving of one's self is an act of love, and love is the essential ingredient of *kiruv* — closeness.

◄§ The Blood Bond of Dedication

On the first Pesach night, G-d Himself scrutinized every Jewish home, passing over those that had the blood of their *pesach* lamb sprinkled on their lintels and doorposts, and He recalled other blood spilled at another time. Then it was innocent blood savagely spilled with the intent to choke off future Jewish generations. It was years earlier, in the same Egypt, when Pharaoh ordered newly born Jewish males to be killed. Many thousands were slaughtered simply because they were Jewish.

He also recalled the blood of the wounds caused by the merciless labor inflicted upon His people. There had been no relaxing of their work load, so the wounds would not heal and the blood lay caked on their scars as they toiled. This constant flow of blood was interpreted by the Egyptians as an ebbing of the strength of the Jewish people.

But on that first night of Pesach, when two other bloods made their appearance — the blood of *milah*, and the blood of *pesach* — G-d said: *Through these bloods will you live and gain strength. Both milah and pesach demonstrate your readiness to be My nation.*

Blood is the life-carrier of man. The Torah refers to it as *"nefesh"* — the soul of man. The blood that invigorates the anatomical heart is also a symbol of the vibrant soul. "Your *mesiras nefesh* to My principles is the manifestation of your boundless dedication."

Thus the passage in *Yechezkel* (15:6): "*And I passed over you and saw you wallowing in your blood and said to you — by your blood (of milah) shall you live, by your blood (of pesach) shall you live.*"

Although they struggled in the blood of brutality, they would live by the blood of their bond with G-d.

◆§ The Harbinger of Redemption

The relationship of these two *mitzvos* to each other and their special meaning for *Klal Yisrael*, is further underscored in another way. There are two times when we set aside a remembrance of *Eliyahu HaNavi* — the prophet Elijah — at a *bris* and at the *Seder*. At every *bris*, a special seat of honor is designated for Eliyahu who is titled "*Malach HaBris*" (the Angel of the Covenant); and at every *Seder* we fill a fifth cup of wine which is known as *kos shel Eliyahu* — the Cup of Elijah.

The prophet Malachi says that Eliyahu will come "before the great and awesome day (of redemption) to return the hearts of the elders to the children and the hearts of the children to their elders." He will unite them in a common cause of repentance, restore their adherence to Torah and elevate them to a level at which they will merit the coming of *Moshiach*.

Eliyahu, who is the "Angel of the Covenant," will insure the people's loyalty to it. This Covenant is reflected in the words G-d spoke to Avraham: "*Go before Me and become perfect.*"

On the *Seder* night, as we commemorate our first redemption, we pray that "the wrath of G-d will be spilled on those who have attempted to devour the Jewish people." We open the door and wait for Eliyahu to come and inform us of the imminent redemption.

◄§ Sefiras HaOmer / *The Sacred Countdown*

nocturnal growth and sublimation
of the beastly ... the unity of counting
together ... the advance from freedom to
spirituality

Adapted from Haggadah Shem MiShmuel
by Rabbi Nisson Wolpin

Sefirah: Three Aspects

Chassidic Insights from
the writings of
the Sochoczover Rebbe
Rabbi Shmuel Borenstein זצ"ל

◆§ Night Trip

I n recounting the travels of the Jewish people across the Sinai
desert, the Torah states clearly that they "went by day and by
night" *(Shemos* 13:21). Since they were "borne on the wings of
eagles," covering 120 *mil* in the brief span of an hour, what need
was there for nocturnal travel? There was no shortage of time to
reach the goals of their travels.

The trek across the desert sands was more than a
geographical trip. It was also a physical enactment of the spiritual
journey from the bondage of Egypt to the freedom of Sinai, each
day bringing an elevation from one spiritual level to the next.
This was a constant climb, and could allow for no interruption in
its ascent to spiritual freedom. Night, as a period of time, is distinct from day and had it been dedicated to rest, the steady climb
to Sinai would have lost its continuity. And continuity is an essential element in every spiritual growth.

There is more involved, however, for not only did the traveling take place at night, it was often *initiated* at night. Night must then be considered for its deeper implications, beyond that of being the period when daylight is absent. Day is indicative of that state of mind when choices are clear, and good and evil stand out in stark contrast to one another. This clarity makes climbing from one spiritual station to the next a clearly defined task, and the ability to interpret events basks in the light of "morning," when one can truly "relate Your acts of kindness" (*Tehillim* 92:3), using them as inspiration for personal growth.

Night refers to the muddled and unclear, when even the right choice appears fraught with hazards, and when what is wrong may appear to be unusually attractive. The wilderness journey to Sinai meant "following Me through the desert in a land not sown with seed" (*Yirmiyah* 2:2), with no visible source of food and sustenance; a journey that was traveled in the "night" of confusion and insecurity. This called upon the Jews to exercise their "faith, through the night" (*Tehillim* 92:3), as they rose to the heights of Sinai.

Whether it be day or night, whether events and choices stand out with clarity or tempt one to retreat from the uncertainty of darkness, one must still advance in his spiritual journey to Sinai.

⋙ Barley Offering

The *Sefirah* count begins on the Second Day of Pesach with the bringing of the *Omer* — a meal offering of barley — to the *Bais HaMikdash*. Every offering expressed the theme of "a soul for a soul"; the person making the offering visualized a portion of himself that embodied the mundane and earthly being rechanneled to spiritual pursuits. This is the highest level of service — converting the mundane to the spiritual, replacing darkness with light.

This principle also applies to the meal offerings of fine wheat flour, which alludes to man's intelligence ("A child does not utter his first word — *Abba, Ima* — until he experiences the taste of grain" — *Berachos*, 40a). Through the medium of the meal offering, the gift of natural intelligence is elevated to the spiritual. But barley is a bovine repast, food from the barnyard, not representative of any ideal human attainment. The only other occasion of a barley-offering in the Temple was the *Minchas Kena'os*, brought by the suspected adulteress. ("Let her who conducted herself as a beast bring the food of a beast as her offering" — *Sotah* 12a.) Yet there is an element usually associated with simple beasts that has spiritual implications.

Domesticated animals as a species possess the attribute of willing subservience. This can also be a wholesome trait in man's Divine service, for its converse, ego-assertion is a troublesome characteristic that is at the root of a host of human transgressions. Yet submissiveness is a character trait with pitfalls. He who willingly bows his head is easily intimidated, and is but a breath away from despair and domination. This aspect of the trait must be avoided.

Ideally, an individual should experience a loss of ego-identity in response to the overwhelming joy and penetrating awe of serving his omnipotent Master — a joyful subservience. At the same time, he should be contemptuous of any concept or action that is in opposition to service to G-d. This is contradictory to natural subservience. Herein lies the sublimating function of the *Omer* offering — the elevation of a natural subservience to the spiritual, channeling it so that it is used solely to express one's relationship with his Creator, still permitting one to challenge the tyranny of the G-dless.

Hence, the timing of the *Omer* offering on the Second Day of Pesach. Liberation from the yoke of Pharaoh and all that he represents thrusts the Jew into a most joyful relationship with his Redeemer. But he does not abandon the subservience imprinted upon his soul by the generations of bondage to Egypt. Instead he refines it, and devotes it completely to G-d — but only to G-d.

G-d said: *"In the past you were servants unto Pharaoh. Now you are servants unto G-d"* (Mechilta).

So *"Sing praise, you servants of G-d"* (Tehillim 113:1) — servants of G-d, but not of Pharaoh.

◂§ Seven Weeks of Mourning

The seven weeks of *Sefirah* are a season of mourning for the twenty-four thousand disciples of Rabbi Akiva who perished during this period. They were punished, we are told, for not having dealt respectfully with one another. It seems strange that Rabbi Akiva's disciples, whose greatness in Torah and in character is far beyond our comprehension — for we still mourn their loss nearly two thousand years after their death — should have suffered so severe a punishment for so mild a sin. Both the sin that earned them their death and the mourning that still follows it need clarification.

Furthermore, there is no element of coincidence in the Jewish calendar, and the commemoration of this national tragedy must somehow be bound with our Sefirah preparations for receiving the Torah.

The *Sefer HaGilgulim* associates these twenty-four thousand disciples with the twenty-four thousand followers of Zimri who died in the plague of *Ba'al Peor*, at the end of the forty years of wandering in the wilderness. The *Zohar* blames their downfall on their ensnarement in *kishuf* — sorcery. The attraction of sorcery, says the *Zohar*, is strongest when one is least aware of the G-dliness of every aspect of one's existence. Shutting out the Divine source of all living things endows the insignificant with the illusion of imposing values and awesome powers that they do not really have. Attempting to manipulate these powers is involvement in sorcery. The less one is aware of G-d, the greater the importance one assigns to his own worth, and the more he is apt to delve in *kishuf*.

The prime preparation for receiving the Law on Shavuos — both at Sinai and today — is to refine one's personal character, as well as to achieve a total sense of unity with all Jewry. Unity is based on recognizing the value of each and every other member of the group for what he can offer — in constructive action, in inspiring word, or even in helpful presence. The less importance one attaches to himself, the more receptive he is to the importance of his fellows, and the faster the bonds of unity can hold. By contrast, inflated self-importance prevents one from appreciating his fellows and their function in complementing his own role in the totality of Israel.

This distorted assessment of one's own worth is akin to the misassignment of values that is associated with the *kishuf* of Zimri's time. And it is this same type of exaggerated self-importance that in some small way served to breed discord among Rabbi Akiva's disciples.

During the days of Sefirah, when we mourn the untimely loss of the disciples of Rabbi Akiva, we endeavor to avoid their shortcomings. Self-examination brings us closer to an understanding of our true worth, and our utter dependence upon one another — nearer to our G-d and closer to Sinai.

Rabbi Moshe Weitman

Sefirah:
Days of Counting

Rabbi Chiya said: "Seven complete weeks shall they be." — When Israel does the will of the Almighty, then are they complete.
Rabbi Shimon ben Lakish said: Let not the mitzvah of Omer be light in your eyes, for through this mitzvah, G-d brings peace between man and wife — that is, in merit of the barley offering. (Midrash Rabbah, Emor)

THE EXODUS from Egypt was undoubtedly history's most dramatic and explicit exhibition of Divine intervention in the events of mankind. The Children of Israel were suddenly and dramatically lifted to the level where they could point their fingers at the majesty of the Almighty and sing: "This is my G-d!" And then as today, on the very next night, they began to count *Sefiras HaOmer* — forty-nine days, seven full weeks — before they were fit to receive the Torah. Notwithstanding the spiritual heights ascended on Pesach night, they were not considered worthy of receiving the Torah until they endured an eternity — a full *yovel*. (*Yovel*, which occurs after a count of forty-nine, is termed by the Torah an eternity.)

The *Pesach* inspiration did not come from within the Jews, but rather as a Heavenly awakening to which they were merely passive recipients.

Indeed, the redemption from Egypt took place years before

its appointed time, with an abrupt suddenness — *bechipazon.* Israel, almost indistinguishable from the Egyptians, could not remain in Egypt for even one additional moment, lest they descend to the point of no return. They had been, in the prophet's words, spiritually naked, clothed neither with Torah nor with *mitzvos.* The greatness of the Exodus experience was unearned, bestowed externally, and as such was subject to fade. The great light they perceived could have become but a momentary flash. With the counting of the *Omer,* the Children of Israel began again from the very beginning, counting day by day, week by week; and through a process of *teshuvah,* they regained the forty-nine rungs from which they had fallen during their enslavement to Pharaoh; each count and each blessing signifying a new step toward *Kabalas HaTorah.*

The Torah tells us of these days: "Complete shall they be." According to the Midrash, only days that are used in their entirety for accomplishing the will of the Almighty are complete.

Sefiras HaOmer is thus not merely a period of counting days in eager anticipation of the Festival of *Kabalas HaTorah.* It is also a time of active preparation — days of spiritual cleansing and purification, before a sacred event.

⋖§ Unfaithful Spouse

The *Sefirah* count is framed by two grain *korbanos.* First is the *Omer* (a measure of barley) brought on the second day of *Pesach.* This *korban* (words such as "sacrifice" or "offering" are poor substitutes for the unique Torah concept of *korban)* permitted general use of the new grain crop. At the conclusion of the *Omer* count, on Shavuos, the *sh'tei halechem* (two wheat breads) were brought. While barley is the food of the beast, wheat is the food of man. The counting, then, is meant to signify our gradual rise from the lowly beginnings of the Jew at Exodus time to his full stature as an Adam — i.e., Man realizing his potential.

Rabbi Shimon ben Lakish, in the Midrash, points out a deeper significance of the barley *korban.* The only other barley *korban* is the *minchas kena'os* brought for the *sotah* — a wife suspected of adultery — as an indication of the low level of her conduct. Should she be found innocent of the alleged sin she nonetheless requires representation by this *korban* of barley, for only because she had behaved improperly could her conduct have been placed under question. Similarly, the Children of Israel had strayed after strange gods during their Egyptian bondage. Just as the *korban* of the *sotah* who is ultimately proven innocent results in peace between husband and wife, reuniting them in love, so too does the barley *korban* of the *Omer* reestablish peace between G-d and Israel, in a relationship often alluded to as that of Groom and Bride.

The *Sefirah* count begins with the *korban* of barley and all that it denotes — reminding Israel, the wife who has gone astray, that she had acted in an unseemly fashion, akin to the beast. Each day filled with *teshuvah* and good deeds is counted towards Shavuos — the day of the bringing of the wheat offering and the day when the relationship between G-d and His people was consummated with the giving of the Torah.

A time interval of ninety-two days is imposed upon a woman when one marital alliance is terminated and she seeks to enter into a new marriage — that is, ninety-one days plus the day of betrothal. The forty-nine day period between the idolatry of Egypt and *Kabalas HaTorah* would seem to correspond to this interval, but it falls short of this count. Actually the *Omer* consists of a double count of the days and weeks (e.g., day forty-seven is counted both as the forty-seventh day and as six weeks and five days). This double count takes place on but forty-three of the forty-nine days, since the first six days of the *Omer* have no weeks to count. These forty-three days, however, consisting as they do of a "day" count and a "week" count, may be doubled to be considered a counting of eighty-six, and with the addition of the six days of single count, the total is ninety-two ... So great is Hashem's love for his bride, Israel, that he shortened the span and allowed us to consider the counting of both the days and the weeks to hasten the ninety-second day when Israel enters the spiritual nuptials with Him.

◄§ Guidance of Fathers

Where does one find guidance for preparing to receive the Torah? The Torah itself precedes the *mitzvos* with a detailed recounting of the lives of the Patriarchs. Their lives form a pattern of action which had to precede, and in fact led to, *Kabalas HaTorah*. *Avos*, the tractate devoted to ethical improvement, is studied during the *Sefirah* period as a means of molding the Jewish personality in the image of our Patriarchs so we, too, may be worthy of the Torah. This is one reason for its very name — "*Avos* — Fathers."

Significantly, *Avos* begins with "Moshe received the Torah

from Sinai." This states the purpose of these teachings: to be fit to receive the Torah.

The acts of the Fathers were meant to foretell the deeds of the Children. Involvement in acts of refinement as a prerequisite to the loftiness of receiving the Torah was expressed in the much-heralded responses of the Children of Israel to the offer of the Law: "Na'aseh VeNishma — We shall do and we shall harken," expressing the precedence that one must elevate his activity before he can receive the Law. We too engage in days of active self-improvement to earn receiving the Law — our own echo of the cry: "Na'aseh VeNishma."

◄§ A Receptacle for Torah

The *Bnai Yisaschar* explains the relationship between Lag B'Omer and Shavuos: Rabbi Yochanan ben Zakai told five of his disciples to determine the best path for a man to follow. Rabbi Elazar ben Aroch, the last of the five, advised that *lev tov* — a good heart — was most desirable. Rabbi Yochanan ben Zakai preferred his conclusion above all others and said that, in truth, it included all others. More than a path in life, Rabbi Yochanan ben Zakai may have been seeking the path that leads to a full and complete commitment to Torah, and this path of *lev tov* is in turn indicated in the Torah.

The first mention in the Torah of the word *tov* — good — deals with light: "And the Almighty saw the light that it was good." This was no ordinary light but, as the Talmud tells us, a spiritual illumination, which enabled man to see from one end of the world to the other. Rashi cites the Talmudic comment: "It was so good that the Almighty hid it for the righteous to enjoy in the world-to-come. And where was it hidden until then? — in the Torah." Consequently, the Torah is often alluded to as "light" — *oraisa;* and similarly, men wise in Torah knowledge are endowed with gifts of vision and perception that enable them to see further and with more clarity than ordinary mortals. When Rabbi Elazar ben Aroch sought ultimate good, he consulted the Torah. The first mention of "*tov*" — good — in the Torah was preceded by thirty-two words. Thirty-two corresponds to the numerical equivalent of *lev* — heart. Thirty-two representing *lev*, plus the *gematria* (numerical equivalent) of *tov* — seventeen — total forty-nine, the number of days we count in preparation for receiving the Torah. These forty-nine days, then, are designated for developing a *lev tov*, as a fitting receptacle for the Torah we receive on the fiftieth day.

The breakup of the count of forty-nine into two periods — the thirty-two days of *lev* and the seventeen of *tov* — is also significant. The thirty-third day of the count is *Lag B'Omer*, the anniversary of the passing of the *tanna* Rabbi Shimon bar Yochai, who wrote the *Sefer HaZohar* — *The Book of Splendor*. The word "*zohar*" means a splendid brilliant light, and the Book indeed offers a glimpse of that bright light which the Almighty had secreted in the Torah. On this thirty-third day, candles are lit in the memory of Rabbi Shimon bar Yochai, a huge bonfire is kindled near his tomb, and the joy and sanctity of the celebration is overpowering. *Lag B'Omer* is also the first of the seventeen days preceding *Shavuos*, and those seventeen correspond to the numerical value of *tov* — the good which the Torah identifies with light. *Lag B'Omer*, then, ushers in days of light and joy, in contrast to the preceding days of sorrow, and fittingly marks the *yahrzeit* of the author of the *Zohar*, who revealed so powerful a light with his *sefer*.

Sefiras HaOmer is not simply a ceremonial counting of days on the evenings between *Pesach* and *Shavuos*. It is also meant to remind us to make these days count, as we prepare ourselves with thought and deed for *Kabalas HaTorah* — the climax and goal of these days and weeks of counting.

Rabbi Aryeh Kaplan

The Omer

*Understanding Sefirah
on many levels*

◄§ When Every Jew Counts

O N THE SECOND night of Pesach each year, Jews all over the
world begin counting the Omer — the days between Pesach
and Shavuos — in accordance with the commandment: "You shall
count from the day after the festival-Sabbath, from the day that
you brought the Omer offering, seven full weeks. Until the day
after the seventh week, you shall number fifty days, and you shall
then bring a new meal offering to G-d" *(Vayikra* 23:15, 16).

Although the *Omer* was a communal offering, the days
between Pesach and Shavuos had to be counted not only by the
communal representatives, but by every Jew *(Menachos 65b)*.

To fully understand the reason for this, we must first explore
another point. Shavuos is known as the anniversary of the giving
of the Torah — for it was on Shavuos, 2448 years after Creation,
that all Israel stood at the foot of Mount Sinai and heard the
declaration of the Ten Commandments, as one can calculate from
the Torah's account of the event.

Yet, nowhere among the Torah's many references to
Shavuos is it mentioned as the anniversary of the giving of the
Torah. Why is this most significant aspect of Shavuos omitted?

A number of explanations are offered for this. The *Alshich* explains that the Israelites reached the highest possible spiritual level with the giving of the Torah, a level that was subsequently lost with the sin of the Golden Calf. To specifically commemorate the initial revelation at Sinai would also mean recalling this great spiritual loss. Thus Shavuos is not explicitly described as marking the giving of the Torah.

The *Abarbanel* offers a somewhat different approach. Remembering the giving of the Torah is a constant obligation upon every Jew. It is therefore not appropriate to designate a single day for specific commemoration.

Nonetheless, it would be very surprising if the Torah provided no hint whatsoever to the great significance of this day. Both the above commentators state that there is an allusion to it in the counting of the Omer: The Omer days are counted because of the outstanding significance in Jewish history of the period between Pesach and Shavuos. On Pesach, the Israelites began as newly freed slaves; and during the ensuing seven weeks they were elevated to a level where they would be worthy of hearing G-d's voice proclaiming the Commandments. The very fact that Shavuos comes at the end of this counting alludes to its importance as the day upon which the Torah was given.

This also explains why every single Jew must count the Omer. The acceptance of the Torah is described with the words, "All the people answered *with one voice,* and said, 'All the words that G-d has spoken, we will do' " *(Shemos* 24:3). The *Sefer Chassidim* explains that the Jews were required to possess perfect unity — to speak "with one voice" — to receive the Torah. If even one Israelite had refused the Torah, it could not have been given.

Moreover, each individual had to rise from the level of slavery to that of revelation. Thus, every individual "counted" those days between the first Pesach and the first Shavuos.

Besides preparation for receiving the Torah, the counting of the Omer also bespeaks the Israelites' eagerness for the Torah, for they had realized that they would receive the Torah seven weeks after the Exodus, and they literally counted the days in anticipation. *(Chinuch* 306). Here, too, each individual shared in this excitement.

◆§ The Advance Toward Freedom

Pesach is known as the festival of our freedom, marking the Exodus, when we were freed from Egyptian slavery. This was only physical liberation — only the first step toward true freedom, which was realized on Shavuos with the acceptance of the Torah. As our Sages teach, "The only truly free man is he who is devoted to the Torah" (*Avos* 6:2).

Many people question this, wondering how total subjugation to the Torah can be equated with complete freedom. But the concept is actually not that difficult. Nothing in the world is truly free. Natural phenomena are bound by laws of nature. And there are laws and rules — natural and man-made — that govern both the individual and society. Further, a man ruled by his passions is also in no sense free. A careful analysis would reveal that true freedom simply does not exist in the material world, for nowhere is any creature free to do whatever it desires.

In the final analysis, only G-d is truly free, for of all that exists, only G-d can do exactly what He wants, at any time that He chooses, with no restraints whatsoever. Stated in another way, true freedom only exists with G-d. Man in search of freedom must seek association with G-d, and his only link to G-d is through Torah — G-d's word. Therefore, ultimate freedom can only be realized through total devotion to Torah.

With the first Pesach, the Israelites had their first taste of freedom. They then eagerly counted the days until they would gain total, absolute freedom, through receiving the Torah.

◄§ Animal Food and Human Food Offerings

In a sense, freedom is an essential ingredient of humanity, for the ability to consider and select his options is a feature peculiar to man. Thus, one can say that with the acceptance of the Torah, the Israelites first realized their potential to be truly human in the fullest sense of the word. They now had the freedom to totally transcend their animal nature.

This is also alluded to in the Omer, which consisted of a sheaf of barley. The *Abarbanel* explains that barley is normally animal food, signifying that immediately after the Exodus the Israelites had not yet transcended their animal nature. On Shavuos, however, the offering was two loaves of bread made from pure wheat flour. Wheat is a human food, indicating that with the acceptance of the Torah, the Israelites gained full human status.

Moreover, the Omer offering consisted of meal, while the Shavuos offering consisted of fully baked breads. Flour is but the first step in converting grain into human food; bread is the final product. On Pesach, the Israelites had taken their first step toward realizing their true humanity; on Shavuos, they took the final step.

⋖§ Chometz as an Offering

Also significant is that the Two Breads of Shavuos were leavened bread (chometz). This is in sharp distinction to Pesach, when chometz is absolutely forbidden.

As the Talmud (Berachos 17a) states, chometz represents the Evil Inclination (yeitzer hara) and on Pesach, the yeitzer hara was totally negated. As long as the Israelites were bound to the yeitzer hara they could not even begin their advance toward freedom. The banishment of the yeitzer hara was represented by the banishment of all leaven from each Israelite's possession.

On Shavuos, however, the Israelites reached a level of true freedom and total self-discipline. On this level, one can make use of the yeitzer hara to serve G-d. Our Sages interpret: "You shall love the Lord your G-d with all (parts of) your heart" — even with the yeitzer hara directing us to harness drives usually associated with evil, and direct them toward good. On that first Shavuos, this was achieved without conscious effort. Since even the yeitzer hara could now be used as a means of coming close to G-d, the Shavuos offering also included chometz.

This can be understood on a deeper level in light of a teaching of the Baal Shem Tov. The Talmud states that in the end of days, G-d will slaughter the yeitzer hara. The Baal Shem notes that the Talmud employs the term normally used for ritual slaughter of kosher animals. He concludes that just as shechitah (ritual slaughter) renders an animal kosher, so too will "slaughter" of the yeitzer hara render it "kosher" — that is, transform it into an angel of good.

Since receiving the Torah raised the Israelites to a level approximating that of the world of the future, they could deal with the yeitzer hara virtually as a good angel. In recognition of this, the Shavuos offering specifically designated the use of leaven. This lofty spiritual level was lost with the Sin of the Golden Calf.*

---

* One may then wonder why the Israelites sinned if they no longer had a yeitzer hara? The Gemara explains that this was part of a Divine plan to teach the ways of repentance to the world (Avodah Zarah 4b).

◄§ Two Loaves, Two Tablets

Also of significance is that *two* loaves were offered, corresponding to the Two Tablets containing the Ten Commandments: and the reason for the number in both cases is very similar.

All through the Book of *Shemos*, the Tablets are referred to as *Luchos HaBris* — Tablets of the Covenant. The generation that had entered the Covenant at Sinai was still alive, and to them the Tablets served as a *tangible sign* of this covenant. In *Devarim* they are referred to as *Luchos HaEidus* — Tablets of Testimony. Since the majority of the people then living were born after the revelation at Sinai, to them the Tablets *bore witness* to this great event.

The Midrash explains that this is one of the reasons that there were *two* tablets. Just as testimony is only valid when taken from two witnesses, so too did the testimony of the Tablets require the presence of *two*.

The paradigm of a covenant *(bris)* was the "covenant between the halves" *(Bris bain HaBesarim)* in which animals were cut in half, and Avraham walked between the sections. Rashi explains that this is the thrust of every covenant: the makers of the covenant accompany each other between the sections of a divided entity. This also is alluded to in the two-ness of the tablets and the loaves.

◄§ The Bridge of Sevens

There is also significance in the duration of the purification process of the Omer — forty-nine days. As Rabbi Samson Raphael Hirsch notes (based on the *Zohar*) many types of impurity are purged in a seven-day purification period. Cleansing can be understood as an act of re-creation and rebirth, with the period of cleansing paralleling the seven days of creation.

Before the Torah was given, however, the Israelites were required to undergo a most thorough cleansing — not only of their own impurities, but of all those that tainted the entire world from the time of creation. Thus, the requisite period of cleansing was seven times seven days.

◄§ Omer: A period of Mourning

All of the themes associated with the Omer — freedom, preparation and anticipation for receiving the Torah — would lead one to think that these particular weeks would be a time of rejoicing and celebration. But instead, it is a period of national mourning when weddings and similar happy events are forbidden, as are haircutting and shaving. This is because the 24,000 students of Rabbi Akiva died during this period (*Yevamos* 62b). It might seem strange that these great men died during these weeks, and even more surprising that this should be enough to endow this entire period with a spirit of mourning.

But the Talmud records that they died because they were somehow faulted for lacking proper respect for one another. The Midrash also states that in some minute way — surely undetectable to us — they were jealous of each other.

Rabbi Akiva's students were the greatest Torah scholars of their time, and as the Talmud states, their death left the world "desolate". During this period of preparation for receiving the Torah, they should have put aside any differences — no matter how minute — that may have existed between them; they should have lived in perfect harmony and unity. Since they maintained their so-called rivalries, even during this period, they were punished precisely during these crucial weeks.

As mentioned earlier, the very act of receiving the Torah required total unity on the part of the Jews. Without such unity, our acceptance of the Torah cannot be complete. And without Torah, we are nothing. It is therefore taught that the Temple was destroyed because of the sin of unwarranted hatred (*sinas chinam*) for in a state of cleavage and rivalry we were without Torah and totally lacking in the merit required for having the Temple in our midst.

Rabbi Levi Yitzchak of Berditchev teaches that since the Temple was destroyed because of hatred, we cannot expect it to be rebuilt unless we purge this hatred from our midst.

We therefore continue to mourn the death of Rabbi Akiva's students, as we continue to mourn the destruction of the Temple. For we know that as long as the Temple is not rebuilt, we have not yet cleansed the stain resulting from these students' lack of unity. Until we do, the Temple cannot be rebuilt, and the *galus* cannot end. Only when we learn to have the fullest measure of respect for one another and live in unity can we be worthy of the true Redemption.

∙⧼ Shavuos / *Receiving the Torah*

the weakness of seeking strength through slumber ... the preservation of one electric moment ... the anticipated initiation of Moshe Rabbeinu ... G-d's revelation and man's discovery ... the lasting bond of receiving the Torah

Adapted by
Rabbi Ben Zion Metzger

The Nocturnal Slumber
of Atzeres

A Shavuos message from
Rabbi Menachem Mendel Schneerson,
The Lubavitcher Rebbe שליט״א

THE MIDRASH relates that the Jewish people slept the entire night prior to the receiving of the Torah "for the slumber of *Atzeres* is pleasant and the night is short," and even a a biting insect did not disturb them. When the Almighty was ready in the early morning to give the Torah and found Israel asleep, it was necessary for Him to arouse them, and this is the meaning of what the Almighty declares:

Wherefore, when I came was there no man?
When I called, was there none to answer? (Isaiah 50:2)

For this reason it is customary to stay awake the entire night of Shavuos engaged in the study of Torah — to undo the slumber of the Jewish nation on the night prior to the giving of the Torah.

Every Torah narrative provides guidance for us in our own spiritual endeavors. Particularly one such as this — the Torah normally goes to great lengths to avoid disparaging or derogatory comment — must assuredly include an inherently significant moral precept, which made it necessary to record these events.

Though there is an obvious implication — the need to undo Israel's having slept on that momentous night — the account of their sleeping would have been sufficient. The enumeration of the various details — that "The slumber of *Atzeres* is pleasant, and the night is short," and that the insects did not bite them — indicates that even these matters have applications to man's spiritual conduct.

◄§ The Slumber of Preparation

When the Jewish people heard that after their departure from Egypt they would be given the Torah, a great longing to receive the Torah was evoked, and they began to count the days till the anticipated time. For this reason we count the days of the *Omer*. If at the onset of the seven weeks they were impatient to receive the Torah, it is self-evident how great the degree of their yearning was at the time immediately prior to the event. How then was it possible that they slept the night before the giving of the Torah?

It should also be borne in mind that their counting was also a means of preparation for the receiving of the Torah. During these forty-nine days, the Jewish people underwent progressive spiritual purification till they were worthy of being the recipients of the Torah. Every day they evoked within themselves the revelation of another of the Gates of Understanding; when they had concluded the evocation of all the Forty-Nine Gates (the maximum degree achievable by human effort), then the Almighty, at the time of giving the Torah, endowed them with the Fiftieth Gate.

If immediately after the departure from Egypt — delivered from the Forty-Nine Gates of Impurity — they longed to receive the Torah, how infinitely greater was their yearning for the Torah after having achieved the lofty degree of the "Forty-ninth Gate of Understanding," after the great spiritual ascent of the forty-nine days, as they became progressively more worthy of receiving the Torah. *How, then, did they permit themselves to slumber?*

We must consequently assume that their sleep is not to be understood in a normal manner, but was rather in itself a manner of preparation for the receiving of the Torah. Further proof that their sleep was a form of preparation is that the insects did not bite them. If their sleep was but a lapse of consciousness and a distraction from their preoccupation with receiving the Torah, then the Almighty would not have caused a *miracle* — that they should not be disturbed during their tranquil slumber.

The *Alter Rebbe* (Rabbi Shneur Zalman of Liadi) notes that the loftiest degree of comprehension and closeness to G-dliness achieved during human existence (when the soul is garbed in human form) is still incomparable to the exalted level of closeness achieved by the soul *prior* to its descent into the human body. This is so because the physical body cannot cope with so high a degree of closeness *(Tanya 37)*.

During sleep, the soul divests itself of the body and ascends to its source; there remains within the body "but a small measure of life" from the soul. Therefore, at the time of slumber, the soul can sometimes achieve loftier conceptions than during the time of wakefulness while vested in the physical garb of its body.

It is known that those who preoccupy themselves with Torah with great dedication and zeal during their waking hours achieve in the course of their sleep even further revelation in matters of Torah — to such a degree, at times, that problems they struggled to clarify while awake which remained unanswered are resolved upon their awakening from a period of sleep, because of the soul's apprehension above.

Therefore, after the Jewish people had achieved all that is possible for the soul in bodily garb to achieve, i.e. — the Forty-Nine Gates of Understanding — they wished to slumber prior to receiving the Torah, for they desired that the soul divest itself from its bodily garb and ascend above to apprehend lofty conceptions. They felt that the exalted concepts they would achieve would be the most appropriate — the culmination of their preparation for the revelation from above at the time of the giving of the Torah.

Therefore the Midrash states — "The slumber of *Atzeres* is pleasant and the night is short" — the more a person strives and refines himself while awake, when the soul is in its bodily garb, to that extent does the soul ascend and achieve loftier conceptions during the period of sleep. At the conclusion of the spiritual labor of counting *sefirah* for forty-nine days, they had already achieved the spiritual preparation for *Atzeres*. And, "The Night" [the spiritual darkness and 'concealment' of the world] is short; there remained but a small degree of concealment, for the entire labor had been completed and in a very short while there would occur the revelation of *Mattan Torah* — at such a time the slumber is "pleasant," for by means of sleep, one can achieve the loftiest spirituality.

The great ascent of the Jewish people at the time of their sleep affected even the surrounding world and nature to the extent that not even an insect disturbed them from their slumber.

◈ To Serve With the Body

Nevertheless, the Almighty was not content with Israel's slumber prior to receiving the Torah, for this was not the appropriate preparation. The preparation for receiving the Torah must be of an entirely different nature.

The purpose of all ascent is essentially spiritual endeavor using the physical human body. It is by this means that the relationship with the essence of G-dliness can be truly achieved. So significant is the importance of laboring *with* the physical body, that the *Heavenly Court* above recognizes the judicial decisions rendered by the Torah scholars on *earth*. Though their opinion be at variance with the Heavenly decision, the Almighty declares, "My sons have triumphed," for the Torah "is *not* in Heaven."

Since the singular importance of the giving of the Torah was the endowment of exalted significance to the soul's labor *within* the body, the preparation for the giving of the Torah had to be in a similar manner. Not to recline in slumber, not the soul's separation from the physical body, but to labor and serve *with* the body.

How does this apply to our spiritual endeavor? There are those who argue: Why should I concern myself with physical matters? Far better to shut myself off from the world, to labor in Torah and prayer in seclusion. I have expended great effort in the learning of Torah and the fulfillment of *mitzvos;* I have already achieved the level of *Atzeres* and — "the night is short" — the darkness within me is greatly diminished; by isolating myself from the world, I will achieve even loftier spirituality.

We are therefore told that even prior to the receiving of the Torah (but on the very day that it was given), such conduct was not in accordance with the will of G-d, and there remains constantly the necessity to undo the slumber of the past. Most assuredly, subsequent to the giving of the Torah, our spiritual labor must be in a manner of "descent below" — the spiritual descending — concerning itself with the physical; preoccupying ourselves with a fellow Jew of lesser degree. Specifically by such means will the scholar succeed in achieving ascent — "and from my students have I derived more than from the others" *(Taanis 7a).*

This is the reason for our custom of not sleeping during the night of *Shavuos.* The preparation for receiving the Torah is not in slumber, but in the soul's ascent and departure from the physical, to achieve the apprehension of lofty conceptions. The primary endeavor for each individual is to labor with the human body, with his baser nature and his share in the material world, and thus to prepare for the receiving of the Torah with inward joy — for the entire year.

Rabbi Mordechai Gifter

The Permanence
of Ma'amad Har Sinai

That singular moment in history
as a dynamic process,
making Israel ever worthy
of receiving the Torah

> *Only, take heed and guard your soul carefully, lest you*
> *forget the things which your eyes saw and lest they depart*
> *from your heart all the days of your life. Make them known*
> *unto your children and your children's children: the day that*
> *you stood before G-d at Horeb [that is, Sinai] ...*

◄§ Sensory Perception of Torah

The greatest single event in the life of *Klal Yisrael* is the
experience of *Ma'amad Har Sinai*, standing at the foot of
Mount Sinai to receive the Torah. In *Ma'amad Har Sinai* all of
Israel, not *Moshe Rabbeinu* alone, became endowed with the
power of prophecy. All Israel became prophets of G-d. The Rabbis have taught us: The first two statements of the Decalogue
were heard directly from G-d by all of Israel, in the way that all
the other statements were heard by Moshe. This fact is the basis
for that which the Torah teaches: "And they shall believe in you

forever." This is the very basis for the authority of Torah in Jewish life. In becoming prophets themselves and thereby becoming the receptors of Torah, the power of prophecy resting in *Moshe Rabbeinu* became an acknowledged fact.

Additionally, in becoming prophets, all of *Klal Yisrael* was endowed with a sensory perception of Torah. *Emunah* (implicit faith) is the result of intellectual perception of knowledge. Human knowledge, if it is to be of value, if it is to be durable, must be experienced through the physical senses of man. In the personal perception of prophecy, therein lay the guarantee for: "They shall believe in you forever," the source and origin of Torah for all eternity, *"because man does not believe that which he does not know" (Ramban).*

It becomes patently clear that we cannot speak of the perpetuity of Torah in *Klal Yisrael* as disassociated from the event of *Ma'amad Har Sinai.* If the Torah is necessary for Israel, if Torah is our life-blood, and the length of our days, then *Ma'amad Har Sinai* must be ever-present among *Klal Yisrael.*

The prime function of the *Mishkan* (temporary Sanctuary) and, afterwards, the *Bais HaMikdash* (the Holy Sanctuary) was to give permanence in the life of our people to *Ma'amad Har Sinai.* The glory of the Divine Presence which descended on Sinai in a form of overwhelming force and magnitude, descended to the *Kodesh HaKodashim* (the Holy of Holies) in hidden form, and the voice which descended from Heaven to speak Torah on Sinai — the same voice descended to the top of the Holy Ark, between the two Cheruvim, to continue to speak Torah (*Ramban, Terumah*). In the presence of this continuity of the *Ma'amad*, Israel was able to rise to the heights of the *Korbanos* services. Three times each year *Klal Yisrael* was called upon to appear, "to see and be seen" before the countenance of G-d. In the proximity of this *Ma'amad* was the chamber of Hewn Stone, the seat of the Sanhedrin, the supreme authority of Torah in Israel.

One of the six hundred and thirteen *mitzvos* is that of *Talmud Torah*, the study and propagation of Torah to hand down, to commit Torah to our children from generation to generation. It is however not sufficient to hand down the word of Torah alone. The *Ma'amad Har Sinai*, the original form of its descent to *Klal Yisrael*, must by sensed be each generation. Only then is it Torah.

This is specifically and explicitly stated in a complete portion of the Torah, worthy of our constant consideration.

Behold, I have taught you statutes and laws ... observe therefore and do them; for this is your wisdom and your understanding in the sight of all peoples, who when they hear all these statutes shall surely say, "Surely this great nation is a wise and understanding people." Only, take heed and guard your soul carefully, lest you forget the things which your eyes saw and lest they depart from your heart all the days of your life. Make them known unto your children and your children's children: the day that you stood before G-d at Horeb [that is, Sinai] ... and you came near and stood under the mountain, and the mountain burned with fire to the heart of Heaven with deep darkness and cloud (Devarim 4:5-11).

Upon these words the *Ramban* comments: The Torah teaches us here that in addition to keeping Torah and *mitzvos*, it is our duty at all times to remember the source and origin of these *mitzvos*; we are exhorted not to forget *Ma'amad Har Sinai*, all that we saw and heard. All that we witnessed in the *Ma'amad Har Sinai* must be handed down to our children forever.

The benefit resulting from this *mitzvah* is very great, for if Torah had come to us through *Moshe Rabbeinu* alone, even though his prophecy was proven, there would be the danger that should a prophet arise to deny the Torah, this would prove to be cause for doubt in the minds of our people. But, since Torah descended directly from G-d to our ears and we witnessed this event with our own eyes, we are able to negate all denial and cast aside all doubts. He who would deny Torah is clearly recognized as a fraud for we are fully conscious of his deception.

This is the meaning of "they shall believe in you forever," for when the *Ma'amad Har Sinai* is handed down to our children, they will recognize it as truth as if they had personally witnessed the *Ma'amad*. For no father will bear false testimony to his son, and no child will doubt the testimony of his parents. They will together believe that which was perceived with the senses.

◁§ The Sinai Element in Teaching

The Rabbis teach us that as soon as a child is capable of speaking, it is the father's duty to teach him Torah; and what must he teach his son — *The Torah which Moshe commanded to us is the heritage of the congregation of Yaakov.* In the light of the *Ramban's* comments, this means that a father bears testimony to his young child:

Hear my son, I am witness to the fact that G-d gave us his Torah. So did I see, so did I hear. This, my child, is our heritage. This is not a 'Bible Story,' this is a fact, which I witnessed on Sinai, and of which you will testify to your children.

Our responsibility, then, is to pass on, not only the teachings of Torah, but the precise details of the manner in which Torah was given to us, *Ma'amad Har Sinai.* Only then is it Torah.

This perhaps is the deeper meaning of *Rashi's* comment, "Then when you shall not forget and you shall perform *mitzvos* in their true form, you will be considered wise and understanding. If through forgetfulness, you shall distort the *mitzvos*, then shall you be considered fools." Even if you do perform the *mitzvos*, but not in the true form in which they were originally given, if the *Ma'amad* is forgotten, it will no longer be Torah. It may be Judaism as a civilization, Reconstructionism perhaps, but it will be idiocy and you will be considered fools.

Even the act of Torah study must reflect the *Ma'amad* Har Sinai. The Rabbis teach us that just as the Torah was given at Sinai through fear and inner trembling, so must it be studied in the same manner (*Berachos* 22a).

Man, the finite being, cannot contain all of the Torah, which is infinite wisdom. He can, however, purify himself and make of himself a receptacle in which G-d, in His Divine Mercy, implants the understanding of Torah. *Ma'amad Har Sinai* is a dynamic process which makes all of *Klal Yisrael* worthy of receiving Torah. For this reason we are commanded to maintain constantly the experience of *Ma'amad Har Sinai* as a living, ever-present fact.

ᵉᵍ ᵉᵍ ᵉᵍ

The Rabbis teach us: G-d has created everything in this world except falsehood and evil, which G-d did neither create nor bring about. G-d is the source of all Creation. Falsehood and evil are the creations of man himself. They are product of human fantasy. The challenge of our day for the Torah Jew is to find the means of reasserting Divine Truth in our daily lives; casting aside our hopeless fantasies and coming to grips with the stark reality of Divine Truth as revealed to us through *Ma'amad Har Sinai.*

Rabbi Chaim Dov Keller

Shavuos
and the Legacy
of Moshe

How are we to understand
Moshe as the giver of the Torah
— as if it were his to give?

S HAVUOS is a time for renewal of our love for the Almighty
through a rededication to the learning of His Torah. Toward
this end let us examine the essence of this bond of love between
Israel and the Almighty. Our Sages tell us: "When a child knows
how to speak his father must teach him Torah ... " What is
Torah? Rav Chanina said, It is the verse: *"The Torah which
Moshe commanded to us is the heritage of the Congregation of
Yaakov" (Succah 42a)*. Each nation has its specific treasure — that
national asset which it prizes above all else as its unique possession. It is its source of pride and it guards it with all of its energies.
Other nations have their crown jewels, their art treasures,
national shrines. But the treasure unique to the Jewish People is
Torah, "The precious vessel of G-d with which the world was
created" (*Avos* 3:18).

Thus the King of Israel is enjoined to write two *Sifrei Torah*,
one to accompany him wherever he goes, and one to be kept in his

treasure house (*Sanhedrin* 21b). That *Sefer Torah* hidden in his treasury serves to remind the king that the treasure of the Jewish people does not consist of precious stones or jewels, but is the Torah. Torah is the unique and priceless heritage of *Klal Yisrael....*

This is the simple meaning of the verse every Jewish child learns when he begins to talk.

Yet, curiously, *Targum Onkelos* renders the meaning differently in his translation: "Moshe *gave* us the Torah; he *bequeathed it as inheritance* to the Congregation of Yaakov." How are we to understand Moshe as the giver of Torah — as if it were his to give?

◀§ Three Innovations

Let us examine a *Gemara (Shabbos* 87a) that may shed some light on the problem:

We have been taught: Moshe did three things on his own and the Holy One, Blessed is He, agreed with him. He added one day to the days of preparation before receiving the Torah on Sinai; he separated from his wife; and he broke the Luchos *(the two tablets of law).* The Gemara asks: *What did Moshe expound? What was his reasoning in each of these incidents?*

He added the day because he interpreted G-d's command, "You shall ready yourselves today and tomorrow" as implying that just as "tomorrow" will be a full night and day, so should "today." As G-d had spoken to him by day, the previous night could not be reckoned as one of the two days. He therefore added another full day. [Tosafos *explains that this was not a true exegesis, because had G-d's intention been that there be three days of preparation, how can we say that Moshe added the day "on his own"?*]

He separated from his wife using a Kal Vachomer *(a fortiori argument) ...* [Again Tosafos *explains that this was not a true* Kal Vachomer.]

Moshe shattered the Luchos, *reasoning that the* Korban Pesach, *which is only one mitzvah, cannot be performed by one who has estranged himself from the Almighty. Therefore, how could he give the Jewish people the entire Torah when they had gone astray after the Golden Calf?* [Tosafos *again explains that this was not an incontrovertible line of reasoning. Moshe might possibly have given them the*

Torah and thus brought them back in teshuvah to the Almighty.]

The *Gemara's* entire discussion seems to defy comprehension. It would seem that the *Gemara* strives to determine Moshe's rationale in each of the three actions, finding some basis in the Torah itself for his apparent departure from Divine command. But if Moshe did indeed understand G-d's words in such a manner, why does the *Gemara* say that Moshe acted "on his own"? This is obviously why *Tosafos* must find ways of explaining the words of G-d as implying otherwise. What, then, is the true meaning of "Moshe acting on his own"? How literally is his rationale to be understood?

◆§ The Unspoken Directive

It would seem that our Sages here reveal to us that there are times when the true will of the Creator is not openly expressed to man. There are situations in which He deems it wiser not to reveal His will directly or even in the conventional Torah form of an incontrovertible *drashah* or a *sevara*. In such cases, the Almighty merely alludes to His intent in a form only to be grasped by an extraordinarily inspired individual. Although an ordinary person will completely fail to grasp the intention of the Creator, this individual will rise to the occasion, and act accordingly.

Thus we find this same discussion in Tractate *Yevamos* (62a) with a slight variation. There the *Gemara* does not say "Moshe did three things and the Holy One agreed with him," but "His reason coincided with that of the *Ribono Shel Olam.*" Actually the two versions are one. When in the Tractate *Shabbos* the narrative states that the *Ribbono Shel Olam* agreed with Moshe, this does not mean that His original intention was different and that He subsequently agreed to Moshe's innovation. Rather, Moshe arrived at that true inner will of the Almighty, which His infinite wisdom decreed was not to be openly revealed. This is implicit in the *Gemara's* question — what did Moshe expound? — Moshe most certainly had a sound basis for his conduct that only *seemed* to contradict the expressed will of G-d. However, the *drashah* that Moshe used was not a *drashah* that others would have arrived at. It could only emerge from the great mind and noble heart of Moshe *Rabbeinu.*

⊷§ Not by Command

Significantly, all three actions that Moshe understood "on his own" were connected with the receiving and transmission of the Torah. The *Ribono Shel Olam* in His wisdom did not choose to command the Jewish people to sanctify themselves in preparation for *Kabalas HaTorah* for more than two days. His true will was that they attain an even greater level of *kedushah* by a longer separation. But this was not to be attained in response to a Divine command — love cannot be legislated. Only one among them who determines on his own the potential for greater sanctification could inspire them to strive for greater heights. Thus, the Sages said Moshe added one day on his own. His understanding coincided with the will of God: that His children should, by their own initiative through Moshe's direction, aspire to greater heights in anticipation of that ultimate manifestation of His love for them — giving them the revelation of Torah.

⊷§ Personal Strivings

Similarly, Moshe's decision to completely separate from his wife also anticipated Divine will. In His wisdom, He knew it self-defeating to command Moshe to completely abandon marital life. For the nature of man is such that were this imposed upon him from without, he would sense himself incomplete, impaired in his ability to serve as a vessel for the acceptance of Torah. However, when Moshe came to the realization that such was the true will of G-d and voluntarily assumed this course, rather than impair his completeness of soul, it endowed him with an additional dimension — his attainment of the level of the Master of all Prophets, who at all times was prepared for a Divine revelation.

⊷§ The Gift of Depth

The breaking of the *Luchos* is a greater enigma. But here, too, G-d's true will was that *Klal Yisrael* not receive the Torah as then inscribed on the Tablets. The sin of the Golden Calf rendered them unworthy of this supreme expression of His love. However, there was a specific gain to be realized should Moshe himself grasp the true purpose of the breaking of the *Luchos*.

Even after Moshe descended the mountain and found Jews worshiping the Calf, he could well have presented them with the *Luchos*. But the Torah it conveyed would have been of a different format. It would have consisted of simple statements of laws and commandments — nothing more. And its primary function would have been to return *Klal Yisrael* in *teshuvah*. The awesome profundity, the sacred mysteries of Torah, would have escaped them. The sublimity, the *pilpul*, and the intellectual *sevara* of the Torah would not have been theirs.

> *Moshe was distressed over the breaking of the* Luchos. *The Holy One, Blessed is He, said to him, "Do not be pained over the first* Luchos, *for they were only the* Aseres HaDibros — *the Ten Commandments. But in the second* Luchos *I will give you* Halachos, Midrashos *and* Aggados" *(Midrash Rabbah, Ki Sisa).*

So the shattering of the *Luchos* was consistent with the Divine will. Nonetheless, G-d did not command that they be broken. It was for Moshe to arrive at this understanding on his own — that these *Luchos* were not to be given to the Jewish people. These were to be broken, allowing them to embark on a new beginning. The Jewish people must be aroused to *teshuvah* on their own — by one of their own — and then express their overpowering desire to attain the highest possible level of Torah. Thus, the closing phrase of the entire Torah refers to the breaking of the *Luchos*, measuring the greatness of Moshe in terms of his ability to take that drastic action.

> *"There did not arise another prophet in Israel like Moshe, whom the Almighty knew face to face, in all the signs and wonders for which he was sent by the L-rd to do ... in all the strong hand and the great terror that Moshe did before the eyes of all of Israel" (Devarim 34:10-12).*

Rashi explains: "the strong hand" — he received the Torah on the two tablets with his hands ... *"before the eyes of all of Yisrael,"* (the last words of the Torah) that his heart lifted him to break the *Luchos* before their eyes and that the Holy One, Blessed is He, agreed with him: the *Ribono Shel Olam* said to Moshe, *Yasher Koach* for having broken them."

In recounting the greatness of Moshe, the Torah equates the breaking of the *Luchos* with the receiving of the *Luchos*. He had arms "strong enough" to accept the *Luchos*, and heart great enough to break the *Luchos* ... making possible a *Kabalas HaTorah* in the dimensions which were the fullest and most sublime expression of the Divine Love.

◦§ The Torah of Moshe

The Gemara *(Nedarim 38a) tells us: "Rabbi Yosi b'Rabbi Chanina said that the Torah was only given to Moshe and his descendants ... but Moshe in his generosity gave it to Israel." Rav Chisda asked, "Does it not say 'G-d commanded me at that time to teach you?' " But (the* Gemara *says) the* pilpul *of Torah, the full understanding and the keen reasoning of Torah were given to Moshe and should have been his exclusive possession. But Moshe in his generosity gave them to all of* Klal Yisrael.

Indeed, were it not for the generosity of Moshe, the first *Luchos* would have been given to the Jewish people in simple form of statutes and judgments. But the depth of understanding — the *sevaros*, the *kushyos* and *terutzim* which are to be found in the words of the *Tannaim* and *Amoraim*, the *Rishonim* and *Achronim* — all of this would have been the exclusive possession of Moshe. However, in breaking the *Luchos*, Moshe determined that *Klal Yisrael* would ultimately receive the Torah in its entirety, in all its awesome grandeur.

Thus the *Targum Onkelos* says: "Moshe gave us the Torah and he bequeathed it as an inheritance to the Congregation of Yaakov." This Torah that we have in all its breadth and depth was the Torah of Moshe.

This the last of the prophets, Malachi, expresses in his final words: "Remember the Torah of my servant Moshe." Speaking in the name of the Almighty, the prophet bids us to remember *Moshe's* Torah. It is *that* Torah (in the words of Rashi in Chumash) that we proclaim "We have grasped on to it and we will not forsake it."*

◦§ A New Receiving of the Torah

Our age has witnessed an awesome, tragic shattering of the tablets — in the form of the destruction of the great yeshivos and Torah centers of Europe. We have also witnessed a miraculous

---

*This is the Rambam's intention in saying (*Hilchos Talmud Torah* III,1): "The Jewish people have three crowns: The Crown of Torah, the Crown of Priesthood and the Crown of Royalty. The Crown of Priesthood has been acquired by Aharon, the Crown of Royalty by David, but the Crown of Torah is open and available to all of Yisrael as it is written: *The Torah which Moshe commanded us is the heritage of the Congregation of Yaakov.* Who ever wishes it let him come and take it."

When our Sages speak of the "Crown of Torah" they do not refer to the perfunctory memorization of Torah Law. They mean the great glory that is the *pilpul* of Torah, which was Moshe's and which Moshe passed on to us. Thus the *Rambam* quotes this verse.

rebirth of Torah in *Eretz Yisrael* and in America. Our generation has been given a Divine opportunity to receive new *Luchos* from the hand of Providence. In response, a new generation is arising in this country and in *Eretz Yisrael* — a generation of young scholars who are willing to dedicate themselves not to a mere perfunctory study of Torah, but to *lomdus* the likes of which flourished in the great European *yeshivos* that were destroyed.

Even more wondrous — a generation of young women willingly forgo personal comfort and financial security so their husbands may pursue the study of Torah. And hosts of *ba'alei batim* (laymen) are emerging, who set aside regular periods for studying the Torah, and who appreciate the crucial role of Torah to the survival of the Jewish people.

Of course, there is much more to be accomplished. To be sure, many shadows darken the Jewish horizon. But for all that has been achieved, and for the promise that the future offers, we must rejoice with our Torah on the *Yom Tov* of *Mattan Torah*.

A. Scheinman

Revelation and Search

*Man's role in seeking
understanding of Torah,
since Sinai*

I.

Accepting the Law — Twice

R EVELATION is the cornerstone of faith, upon which all of
Judaism rests. As the *Rambam* points out, it is not simply a
proof of faith, but the perception of the Divine in the most direct
way possible. While other miracles served to prove Divine existence, pointing to such, revelation was the experience of the
Divine itself. For one brief moment, the curtains of concealment
were parted, letting in the rays of the Divine in all its brightness.

Yet, strangely enough, *Chazal* tell us that the experience of
Revelation at Sinai was somehow not the ultimate in acceptance
of G-d's dominion. The *Gemara (Shabbos* 82) tells us that at Sinai
"the mountain was poised over the Jews like a barrel." The Jews
were forced into accepting the Torah; and it was not until the
miracle of Purim, a thousand years later, that the Jews willingly
reaffirmed their commitment to Torah. Besides the strangeness of
having to be forced to accept the Torah when one has beheld and

experienced the Divine in all its glory, the literal description of these events in the Torah does not mention this tradition. The passages describing *Mattan Torah* make no mention of force, while prior to the original Purim, the Jews were indeed threatened with extinction, until they did *teshuvah* and returned to G-d.

II.
Searching — to Fill the Void

IN TWO WAYS does one become cognizant of the sun. One can behold the sun in its dazzling glory. Or one can be locked into a pitch-dark room wherein every minute of waiting for a crack of light makes one even more aware of the joy of basking in the sun. Similarly, a father-son relation peaks with a warm embrace at the height of a moment of joy. Yet it can be outranked by the feelings of yearning and pining that accompany a prolonged absence from home. Many a son who has not responded to a warm embrace has found the pangs of absence unbearably strong.

This phenomenon is explained in the discussion by the *Maharal* on the importance of the Four Questions, and why someone who conducts his *seder* in a monologue fashion, not following a question-and-answer format, does not fulfill his obligation to retell the Exodus on Pesach. He explains that when one merely hears a statement, he does not incorporate it into his personality. It is just tagged on to his awareness. This is not the case when one receives an answer to a question. For by having posed the question, he opens a void, so to speak; and the answer fills it, forming a unified entity with the person rather than adding on a superfluity.

The Vilna Gaon's commentary on *Shir HaShirim* makes a similar observation. The pleasure a person derives from a food is in direct proportion to his hunger. A sated person can be presented with the tastiest of dishes, and he will reject it in disinterest; and should he force the food in, it will not easily find its way down.

The *Sfas Emes (Vayeitzei)* also refers to this principle in explaining why *Yaakov Avinu* did not receive his dream and prophecy until *after* he had left the yeshivah of Shem and Ever. When a man is in an atmosphere of *kedushah* (sanctity), his thirst for *ruchniyus* (spirituality) is not comparable to the thirst that wells up within a person stumbling through the desert. He bases this on a *Midrash:* "My soul thirsts for you — *where?* in a barren and arid land."

⋖§ Compulsion Through Clarity

This, then, is the difference between *Shavuos* and Purim — the festival of Receiving the Torah at Sinai and the holiday of its reaffirmation in Shushan. In the first instance, *Klal Yisrael* was compelled to accept the Torah — but not simply by a physical force; the impact from the enormity of the event of revelation was so immense that it was likened to the mountain poised over their heads. The brilliant light of revelation left no room for doubt, and under the circumstance it was impossible *not* to accept the Torah. At Purim, however, it was not the threat to life in itself that inspired *Klal Yisrael's teshuvah* and its return to pristine purity. Rather the *hester panim* — the feeling of abandonment — bestirred powerful yearnings for a Sinai-like encounter with the divine.

Our *Chazal* tell us that when Queen Esther was to confront Achashveirosh, she cried: "*My G-d, my G-d why have You abandoned me?*" To this day the designated psalm of Purim (according to the Vilna Gaon) is the one in which this outcry appears; and as *Chazal* explain, the psalm refers to the darkest hour of the night. Thus, while *Shavuos* marks the cognizance of G-d through revelation, Purim celebrates the cognizance of G-d that follows a desperate search in the darkness.

⋖§ The Gift and the Acquisition

Torah itself consists of these two parts: One, the Written Law, which is "G-d's Torah" so to speak, was given to us as revelation. Yet, as it reads, it would remain closed to us. We must refer to the second part of the Torah, the Oral Law, also given at Sinai, to understand the written word. This encompasses the Divine interpretations and expositions, which are accessible to human comprehension; and it includes the rules of exegesis by which G-d instructs man in how to delve more deeply into the law, and teaches him how to apply it to evolving circumstances. *Chazal* describe the long and tortuous system of analyzing every word and nuance of Torah recorded in the Babylonian Talmud as "You restored me in the darkness," for struggling through passages of the Talmud is "grappling in the dark." The Oral Torah, therefore, has special properties: it introduces queries and leads the student to conclusive answers, which become integrated into his personality. The results are deeply satisfying — not unlike the end result of the *Pesach Seder*, as described by the *Maharal*.

Thus, it has been pointed out, *Mishnayos* opens with a question: "When does one begin reciting the *Shema?*", and ends with the word "*Shalom*" — harmony. Understanding the Oral Law is not a matter of absorbing a statement. It is an answer derived from a query, and that is why the Oral Law (and not the Written Law) has been described as the human portion in Torah.

The same principle can be applied to explain the *Maharal's* statement: while the Torah was given on *Shavuos*, *dvaikus b'Torah* (clinging to the Torah) was the result of Purim. True enough, Torah can be presented to people — and it was on *Shavuos* — but it can only become integrated within one's personality *(dvaikus)* if first he searches.

III.
Revelation Again

SEARCH is deeper than revelation, and its findings more permanent. What need, then, is there for revelation? To be sure, we must refer to the *Kuzari's* answer — that not everyone, and not at every time, can a person reach G-d through a higher level of contact through personal search; nor will G-d reveal Himself to every generation. Thus G-d's original revelation at Sinai gives all subsequent generations — especially those unable to reach spiritual heights on their own — a tradition to fall back on.

There is yet another profound thought involved ... one that concerns our discussion. The *Yerushalmi* explains the verse "It is not an empty thing from you," to mean that if a person finds any part of the Torah "empty" — without meaning — it is "from you." That is, Torah cannot be faulted as being meaningless. Rather, this vacuous feeling in the student is an indication that somewhere within him, he is lacking receptivity to that part of Torah. When a work of art is meaningless to a blind man, or a concert uninspiring to a deaf person, the fault is in the viewer, with the audience, not in the composition.

The revelation at Sinai created an indelible impression on the Jewish personality, giving us, as a people, a point of reference for all future searchings for truth. Thus, all the individual *neshamos* of *Klal Yisrael* had to be at Sinai — even a proselyte had to be there. Had we not the memory of Sinai deep within us to drive us in our exhaustive search for meaning and understanding in Torah, we could not persevere in mastering Torah; and we would not succeed. We would be "empty" from ourselves. It is for this same reason that (the Talmud tells us) a person learns the entire Torah when in his mother's womb, even though he is destined to forget it prior to birth; for if he had not first learned the Torah, he would not be able to relate to it later.

◅§ Return to Torah

Studying Torah, then, is always a return of sorts. This is expressed in our daily prayers: "Return us ... to Your Torah." Indeed, parts of the Oral tradition — such as *Targum Onkelos*, the Aramaic translations of Onkelos — were forgotten and later rediscovered. Human endeavor alone would have proven insufficient for composing the *targumim*, had it not been for the spark of Sinai buried deep within the *neshamah*. This creative endeavor was not one of initial discovery; it was a return.

There are other instances of creative recall:

The *Gemara (Menachos)* relates that when *Moshe Rabbeinu* saw Rabbi Akiva teaching his disciples, he became envious of Rabbi Akiva's vast knowledge. The *Ohr HaChaim* explains that, to be sure, *Moshe Rabbeinu* knew all of *Torah she'be'al peh*, the Oral Law that Rabbi Akiva had mastered; but Rabbi Akiva's level of attainment was such that he was able to discern how the Oral Law is derived from the Written Law ... It has been said that in his last years the Vilna Gaon studied only *Chumash* — his encyclopedic grasp of Oral Law was such that he was able to deduce which of the myriad teachings of the Oral Law are implicit in the Written Torah. In a similar vein, the Gaon is reported to have said: "There are three levels of understanding: *pshat* (simple explanation), *amkus* (depth), and again *pshat* (simple explanation). There is however an infinite difference between *pshat* before depth, and *pshat* after depth. The revelation one discovers after "search" is worlds apart from the revelation one starts with.

◅§ ◅§ ◅§

A *shliach* (emissary) sent to strengthen Judaism in an outlying community later reported to his *Rebbe* that an estranged Jew had asked him to explain his mission. He told him a parable: "In the days of yore, scribes would go from town to town filling in 'letters' that have been rubbed out from Jewish *neshamos.*"

After the *shliach* told the *Rebbe* his parable, the *Rebbe* shook his head: "*Chas VeShalom* that a letter of a *Yiddishe neshamah* becomes erased! It is rather like an engraving that becomes filled with dust: blow the dust away and the *original* letter reappears."

We must think of our *avodah* as circular, not linear. We do, indeed, start with revelation. But that which is not earned has no permanence. We must toil on our own until we rediscover the revelation imbued within each of us. For when we do arrive at our goal, it is not a new enlightenment that awaits us; rather we unearth that which has driven us so relentlessly — the eternal flame of Sinai.

Rabbi Avrohom Chaim Feuer

To Kiss
— Or to Embrace?

*The principals of
the Book of Ruth
and our role in
accepting the Torah*

A T THE CROSSROADS of time and eternity stood two widowed sisters-in-law and a bereaved mother. The widows cried bitterly, moved more by compassion than by self-pity. And one, Orpah by name, kissed her sorrowful mother-in-law and turned her back to take the shorter path of time. But Ruth embraced Naomi for all eternity.

Orpah's tears did not dry and fade — forgotten. The Almighty G-d counted them; they watered her future seed. In merit of the four tears shed in the fullness of love and compassion, she was rewarded with four sons: all heroes and great warriors. The colossal Goliath was one. But the four brothers forgot their mother's tears and kisses and challenged their cousins of Israel. "Said the Holy One, Blessed is He, the sons of the one who kissed shall fall into the hands of the one who embraced" *(Sotah* 42b). And so, they fell before David, the descendant of Ruth.

Great is the reward of a kiss, but greater is the strength of an embrace. The kiss was motivated by love and pity — but it was impulse. It was the uncontrolled response to an attraction, the unmeditated reflex reaction to a stimulus. It was limited by the fickleness of a fluctuating emotion; it was terminated by time. Aroused in a moment, it subsided in a breath. Swiftly kindled, it swiftly sputtered to extinction.

Ruth, however, was not seized by an urge: *she* seized the moment. She was not overwhelmed by the circumstance: she *mastered* it. One who is not helplessly captivated is not prey to easy release. Ruth was not merely touched; she was forever converted: transformed to her very depths.

No wonder, then, that the titans fell before young David. The small David *possessed* his power; *he* was not possessed. Bound to the will of the Almighty, he held the strongest force. The giants were captives of time — no match for the boundless energy of the Eternal. The kiss evokes no confidence. It is unstable and unsure; witness the love of Orpah, which soured into acid hatred in her sons. From the Hebrew root for "kiss," נשק, stems also the word for weaponry. The impulsive kiss can easily become a dagger of death, hence the expression "kiss of death." Life is embraced: "And you who cling to G-d — you are all alive today."

"The acts of the fathers are a sign for the sons." Orpah and Ruth, the Moabites, were descendants of Lot. It is difficult to describe the true character of this conflicted man. As a devoted disciple of his uncle, Avraham, he faithfully followed the master on his arduous journeys. He learned hospitality from his uncle; risked his life in order to provide for total strangers. To protect his guests, he was ready to sacrifice his daughters. And yet he chose to live surrounded by the evil of Sodom.

He was torn between two opposing worlds. Pious enough to bake *matzos* for Pesach, yet even after his miraculous rescue from the destruction of Sodom he did not rise to pious devotion — instead he sank to the depths of drunkenness permitting himself to be trapped into incest with his daughters. Lot's lack of control and discipline drained his life of the glory he could have realized. He oscillated between sublime heights and murky depths. Spurred by a whim and desire, he "kissed" many worlds. Lot never achieved fulfillment: unbridled desire and holy love cannot combine. They can meet as a superficial kiss, a casual and clumsy relationship.

The deeds of Lot were signs for Orpah who inherited his traits. On the one hand, she was capable of profound sincerity. The Midrash teaches that all kisses mentioned in the Torah are frivolous and trivial except for three, one being the sincere and meaningful kiss of Orpah's departure. Yet the Midrash tells us that on the night following Orpah's departure from Naomi, she had promiscuous relations with a number of men. She stumbled from extreme to extreme.

◆§ The Discipline of Ruth — and Torah

The Book of Ruth complements so perfectly the Shavuos experience of *Kabalas HaTorah*. To accept Torah is to accept *hora'ah;* rules and instructions. Divinity demands discipline and training.

In our time, we hear of "situational ethics" and "emerging morals." This means, simply, that there can be no pre-ordained rules. Man must formulate the ethics of behavior according to each emerging situation. Follow your impulse. Play the game of life by ear — forget about the notes. There is no reason to cling to a rigid, intransigent set of rules; no need to tackle a problem if we can just touch it; no need to embrace forever; we can live freely for the moment. Virtue is not a "virtue"; it is at best a social contract, as easily broken as made.

The words are new — the philosophy is old. It is a recapitulation of the response of the nations when the Almighty offered them the Torah millennia ago. Each had its own reason to refuse the Torah. "Outlawing theft would disrupt our economy." "Restrictions against murder would radically alter the foundations of our tribal society." But *Klal Yisrael*, each Jew, was willing to radically alter not only his way of life, but his very being, in order to be worthy of Torah, of Eternity. "We will do," they said, "and we will listen." The temporal will give way to the Eternal.

This declaration of eternity is forever the life force of our People. It will sustain us until one day soon — any day soon — the children of the one who could only kiss will be delivered to the hands of *Moshiach, scion of David*, the son of the one who embraced.

~§ **The Three Weeks** / *Mourning and Hope*

appointments with the Divine ...
realization and recognition from tears
of despair ... the scenario for redemption
... renunciation of the material, and the
man on a donkey

Moreinu Yaakov Rosenheim

Tishah B'Av
... A Festival?

Understanding the
Jewish calendar's darkest day
which is described
as a mo'ed in sacred literature

A MONG the various regulations for the liturgy of *Tishah B'Av*, distinguished by their simplicity and far-reaching effects, every one of us has certainly noticed the amazing provision that on the Ninth of Av, the day of the deepest national mourning, *Tachanun* is omitted, in astonishing similarity to festivals and days of happy memories. One might perhaps think that this amazing fact could be explained in a similar way to a reverse provision that, for example, during the days of *Chol HaMoed* no wedding should take place, so that the national joy of the festival should not be diluted by a personal *simchah*. In a similar way, one might think, the sad feelings expressed by *Tachanun* based in their major part on the consciousness of sin and moral incapability of the *individual*, should not mingle with the huge stream of *national* mourning. However, the Talmud and Midrash in no way explain the omission of *Tachanun* on the Ninth of Av by some principle like "one does not intermingle various types of mourning,", but they quote a verse from Jeremiah's *Eichah* in which he classifies the day of our national disaster as a *mo'ed* i.e., a festival: "He hath called a 'solemn assembly' *(mo'ed)* against me to crush my young men." It is therefore a festival that this black day of annual national mourning is called — this day which weeks before makes every sound of joy die on our lips;

which quenches the lights in our homes and houses of worship, and makes us sit down on the ground, bewailing our lost pride.

A simple linguistic consideration might perhaps offer a solution to this puzzle of calling *Tishah B'Av* a festival. The word *mo'ed* means both festival and assembly, or finding each other, as demonstrated by Rabbi S. R. Hirsch. Thus, the word means simply a place or time in which "G-d finds Himself together with His people." Thus every day bringing us that sense of nearness to G-d, making us feel His presence coming out to us from behind its cloak of natural laws and accident, is a *mo'ed*, a day of Divine presence in our life, and therefore — a festival.

Had accident governed the history of Israel, had the reason for the breakdown of Judea and its Bais HaMikdash been rooted in the fact that in nature the materially weaker is subdued by the stronger, then the day on which we renew our awareness of that historic event with all its dreadful consequences would be filled with thought of the abandonment of the individual and the nations to the malice of a blind fate. No glimmer of festivity could then have fallen into the darkness of such a thought.

It is, however, because Divine Providence, deciding our fate, is expressed also in His wrath; because the Ninth of Av had already been determined as a fateful day for all time, as early as a thousand years ahead, before Israel's tribes had ever entered the Holy Land; because in the repetition of all great catastrophes in Jewish history on that same day, there lies the strongest negation of all "accidental occurrence," and the strongest proclamation is voiced of our profound security in the reign of our G-d — it is thus that the Ninth of Av is promoted to the degree of a *mo'ed*, a day of Divine presence, and, all mourning notwithstanding, it becomes a festival.

An echo of this concept can be detected in a profound saying of our Sages in *Midrash Eichah* commenting on the verse, "He has filled me with bitter herbs, he has sated me with wormwood." The first part of this verse is interpreted as relating to the night of Pesach (bitter herbs) while the second part is connected with night of *Tishah B'Av*. On that first night of protection, the outstretched arm of G-d was raised in punishment over Egypt and in salvation over the Jewish people; in both cases demonstrating His nearness. In the same way, we feel in the primitive verdict of the Ninth of Av, the eternal Providence of G-d, the same concept makes the mourning of the Ninth of Av become a supporting staff for the Jewish people in its long journey through the *Galus*.

adapted from Michtav MiEliyahu
by Rabbi Nisson Wolpin

Weep for the Destruction
... Weep for the Redemption

Confrontation or Circumvention?

DAVID THE KING spelled out the formula for a virtuous life
in a simple verse in his *Tehillim*: *"Turn away from evil and
do good ... "* When this aphorism is translated into a *modus
operandi*, however, it becomes amazingly complex. One might assume that to "turn away from evil" one must first identify the
threat in a confrontation of sorts — recognizing one's personal
shortcomings, labeling them as evil, and defying them by overpowering the "evil inclination." Yet this is not always the recom-
mended course. There are times when it is better to flee, to evade
identifying the challenge, or to simply postpone dealing with the
problem. Confrontation may over-tax one's resources.

A classic case is a *Midrash Tanchuma* that describes a
meeting of Avraham and Yitzchak on their way to the *Akeidah*
(the Binding), with a satanic old man.

> The old man asked: *"Where are you going?"*
> Avraham: *"To pray."*
> Old man: *"And since when does a man carry fire and
> slaughtering knife in hand and kindling wood on his back on
> his way to prayer?"*
> Avraham: *"We may tarry a day or two, and find need
> to slaughter an animal and prepare it as food to eat."*
> Old man: *"Ha! Do you think you deceive me? Wasn't I*

*there when G-d told you to take your son, your only son ...
and bring him for a sacrifice?"*

It seems odd that Avraham should appear to be devious when asked about the nature of his mission and not tell the challenger outright where he was going and why. Yet there are times when a person senses that a challenge may prove too overwhelming if met head on. In Avraham's case, he might have found his zeal to perform G-d's command somewhat dampened if he would have been forced to rationalize it to the satisfaction of the "old man."* In a case such as this, it is better to sidestep the challenge ... In fact, even if untruths are uttered as part of such a tactic, they are spoken for a sacred purpose, and as such can be condoned as serving a higher truth (Rabbi Simchah Zissel Ziv of Kelm).

◆§ ◆§ ◆§

[*A classic case of the reverse situation, when a confrontation with evil almost proved counterproductive, is Yoseif's refusal to consent to the adulterous invitation of Potiphar's wife. Commentaries say that rather than utter a terse "no", Yoseif went into lengthy explanations as to why he would not enter a relationship with her. In the process of justifying his refusal, he became so involved in the proposition that he felt weakened in his resolve, and was even prepared to yield — but for the sudden envisioning of his father Yaakov's presence ... It is often better to flee a compromising situation than to lock horns with an evil impulse in expectation of overpowering it. The would-be victor can become a victim in the process.*]

◆§ Coming to Grips with Spiritual Alienation

There is an obstacle to complete service to G-d that man can neither flee, evade nor circumvent, and that is the condition described as *Shechinta begelusa* — literally: the Divine Presence in Exile. The term seems to portray a condition of G-d's choosing rather than a human failing, and as such would leave man little to act upon. But it is a condition that man creates and the onus of response is on him.

The formal repository of the Divine Presence is the *Bais HaMikdash (sanctuary)*, but the commanding passage in the

---

*Thus is "the *yeitzer hara* (the evil inclination) an old and foolish king." A king — for he is sovereign over every man. Old — for he has amassed vast experience. A fool — because he falls prey to his own brand of deception.

Torah states: *"And build for Me a Mikdash that I may repose in their midst."* The implication is that once the People stretched out their arms to participate in the building of the sanctuary, G-d established His presence in them — within each and every person — and there it continues to repose.

In every situation, under all conditions, a spark of Divinity will always smolder within every Jew. In spite of egocentricity, materialism, or hedonism — all of which serve to block out one's awareness of this Divinity — the spark is never smothered and the presence stays on. G-d's vow: *"I shall not reject you nor despise you to the point of obliteration,"* is a reassurance that no matter how numbed a person's spiritual sensitivity may become, and regardless of the extent of his alienation from the Divine, he always has the capacity to come back. The spark is there.

◆§ The First Step into Exile

"Because on the Ninth of Av you wept for nothing (when the spies returned from Canaan) and you listened to their fearful description of the conditions there, that day will remain for you as a time of weeping for generations to come." The first time the Jews erected a barrier of insensitivity between themselves and that Divine Presence was on a *Tishah B'Av*, when Moses' twelve scouts returned from their tour of the Holy Land. Their glowing report of the fertility of the land was exceeded by their pessimistic view of their ability to conquer it. The omnipotence of the G-d Who led them from Egypt diminished in the eyes of the people, and a barrier arose between their awareness and G-d's reality. They wept bitter tears of hopelessness, further encrusting the barrier they had erected. *"The people of Canaan are mightier than us. (Read: Mightier than our Divine Leader.)"* And they were further isolated from their awareness of the Divine Presence — the prototype *galus* situation for the Jewish people, the individual Jew, and the *Shechinah*.

When a person is uninspired in his study or his prayer, feels estranged from his immediate and lifelong goals or purpose, then there can be no point in sidestepping the issue of postponing confrontation with it. He must face it fully and immediately: He and the *Shechinah* are suffering a mutual alienation.

By tradition there are many approaches to restoring contact with the Divine. All these approaches were sealed off with the destruction of the *Bais HaMikdash* — all save one: the Gates of Tears. If one so despairs over his spiritual alienation that he finds every means of expressing this despondency inadequate, then tears as the ultimate expression can penetrate the wall of indifference that shuts out the Divine Spark. Barriers that are impervious to all other attempts at entry dissolve in tears.

When *Tishah B'Av* approaches on our yearly calendar cycle, the very season endows the Jew with a lonely realization of how he has fallen from earlier attainments. Should reminiscence alone prove insufficient to awaken him to awareness of his state of spiritual alienation, should recall of past national and personal tragedies fall short of the impetus required to bring him to tears, then G-d supplies him with with new reminders: The destruction of the First *Bais HaMikdash* ... the destruction of the Second *Bais HaMikdash* ... the massacre at Betar ... the expulsion from England ... the expulsion from Spain ... the outbreak of World War I ... and many more national tragedies all of which befell the Jews on *Tishah B'Av*. These tragedies came not merely as punishments, but as stimulants to force an agonizing appraisal upon the Jew of his lonely spiritual state — an appraisal that brings to weeping, which brings forth those tears that wash away the crusty barriers between the Jew and the Divinity. The *Shechinah* responds to tears of yearning, and rays of light, warmth and hope, break through the walls of opacity.

The tears for the destruction are the tears that bring redemption.

Rabbi Nachman Bulman

Redemption
of Mourning

A search in sacred literature
for a clue to our era
as the time of Moshiach

W HEN the *Seventeenth of Tammuz* heralds the advent of our
Three Weeks of mourning, our remembrance of the destruction of G-d's dwelling place on Earth culminates once again in the
soul searing tones of *Tishah B'Av's* lamentations. In some, the
discomfort enjoined during this period, the restraints we practice,
awaken a glimmer of recollection for the historic tragedy which
stands behind our customs of mourning. Some will even recall the
blueprint of historic anguish which was drafted in the earliest
days of our history during these very weeks.

On the *Seventeenth of Tammuz*, the fortified walls of
Jerusalem were pierced and torn open by our enemies. On the
same *Seventeenth of Tammuz*, so many centuries earlier, the
Tablets of the Law were shattered by *Moshe Rabbeinu*. On the
evening of the *Ninth of Av* our forefathers wept, in loss of faith,
when they heard the slanderous report of the spies on the
promised land. On the same *Ninth of Av* so many centuries later,
the light of our life was twice extinguished — the *Bais HaMikdash*
was leveled. *But to the masses of our people, the experience of
these weeks has almost vanished from living memory.*

◄§ Mourning as Guidance to Aspirations

For many centuries our fathers experienced the deepest
pangs of mourning during these days. But their mourning was

not one that paralyzed their spiritual energies. It rather awakened those energies. They knew why they mourned. And they knew the meaning of *Galus*. And they also knew what the Torah wished them to know of the meaning of *Geulah* (redemption). Their fathers had sinned, and had therefore been driven into exile from their beloved land — an exile whose termination they had not yet merited. They knew wherein they had committed wrongdoing. They acknowledged their transgressions honestly. They grieved over them sincerely.

They responded with gratitude to the peoples who extended humane treatment to them in the lands of exile. But they never mistook, even under the best of circumstances, those lands of exile for home. Their political allegiances were forthcoming to no lesser extent than that of other citizens of the lands in which they lived. But their highest spiritual allegiances they gave to their portable homeland, the Torah, while never ceasing to yearn, with every nerve of being, for restoration to their own beloved land, the Land of the Fathers. They adjusted themselves to their contemporary surroundings, but never completely. They rooted themselves in the societies which enveloped them, but never completely.

The bitterness and the length of exile sometimes caused them to fall prey to the delusions of false messiahs. Their awakening was not long in coming. Those who refused to part company with those delusions became as withered branches of Israel's tree, and in time fell away completely from the stem. For our people as a people, the Messianic vision shone true and pure during all these centuries of exile.

In recent generations, however, the vision has become clouded for ever larger segments of our people. Reform came, and tore Zion out of the *Siddur*. Secular Zionism came and tore the *Siddur* out of Zion. An inscrutable Divine wrath tore out of our midst millions of Jews in whose souls both the *Siddur* and Zion refused to be torn apart.

And we, the sad remnants of those millions, have become subject to confusion. Upon us the curse of the *tochachah* (admonition) has fallen: "*And I will surely hide My countenance from you on that day.*" The illumination of Divine meaning for our times has been taken away from us, and our faith in the coming of the *Moshiach* has become pale ... . In some countries our material blessings are so bountiful that some of the best of us are lulled into forgetting that: the best *Galus* is still *Galus*. And there, in the Land of the Fathers, such mighty events have transpired ... How shall we look at them? What is the meaning of *that* test? Are we in the midst of the Messianic age?

Let us read together:

'The king, the Moshiach, will arise and restore the Kingdom of David to its ancient first dominion. He will build the Bais HaMikdash and he will ingather the dispersed of Israel. And the laws will be restored in his days as they were in times of old. Sacrificial offerings will be brought. And Shmittah (every seventh year) and Jubilee years (every fiftieth year) will again be observed according to all their commandments that are stated in the Torah. And whoever does not believe in him, or does not await his coming, denies not only the other prophets alone but also the Torah and Moshe Rabbeinu ... And if a king will rise from the house of Davi₫ who will dwell in the study of Torah and will be engaged in mitzvos like David his father, in accord with the Written Torah and the Oral Torah, and he will incline all of Israel to walk in it and to strengthen its foundation, and he will wage the wars of Hashem then there is the certainty that he is the Moshiach. If he did and succeeded, and built the sanctuary in its place and ingathered the dispersed of Israel, then he is certainly the Moshiach. And he will perfect the entire world to serve Hashem together for it is said: 'Then I will transform unto the peoples a pure speech so that they should all call in the name of Hashem and serve Him as one'. "
(Rambam, Hilchos Melachim, Chapter 11).*

We learn from these words of the *Rambam* — and in this matter his viewpoint is the unanimous viewpoint of all of Israel's sages — a number of basic insights.

□ The fulfillment of the Messianic faith entails the restoration of the House of David, the rebuilding of the *Bais HaMikdash*, the ingathering of Israel's dispersed and the total restoration of Torah law in the areas of the sanctuary and the land. If any of these elements are missing, we know clearly that the Messianic vision has not been fulfilled.

□ One who does not believe in the *Moshiach*, or, even if he does believe in him, but *does not* wait for his coming, denies not only the teachings of the prophets but the teachings of the Torah and of *Moshe Rabbeinu* as well. This faith is then primary in the Torah, and is not derived merely by implication, or through sources secondary in importance to the Torah.

☐ What are the qualifications by which the claims of the *Moshiach* may be judged? First and foremost he is a person who is descended from the house of David. He is neither a deity, nor a movement, nor a process. *He is a person.* Secondly, he is infinitely more than a gifted statesman or a military leader. He is a scholar of the Torah and observes its *mitzvos*. His study and observance are in accord with both the Written and the Oral Torah.

☐ He is not neutral with reference to the observance of the Torah on the part of the people of Israel. *"He inclines all of Israel to walk in its ways."*

☐ He does not see himself as a military leader whose military fortunes are unrelated to G-d's will. *"He wages the wars of Hashem."* When do we know definitely that his Messianic claim stands confirmed beyond doubt? His having brought about the ingathering of even all of the exiled Jews in the world is insufficient testimony. In addition to having brought about the ingathering of the exiles he must also have *"rebuilt the Bais HaMikdash"* in its place.

☐ What is his relation to the rest of humanity? It will be vastly more than to project an example of great technological progress with limited means or even of the application of the ideals of social justice to the life of a society. His proper function will be *"to perfect the whole world to serve Hashem in unity."* As long as all of humanity has not been brought to the service of G-d, we know that the Messianic vision has not yet been fulfilled.

◄§ The Inner Life of Jewry

What will be the character of the inner life of the people of Israel during the days of the *Moshiach*?

> *"The Sages and the Prophets did not yearn for the days of the Moshiach so that they might rule over all the world or that they might rule over the nations, or that the nations might hold them in esteem, or that they might eat and drink and rejoice — but rather that they should be completely free for the pursuit of wisdom of Torah; so that there would be none to oppress them or to distract them in order that they might merit the life of the world to come ... "* (Rambam, Hilchos Melachim, Chapter 12).

The Messianic faith of the people of Israel was not motivated by imperialistic designs of any sort. (Of such designs we are innocent, thank G-d, to this day.) Nor was it motivated by the desire for good public relations, nor the desire that the nations of the world extend honor and glory to us. Nor was it motivated by the desire for material pleasures or joys. It was motivated solely by the yearning for the building of a Jewish society which was to be suffused and enveloped totally by the life of Torah and its wisdom.

A Jewish society whose fundamental life principle is not that of Torah has not yet experienced the fulfillment of the Messianic vision.

What will be the moral and economic situation of humanity in general during the Messianic age?

> "And at that time there will be neither famine nor war, neither jealousy nor competition, for the good will be bountiful and all pleasures will be abundant as the earth. And the entire world will be engaged solely in the quest for the knowledge of G-d alone. And therefore the people of Israel will be great sages — they will know things that are concealed — and they will grasp the knowledge of their Creator to the extent of Man's capacity. As it is said: 'for the earth is to be filled with knowledge of G-d as the waters cover the ocean.' " (ibid).

As long as the world still suffers the pain of famine, the anguish of war, the curse of jealousy, the destructiveness of competition — as long as the world is engaged, with all too few exceptions, in the pursuit of the knowledge of everything to the exclusion of G-d — as long as the people of Israel itself is sadly lacking in the "grasp of the knowledge of the Creator" of the universe — we know that the Messianic age has not yet arrived.

When we say Kinos, let us strive a bit harder to experience the agony of Galus through a renewed understanding of how far we are from Geulah. And let us resolve to prepare ourselves and our surroundings, so that we might be a bit more worthy to receive the consolation of the coming of Moshiach, for whom our people has pined unto its last breath through all the centuries of exile.

And surely, no small part of such preparation would be the commitment of our utmost capacity to building a Torah society in the Land of Israel.

Rabbi Avrohom Chaim Feuer

When the Penny Vanishes
from the Purse ...

*The key to
the Temple's ruin
and its future reconstruction*

D URING THE SUMMER months of Tammuz and Av we
painfully review the events which caused the *Bais
HaMikdash*, the House of G-d, to be destroyed. We are told that
the furious flame of senseless hate, *sinas chinam*, burned our second Sanctuary and turned its splendor into ashes. One might fail
to comprehend what could have stoked the flames of hatred to
such destructive force. *Chazal*, our Sages who penetrate the surface of events with their Torah vision, offer:
>*"For their love for money, they came to hate one
another"* (Yerushalmi Yoma).

This answer touches on man's basic nature — for man, compared to most lesser creatures, is almost totally lacking in natural
defenses and thus desperately craves for a sense of safety and
security. Men are powerfully drawn to whatever seems to
promise them this protection and insurance. In the time of the
First *Bais HaMikdash* pagan forces impressed many Jews as being
their guardian angels, and they placed their confidence in *avodah
zarah*. The sun, the moon, the wind, the trees and other natural
phenomena provided security in a panic-filled present and against
the perils of an unforeseeable future.

☙ Deflected Desire

The destruction of the First Temple and the Babylonian *Galus* shook the people back to their senses, and they came to recognize that the Creator is the supreme and exclusive protector. Thus, they merited their return to Zion. But the attraction of *avodah zarah* continued to taunt them and they felt too weak to withstand it. So the leaders of the time, under the guidance of the Prophet Zachariah, took drastic and extraordinary action: They prayed that this *yeitzer hara* (evil inclination) be eradicated from their passions and their hearts. Their unusual request was granted *(Yoma* 69b). But the *yeitzer hara* of *avodah zarah* could not be removed without a different temptation taking its place, for the balance between the attractions of good and evil must be maintained to present man with free choice. The *Ari HaKadosh, Rabbeinu Chaim* (the brother of the *Maharal),* and the *Chida,* among others, tell us that desire for money took its place. This desire for possessing money proved insatiable — an appetite impossible to still. Even if a man's needs be few, his possessions — no matter how vast — never seem sufficient.

"He who loves silver will never be content with silver" *(Koheles* 5:9).

"He who possesses one hundred, desires two. He who possesses two hundred, desires four" *(Koheles Rabbah* I:34).

An endless, vicious, frustrating cycle. When one owns nothing, he has nothing to lose and nothing to protect. But he who has tasted the sweetness of having one hundred is concerned that his hundred remain with him. The only way he can ascertain that is to prove that he can duplicate this amount. Once he has demonstrated this ability to his satisfaction, he has also experienced the incomparable thrill of possessing two hundred, and he cannot be secure with perpetuating this sensation until he duplicates this sum again ... and again ... .

As a wise and audacious beggar once said to a king: "Your Highness is really needier than I am, for I need so little to be comfortable and secure, and you need so very much to be at ease." Insecurity is without limits and so is greed.

Man's true source of security, his *bitachon* (trust), should be with his Creator. G-d is boundless and so is His protection boundless. No security can compare with this. But man, in his foolishness, has transferred his account; he has withdrawn from G-d and has deposited his faith with his funds and his finances. It follows that to replace a boundless, protective Creator he must forever seek endless, unlimited supplies of money. Thus did the Sages comment: "Man does not die with even half of his desires in his grasp."

As long as man seeks his security in tangible possessions, he will never realize complete security until he has every last cent in the world in his grasp. And more. As long as his neighbor has any personal possessions, he is reduced to a ruthless rival, a competitor who jeopardizes his security and must be quashed. It is not difficult to see how "Because they loved money, they despised one another."

"On account of Kamtza and Bar Kamtza Jerusalem was destroyed."

While this tragic tale of intense hatred is well known, it is interesting to note that Kamtza (kamtzan) literally means a miser whose fist is clamped over his coins. It was this obsession with money that aroused men to horrible feuds and bitter vendettas.

◄§ The Ultimate Defilement

The fate of the Second Bais HaMikdash was irrevocably sealed when the gold rush entered the Temple grounds. This was the ultimate defilement. For this House had been set aside as a spiritual haven, a refuge from worldly pursuits and greed: "One may not enter the Temple Mount wearing a money belt" (Berachos 62b).

In the administration of the Sanctuary, a cost-consciousness had no place: "Poverty is not befitting an abode of wealth" (Menachos 89b).

The Kohanim themselves were personally divorced from the pursuit of personal profit, for they possessed no real estate or farms. The priestly gifts they received were not even considered "dividends" or tokens of gratitude from the people. "The priests eat from the table of G-d."

In the Second Temple this changed. The post of Kohen Gadol — the High Priest — was sold annually to the highest bidder. The High Priest in turn misused his power to enhance his personal standing (Yoma 8b-9a).

Rabbi Yoseif said: I discern a conspiracy here. Marsa bas Baysas brought King Yanai three pots of dinarim in order that he appoint her husband, Yehoshua ben Gamla, Kohein Gadol (Yevamos 61a).

Religion became profit-oriented, and the Temple as its focal point had to be destroyed.

Is there any hope for reconstruction? Is there anything we can do to speed its advent? Listen to the prophetic voices of old as they describe a new order which will someday reign:

Rabbi Michel of Zlotchov would point to the prophetic vision of *Parshas Ha'azinu*: *"And there is no strange god with Him"* (*Devarim 32:12*). "This is an assurance that there will be no idolators in your midst. Another explanation: there will be no one engaged in commerce in your midst" (Sifre: ibid.).

If one invests all his trust in merchandise this too can become an object of worship: *"As for the merchant, the balances of deceit are in his hands; he loves to extort"* (*Hoshea 12:8*).

"They rely on dishonest profits for they are dealers in fraud. Therefore do they proclaim: I have waxed rich, what need have I for G-d?" (*Rashi: ibid.*)

The very last words of one of the three last prophets, Zachariah, predict a new era in the Temple. (It was he who was responsible for eradicating the *yeitzer hara* for *avodah zarah*.)

"And on that day there will no longer be a merchant in the House of the L-rd of Hosts" (*Zachariah 14:21*).

"No longer will there be traders in the Bais HaMikdash" (*Targum*).

The Temple will be rebuilt when we become like the *Kohanim* — who depend on G-d's table, rather than on their own.

◦§ Footfalls of Moshiach

There was, until recently, an old *tzaddik* residing in the Holy Land, whose words of *mussar* disciplined thousands from far and wide, and whose personal life exemplified this trait of utter dependence on G-d's table. He was a gravely serious man, earnest and composed. One day his students observed that their master was extraordinarily light-hearted, and they who dared inquired: "Rebbe, why the unusual gaiety?"

The *tzaddik* replied, "All of my years I had depended on a meager income and even this was erratic in coming. I knew full well that I could not depend on those irregular payments for my subsistence, and I came to realize that I existed only by the grace and direct generosity of G-d. I lived from His open hand. Some time ago, however, I began to prosper, my income increased and became more regular — I began to count on the constant unfailing payments. This became my security, my support, and I slowly slipped out of the arms of G-d. But now, *Baruch Hashem*, I have slipped behind and I have not received any income in months. How wonderful it is to be back at G-d's table! And you wonder why I rejoice?"

Such men can hear the *ikvesa d'Meshicha* — the footfalls of *Moshiach* — drawing near in our time. The rest of us are deaf to these steps, for the coins jingling in our pockets are drowning out this long-awaited sound. But G-d wants us to pay attention and hear.

As the entire world was plunged into the great depression of 1929, the Chofetz Chaim observed that this economic crisis did not result from a shortage of money or food or goods. This was evident because all nations, both rich and poor, industrialized and primitive, suffered alike. The *tzaddik* of Radin explained that a stable thriving economy is not based solely on money. Credit is the cornerstone of world finances, and credit is based on mutual trust. In 1929, there was no shortage of money — only a breakdown in the confidence that businesses and banks ordinarily place in one another. This abnormal crisis situation, this hostile climate of suspicion and doubt, was an act of Heaven punishing the world, measure for measure: When men abandon faith in *Hashem* and place all of their security in cash and credit, then G-d eventually destroys this false depository of trust. Men questioned the integrity and endurance of once-sacred contracts. Panic ensued, with the long, dark depression in its wake.

We witness this in everyday life. Men who put their lives in G-d's hands know that no other man can do them harm, and so their thoughts and acts are not clouded by fears and suspicion of their neighbors. Those who lack this belief are bundles of jagged quivering nerves, for every man is a potential threat to their security.

In the time of *Moshiach*, international peace, understanding, cooperation, and trust will be universal. As faith in G-d is restored, men will regain faith in one another. When men will cease to be enamored with their money, they will cease to hate one another.

◆§ Rude Awakening for Moshiach's Arrival

Ideally, we should recognize our utter dependence on G-d and — whether penniless or endowed with a generous abundance of resources — we should conceive of every cent we possess as bread from His table. Any measure of affluence would be understood as a Divine trust for us to execute with responsibility and fealty to His wishes. Failing this, G-d resorts to tactics of shock to awaken us to the bankruptcy of the faith we have invested in our own powers of self-support. He then shakes the confidence we have placed in our bulging coffers and fat bank accounts. *Depression ... recession ... inflation ... devaluation ... price freeze ... profit squeeze ... wage slash ... stock market slips ... unemployment rise ... petro dollars ... gold craze ... soaring taxes* — all of these elements of economic instability have a definite purpose and are part of a Divine plan. *Chazal* tell us with great emphasis that the confusion, the anarchy, and the audacity that mark the era preceding *Moshiach's* arrival are designed to shake our self-confidence and to make us realize that *" ... we have no one to lean upon except our Father in Heaven" (Sotah 49b).*

Moshiach himself will come empty-handed, *"a pauper riding on a donkey" (Zachariah 9:9).*

"The Son of David will not come until the penny vanishes from the purse" (Sanhedrin 97a).

Only then will we hear the footfalls. Only then will our mourning turn to joy and will the ruins of the Temple be rebuilt.

Glossary

ABBA
daddy

ACHARIS HAYOMIM
the End of Days; the time of ultimate justice

ACHRON (ACHRONIM)
Torah scholar of the last 500 years (approx.)

ADMOR (ADMORIM)
title given Chassidic *rebbes*; acronym of the Hebrew for, "our master, our teacher, our rabbi"

AFIKOMAN
last piece of matzoh eaten at the conclusion of the Passover seder meal

AGGADAH (AGGADOS)
sections of the Talmud not directly relating to *halachah*

AGUDAH ACHAS
lit. one bundle; one harmonious body comprising all of Israel united in the service of G-d

AHAVAH RABBAH
lit. great love; blessing recited during daily morning service

AIS RATZON
time of grace; propitious time for prayer

AKEIDAH
binding of Isaac

ALEPH-BAIS
the Hebrew alphabet, named for the two first letters א and ב

AMAL
labor; toil

AM HANIVCHAR
Chosen Nation

AM HASHEM
Nation of G-d

AMKUS
lit. depth; in-depth study of Torah

AMORA (AMORAIM)
sage of the *Gemara* era (approx. 1500 - 1700 years ago)

ANANEI HAKAVOD
the Clouds of Glory which accompanied the Israelites through their forty-year sojourn in the Wilderness

ARAVAH
willow; one of the four species of the Succos service

ARBA'AH MINIM
four species: *esrog, lulav, hadas* and *aravah,* used in the Succos service

ARON HAKODESH
lit. holy ark; the ark containaing the Torah scrolls; also called *aron*

ASARAH B'TEVES
tenth day of Teves

ASERES HADIBROS
the Ten Commandments

ASERES YEMEI TESHUVAH
lit. ten days of penitence; from Rosh HaShanah until Yom Kippur

ASHAM
1. guilt; 2. *korban asham*

ASHAMNU BAGADNU
lit. "We are guilty! We rebelled!"; first two words of the *vidui* litany

ASHER YOTZAR
thanksgiving blessing for the bodily functions

ASTIR
lit. "I shall hide!;" the word used by the Torah to describe the attribute of *hester panim*

ATTA HORAISSA
prayer said before Torah is removed from the Ark on the Sabbath and festivals

ATZERES
lit. gathering or restraining; Talmudic name for Shavuos

AV (AVOS)
father

AVEIRAH (AVEIROS)
sin; opposite of *mitzvah*

AVODAH or **AVODAS HASHEM**
1. service of G-d especially through prayer, charitable acts, kindness, Torah study, etc. 2. the *Bais HaMikdash* service; 3. the liturgical recital of that service

AVODAH ZARAH
idolatry

AVRAHAM AVINU
the Patriarch Abraham

BA'AL
lit. master; used as an author's title relative to his works

BA'AL HABAYIS (BA'ALEI BATIM)
layman

BA'AL PEOR
a Moabite deity (see *Bamidbar* 25)

BA'AL TESHUVAH (BA'ALEI TESHU-VAH)
penitent; one who has either strayed from Orthodoxy and returned, or has not been raised according to Orthodox tradition but has found his way back to the time-honored path

BACHUR (BACHURIM)
post-adolescent unmarried man; especially, *yeshivah bachur*, a student of a yeshivah

BAIS DIN (BATEI DIN)
court of Torah law

BAIS HAKNESSES
synagogue

BAIS HAMIDRASH (BATEI MIDRASH)
study hall; especially a synagogue used for both prayers and study

BAIS HAMIKDASH
the Holy Temple

BAMIDBAR
Book of Numbers

BARUCH HASHEM
lit., G-d be Blessed; a common expression of thanks to the Creator for any bit of good fortune one may enjoy

BECHIPAZON
suddenly; in a rush

BEREISHIS
Book of Genesis

BIKKURIM
first fruits; brought to *Bais HaMikdash* and presented to the *Kohen*

BIMAH
platform in center of synagogue where Torah is read; also used for communal announcements after or during a pause in the synagogue service

BIRCAS HAMAZON
Grace After Meals

BITACHON
trust; faith

BITUL HAYESH
lit. negation of what is; a negation of the primacy of the material in favor of the spiritual

B'NEI EPHRAIM
Children of Ephraim; one of the Israelite tribes

B'NEI TORAH
lit. sons of Torah; those who strive to study the Torah and apply its teachings to every phase of their life

BRACHAH (BRACHOS)
blessing

BRIS
1. *bris milah*, the covenant of circumcision; 2. the covenant of Torah

BRIS BAIN HABESARIM
Covenant Between the Parts (*Genesis* 8:7-21)

BRIS KODESH
lit. the sacred covenant; circumcision

CHACHAM (CHACHAMIM)
1. wise man; in Sefardic circles the equivalent of "Rabbi"; 2. the wise son of the Haggadah

CHAG HAASSIF
the harvest festival, i.e., Succos

CHAG HAAVIV
the spring festival, i.e., Passover

CHAG HAKATZIR
the reaping festival, i.e., Shavuos

CHANUKAH GELT
(Yid.) gifts of money given to children on Chanukah

CHANUKAS HAMIKDASH
dedication of the *Bais HaMikdash*

CHAROSES
a mixture of nuts, apples, cinnamon, and wine into which the bitter herbs are dipped at the Passover Seder

CHASHMONAIM
Hasmoneans

CHASSAN
bridegroom

CHASSID (CHASSIDIM)
1. righteous one; 2. Chassidic Jew

CHAS VESHALOM
"G-d forbid!"

CHATZI
half

CHAVRUSA
study partner; study group

CHAZAL
1. Talmudic sages; 2. a statement by the sages

CHAZAN (CHAZANIM)
cantor; prayer leader

CHESHBON HANEFESH
soul-searching; spiritual inventory

CHESSED
deeds of kindness

CHINUCH
education

CHOCHMAH
wisdom

CHOK (CHUKIM)
Torah commandment whose ultimate rationale is beyond human comprehension

CHOL HAMOED
the Intermediate Days of Passover and Succos

CHOMETZ
leavening; yeast; leavened dough

CHOSHECH
darkness

CHUMASH
set of the five books of the Torah; any of the five books

CHURBAN
destruction; especially *churban Bayis*, destruction of the Holy Temple

CHUTZPAH
audacity

DAVEN
(Yid.) pray

DERECH HASHEM
lit. path of G-d; life-style in accordance with the Torah

DEVARIM
Book of Deuteronomy

DIVREI HAYOMIM
Book of Chronicles

DRASHAH
1. learned discourse; 2. Scriptural exegesis

DVAIKUS
cleaving to G-d

DVAR TORAH (DIVREI TORAH)
a Torah thought

EICHAH
Book of Lamentations

EIDAH
assemblage

EIDUS
testimony; witness

ELIYAHU HANAVI
the prophet Elijah

ELOKAI NESHAMAH
thanksgiving blessing for the soul, recited every morning

EMUNAH
faith; belief

EPHOD
apron-like garment; one of the eight articles of the uniform worn by the *Kohen Gadol* while performing the *Bais HaMikdash* service

ERETZ YISRAEL
the Land of Israel

EREV SHABBOS
the eve of the Sabbath

ESROG
citron; one of the four species used in the Succos service

GALUS
exile; Diaspora

GALUS YAVAN
the Greek Exile

GAN EDEN
the Garden of Eden

GEHINNOM
Hell

GEMARA
1. section of Talmud which elucidates the Mishnah; 2. a Talmudic tome

GEMATRIA (GEMATRIOS or GEMATRIOT)
numerical equivalencies of the Hebrew alphabet

GEULAH
redemption

GOLAH
galus

GRAMMEN
(Yid.) rhymes; esp. those composed in honor of Purim which satirize the shortcomings of the audience

GREGGER or GRAGGER
(Yid.) noisemaker used by children to drown out Haman's name at the public Megillah reading on Purim; Heb. *ra'ashon*

HADAS
myrtle; one of the four species of the Succos service

HAFTARAH (HAFTAROS)
portion of Prophets read at the completion of the public Torah reading on the Sabbath and festivals

HAGOMEL LECHAYAVIM
first words of the blessing recited by a person who either crossed the desert or ocean, arose from a sick bed or was released from captivity

HAKAFAH (HAKAFOS)
lit. circuit; the joyous dancing and singing which accompanies the seven circuits of the Torah around the *bimah* on Simchas Torah

HALACHAH (HALACHOS)
Torah law

HALLEL
1. praise; 2. esp. *Psalms 113-118*, recited on the Pilgrimage Festivals, New Moon and Chanukah during morning services

HANEIROS HALALU
lit. these flames; a prayer recited after kindling the Chanukah menorah

HANESHAMAH LACH
lit. "The soul is Yours!"; expression of yearning for nearness to G-d which is a theme of the *Slichos* prayer

HASHEM
lit. The Name; a respectful reference to G-d and His Ineffable Name

HASHGACHAH (HASHGACHOS)
supervision; especially, *hashgachah peratis*, Divine supervision and intervention in the affairs of the individual

HASHKIVEINU
blessing recited during daily evening service

HASKALAH
lit. enlightenment; Reform Judaism

HAVAYAH
lit. existence; an anagrammatic form of the Ineffable Name of G-d

HAVDALAH
1. separation; 2. the service at the close of the Sabbath or a festival which sets that Holy Day apart from the weekdays

HEDYOT
layman; common; ordinary

HESTER PANIM
lit. hiding of the face; G-d's hiding of any manifestation of His Presence, a form of punishment to a wayward generation

HIDDUR (HIDDURIM)
enhancement, esp. of *mitzvos*

HODA'AH
gratitude

HORA'AH
decision of law; *p'sak*

HOSHANA (HOSHANOS)
special prayers for salvation recited during the Succos festival

HOSHANA RABBAH
last day of Succos, so called because of the many *hoshana* prayers recited that day

IKVESA D'MESHICHA
lit., footsteps of the Messiah; the period immediately preceding the advent of *Moshiach*

IMA
mommy

KABALAS HATORAH
receiving of the Torah at Mount Sinai

KABTZON (KABTZONIM)
beggar

KAHAL
congregation

KAMTZAN
miser

KAPARAH
forgiveness

KAROV
to draw close

KASHRUS
kosherness

KAVANAH
intent; concentration; purpose

KAVEYACHOL
lit. "As if it were possible to be!"; used to introduce an anthropomorphism or anthropopathism

KAVOD HATORAH
respect for the Torah

KEDUSHAH
holiness

KEHUNAH GEDOLAH
office of the *Kohen Gadol*

KIDDUSH
sanctification blessing recited over a cup of wine at the onset of the Sabbath or a festival

KIDDUSH HASHEM
sanctification of G-d's Holy Name; martyrdom

KINOS
laments; esp. the order of liturgical lamentation of *Tishah B'Av*

KIRUV
closeness

KISHUF
sorcery

KLAL YISRAEL
the community of Israel, i.e., all of Jewry

KODESH (KODASHIM)
sacred

KODESH HAKODASHIM
lit. Holy of Holies; inner sanctum of the *Bais HaMikdash*

KOFRIM
deniers; non-believers; heretics

KOHELES
Book of Ecclesiastes

KOHEN (KOHANIM)
one descended from the male line of the priestly family of Aaron

KOHEN GADOL
chief *Kohen*

KORBAN (KORBANOS)
sacrifice; Temple offering

KORBAN ASHAM
guilt offering; a *korban* brought in atonement for certain specified sins

KORBAN CHATTOS
sin offering; brought in atonement for certain inadvertent transgressions

KORBAN OLAH
burnt offering

KORBAN PESACH
the Passover offering; a young lamb or kid sacrificed during the afternoon of the eve of Passover, and eaten that night at the Seder

KORBAN RE'EYAH
burnt offering mandated for the pilgrim to the *Bais HaMikdash* during the *Shalosh Regalim*

KORBAN SHLOMIM
peace offering

KORBAN TODAH
thanksgiving offering

KOREIS
spiritual excision manifested either by a shortened life span or the premature loss of children

KOS SHEL ELIYAHU
Cup of Elijah; the fifth cup poured at the Pesach Seder in honor of the prophet Elijah

KREPL (KREPLACH)
(Yid.) turnover filled with meat, chicken liver, kasha or the like and boiled

KULO TECHEILES
lit. entirely blue; completely noble

KUSHYA (KUSHYOS)
questions

LAMED-VAVNIK
(Yid.) one of the thirty-six (*lamed-vav*) *tzaddikim* who, Kabbalists teach, are hidden in every generation

LASHON HARA
evil talk, i.e., slander, gossip, etc.

LAVUD
a legal fiction which considers a gap of less than three handbreadths as closed

LECHAYIM
lit., "To life!"; traditional toast over a glass of spirits

LEHAVDIL
lit. to separate; a word inserted into a sentence to prevent speaking the profane and the sacred in one breath

LEV TOV
a good heart

LISHMAH
purity of motivation

LIVYASAN
Leviathan, of whose meat the *tzaddikim* in *Gan Eden* will partake, and whose skin will be fashioned into a *succah* for their comfort

LOMDUS
Torah scholarship

LUCHOS
tablets; especially the twin tablets upon which the Ten Commandments were inscribed

LULAV (LULAVIM)
palm branch; one of the four species used in the Succos service

MA'AMAD HAR SINAI
lit., the station at Mount Sinai; the receiving of the Torah

MA'ARIV
evening prayer

MAGI'A LI
lit. "It's coming to me!"; a euphemism for insatiable materialistic desire and self-indulgence

MAHARAL
acronym for Moreinu HaRav Loewy "our teacher Rabbi (Yehudah) Loewy" (1512-1608)

MAI CHANUKAH
lit. "What is Chanukah?"; the opening phrase of the Talmud's discussion of Chanukah, its origin and its laws

MALACH (MALACHIM)
angel

MALACH HABRIS
lit. angel of the covenant; an appellation of Eliyahu HaNavi, the prophet Elijah

MALBIM
acronym for Rabbi Meir Leibush Ben Yechiel Mechel (1809-1878), author of a commentary on all of Scripture

MARROR
bitter herbs eaten at the Passover Seder

MASHGIACH (MASHGICHIM)
dean of students in a yeshiva who acts as guide and advisor

MASMID (MASMIDIM)
student displaying more than the usual diligence in his studies

MATANOS LA'EVYONIM
gifts distributed to the poor on Purim

MATTAN TORAH
Giving of the Torah at Mount Sinai

MEHADRIN
those who seek to enhance and embellish the scrupulous performance of mitzvos both physically (a beautiful menorah, a beautiful tallis) and spiritually (with purest of intentions)

MEHADRIN MIN HAMEHADRIN
those who outdo even the mehadrin in their performance of mitzvos

MESIRAS NEFESH
self-sacrifice; especially in refusal to renounce a principle of religious faith;

devotion to a cause beyond the call of duty

METZORA
one afflicted with the spiritual disease tzara'as, the physical manifestations of which are described in Leviticus 13

MEZUZAH (MEZUZOS)
parchment inscribed with two Scriptural passages (Deuteronomy 5:4-9 and 11:13-21) and attached to the doorposts, usually encased in a decorative holder to protect it from the elements

MIDAH (MIDOS)
1. character trait; 2. attribute of G-d

MIDAH K'NEGED MIDAH
lit. measure for measure; retribution, both reward and punishment, which exactly fits the deed

MIDRASH (MISRASHOS)
compilation of homiletic Scriptural interpretations of the Amoraim

MIL
distance measure equal to 2,000 cubits

MILAH
circumcision

MINCHAS KENA'OS
meal offering brought in the Bais HaMikdash by a suspected adulteress who denied the charges against her

MINHAG (MINHAGIM)
custom

MINYAN (MINYANIM)
quorum of ten adults males needed in the performance of certain religious practices; also used as a unit of counting people in general

MISHKAN
Tabernacle; the portable Bais HaMikdash which accompanied the Israelites through their forty-year sojourn in the wilderness

MISHLEI
Book of Proverbs

MISHLO'ACH MANOS
sending of food packages to friends on Purim; also called shalach manos

MISHNAH (MISHNAYOS)
1. the teachings of the Tannaim, as compiled by Rabbi HaNassi, and forming the basis of the Talmud; 2. a paragraph of that work

MISHPACHAH
family

MISYAVNIM
   1. Hellenists; 2. assimilated Jews

MITZRAYIM
   Egypt

MITZVAH
   1. a commandment of the Torah; 2. any good or exemplary act

MODEH ANI
   lit. "I give thanks"; prayer recited immediately upon awakening in the morning

MO'ED (MO'ADIM)
   lit. appointed time; festival or holiday

MOSHE RABBEINU
   our teacher Moses

MOSHIACH
   the Messiah

MUCHAN
   prepared

MUKTZAH
   lit. set aside for a specific purpose; items which may not be handled on the Sabbath or festivals, usually because of the secular nature of their function

MUM
   blemish; imperfection

MUSSAR SHMUESS
   (Yid.) lecture on ethics

NA'ASEH
   lit. "We will do!"; the first half of the formula "Na'aseh VeNishma! We will do! We will listen!" used by the Israelites in accepting the Torah

NACHAS
   pleasure in accomplishment

NASSI
   president or prince

NAVI
   prophet

NAZIR
   one who has taken nazirite vows, i.e., not to consume any products of the grape vine, not to cut his hair, not to become contaminated by contact with a dead body (*Numbers* 6:1-21)

NECHAMAH
   assuagement; comfort

NE'ILAH
   final, additional prayer of Yom Kippur

NEIR (NEIROS)
   light; candle; flame

NEIR ECHOD ISH U'VEISO
   lit. one candle for each man and his household; the minimal requirement for each night of Chanukah

NEIR TAMID
   eternal light

NEIS
   miracle

NEIS NIGLAH
   overt miracle; obvious reversal of the laws of nature

NEIS NISTAR
   covert miracle; event in which the miraculous is disguised as natural

NESHAMAH (NESHAMOS)
   spirit; soul

NETZACH
   eternality; esp. as an attribute of God

NISHMA
   lit. "We will listen!"; the latter half of the formula "Na'aseh VeNishma! "We will do! We will listen!", used by the Jews in accepting the Torah

NISHMAS
   lit. the soul of ... ; a prayer recited during the morning services on *Shabbos* and festivals

OLAM HABA
   World-to-Come; the reward awaiting the righteous as the fruits of their labors in *Olam Hazeh*, this world

OLAM HAZEH
   this world, as opposed to *Olam Haba*, the World-to-Come; often used as a metaphor for material assets

OMER
   1. a dry measure equivalent in volume to 43.2 eggs; 2. a meal offering consisting of an *omer* measure of barley, brought in the *Bais HaMikdash* on the second day of Pesach; 3. *Sefiras HaOmer*

ORAISA
   lit. light giver; Aramaic for Torah

OS
   a sign; esp. *os bris*, the sign of the covenant, i.e., circumcision

PESACH
   1. Passover; 2. the *Korban Pesach*

PILPUL
   keen dialectic analysis of a difficult portion of Torah

PIRSUMEI NISA
   publicizing the miracle; one of the major precepts of Chanukah

PSHAT
simple explanation of Scripture

RABBEINU
our teacher; especially used in alluding to Moses

RAMBAM
acronym of Rabbi Moshe Ben Maimon (Maimonides, 1135-1204)

RAMBAN
acronym of Rabbi Moshe Ben Nachman (Nachmanides; 1194-1270)

RASHA GAMUR
totally wicked person

RASHI
acronym for Rabbi Shlomo Yitzchaki (1040-1105), greatest of all commentators on Scripture and Talmud

REBBE (RABBEIM)
rabbi; especially, a Torah teacher, or a Chassidic leader

RIBONO SHEL OLAM
Master of the Universe

REGEL (REGALIM)
pilgrimage festival; Pesach, Shavuos or Succos

RISHON (RISHONIM)
Torah scholar of about 500-1000 years ago

RISHON L'CHESHBON AVEIROS
lit. the first day for reckoning sins; an allusion to the first day of Succos — on Yom Kippur past sins are forgiven, the next four days are ripe with preparation of the succah and the four species, leaving no time for sin — when one must be extra careful not to allow the tranquility of day to lull him into sinfulness

RODEF SHALOM (RODFEI SHALOM)
one who pursues peace

ROSH CHODESH
lit. the new moon; the first day of each month, celebrated as a quasi-festival

ROSH YESHIVAH (ROSHEI YESHIVAH)
dean of a Torah academy

RUACH HAKODESH
lit. Holy Spirit; divine knowledge which falls just short of prophecy

RUCHNIYUS
spirituality

S'CHACH
succah covering

SANHEDRIN
highest Rabbinic Tribunal

SCHLIMAZEL
(Yid.) lit. hapless; a hapless individual

SCHMOOZERS
(Yid.) conversationalists

SEFER (SEFARIM)
book; esp. holy book

SEFER TORAH (SIFREI TORAH)
Torah scroll

SEFIRAH or SEFIRAS HAOMER
lit. counting (of the Omer); 49 day period, beginning the second day of Passover ending the day before Shavuos; each night during this period a special blessing is pronounced followed by the count of that day, e.g., "Today is the 20th day, making two weeks and six days of the Omer."

SEUDAS PURIM
festive meal, eaten on the afternoon of Purim

SEVARA (SEVAROS)
rationale

SHA'AILAH (SHA'ALOS)
halachic queries

SHABBOS (SHABBOSOS)
the Sabbath

SHABBOS HAGADOL
lit. The Great Sabbath; the Sabbath preceding the Passover festival; usually marked by a scholarly lecture-sermon, of long duration, pertaining to the laws of Passover

SHABBOS TESHUVAH
lit. Sabbath of Repentance; the Sabbath falling between Rosh Hashanah and Yom Kippur; usually marked by a scholarly lecture-sermon of long duration on the theme of repentance

SHALACH MANOS
sending of food packages to friends on Purim; also called mishlo'ach manos

SHALOSH REGALIM
the three pilgrimage festivals: Pesach (Passover), Shavuos, Succos

SHALOSH SEUDOS
lit. three meals; the third Sabbath meal, usually begun just before sunset and lasting until nightfall or later

SHAMASH or SHAMMOS
synagogue caretaker; rabbi's assistant

SHECHINAH
manifestation of the Divine Presence

SHECHITAH
  slaughter of animals according to Torah law

SHEHECHEYANU
  lit. "Who has kept us alive!"; a blessing recited on certain festive occasions

SHELOCH SHELI
  lit. "What's yours is mine!"; an expression connoting self-indulgence at the expense of another

SHELO LISHMAH
  selfishly motivated

SHEMA
  the verse "Hear, O Israel, HASHEM, our G-d, HASHEM is One!" which forms the basis of the daily proclamation of G-d's Unity

SHEMA KOLEINU
  lit. "Listen to our voices!"; the opening words of the central *slichos* prayer

SHEMONEH ESREI
  lit. eighteen; the Amidah prayer which originally comprised eighteen blessings

SHEMOS
  Book of Exodus

SHIR HASHIRIM
  Song of Songs

SHLIACH
  messenger; emissary; proxy

SHLIACH TZIBBUR
  lit. messenger of the congregation; prayer leader; cantor

SHLOMO HAMELECH
  King Solomon

SHMIRAS HAMITZVOS
  observance of the *mitzvos*

SHMIRAS SHABBOS
  Sabbath observance

SHMITTAH
  the Sabbatical year; each seventh year the earth in Israel must not be worked (*Leviticus* 25:1-7)

SHMUEL
  Book of Samuel

SH'TEI HALECHEM
  lit. two loaves; a *Bais HaMikdash* offering consisting of two leavened wheat breads, brought on Shavuos

SHTIEBEL (SHTIEBLACH)
  (Yid.) lit. small room; small local synagogue

SHUL
  (Yid.) synagogue

SHULCHAN ARUCH
  compilation of practical Torah law

SIMCHAH
  rejoicing

SIMCHAH SHEL MITZVAH
  rejoicing while performong, or at the opportunity to perform, a *mitzvah*

SIMCHAS BAIS HASHO'EIVAH
  rejoicing in the *Bais HaMikdash* accompanying the water-drawing service each evening of Succos

SIMCHAS TORAH
  the last day of Succos on which the concluding portion of the Torah is read, to the accompaniment of joyous dance and song

SINAS CHINAM
  unjustified hatred

SLICHOS
  penitential prayers recited before and during the *Yomim Noraim* and on fast days

SOFER (SOFRIM)
  1. scribe; 2. statistician

SOTAH
  a wife who brings suspicion of adultery upon herself by disregarding her husband's admonition not to go into a secluded place with a particular man

SUCCAH (SUCCOS)
  temporary dwelling; specifically, that used during the Succos festival

SUCCAS SHALOM
  lit. *succah* of peace; Divine protection

TAAM
  1. reason 2. taste

TACHANUN
  1. supplication; 2. a part of the weekday morning and afternoon prayers

TALMID (TALMIDIM)
  1. disciple; 2. student

TALMID CHACHAM (TALMIDEI CHACHOMIM)
  Torah scholar

TALMUD TORAH
  the precept of Torah study

TANACH
  Scripture

TANNA (TANNAIM)
  Sage of the Mishnah

TARGUM (TARGUMIM)
  lit. translation; esp. the Aramaic translation of the Pentateuch by Onkelos

TARGUM HASHIVIM
lit. translation of the seventy; the Septuagint

TEFILLAH (TEFILLOS)
prayer

TEFILLIN
phylacteries

TEHILLIM
Book of Psalms

TERUAH
staccato shofar blast

TERUTZ (TERUTZIM)
response; answer; reply

TESHUVAH
repentance

TEVA
nature

T'HOM
abyss; great depths

TIFERES
glory; esp. as an attribute of G-d

TIKUN
emendation; correction; bringing to perfection

TIMTUM HALEV
callousness of the heart in the performance of *mitzvos*

TISHAH B'AV
ninth of Av; date on which the first *Bais HaMikdash* and, 490 years later, the second *Bais HaMikdash*, were destroyed

TOCHACHAH
admonishment

TOHU
nothingness; void; descriptive of the universe before its creation

TOV
good

TYERE BRIEDER
(Yid.) "Dear brothers!"

TZADDIK (TZADDIKIM)
lit., righteous one; used of Chassidic *rebbes* and other extremely pious and caring people

TZEDDAKAH
charity

TZIBBUR
congregation; multitude

TZILUSA DEMEHIMENUSA
lit. shade of faith; and epithet for the *succah*

VAYEHI
lit. "It was!"; common Scriptural paragraph opener

VAYIKRA
Book of Leviticus

VEHAYAH
lit. "It will be!"; common Scriptural paragraph opener

VIDUI
confessional prayers

VOHU
emptiness; formlessness; descriptive of the universe before its creation

YAAKOV AVINU
the Patriarch Jacob

YAHRZEIT
(Yid.) anniversay of a death

YASHER KOACH
lit. "May your strengths be aligned!"; a blessing given to one who has done a personal favor, performed a particular *mitzvah*, or accomplished a difficult feat

YECHEZKEL
Book of Ezekiel; the Prophet Ezekiel

YEHUDAH
Judah

YEITZER HARA
evil inclination; personification of evil influence

YERUSHALAYIM
Jerusalem

YESHAYAH
Book of Isaiah; the Prophet Isaiah

YESHIVAH (YESHIVOS)
torah academy

YESHNO AM ECHAD
lit. "There is one nation!" (Esther 3:8); homiletically interpreted as "one nation which sleeps", a play on the words *yeshno*, there is, and *yashno*, they sleep

YIDDISHE NESHAMAH
(Yid.) a Jewish soul

YIDDISHKEIT
(Yid.) Judaism

YIRMIYAH

YIRAS SHAMAYIM
fear of Heaven
Book of Jeremiah; the Prophet Jeremiah

YIUSH
despair; sense of abandonment

YODE'AH TA'ALUMOS
  lit. the One wh knows the secrets; an allusion to G-d's omniscience and His
  plumbing the depths of the heart
YOFI
  beauty
YOMIM NORAIM
  lit., Days of Awe; the Ten Days of
  Penitence, beginning Rosh Hashanah
  and ending Yom Kippur
YOM TOV (YOMIM TOVIM)
  lit. good day; festival
YOM TOV SHEINI SHEL GALUS
  second day of the festival in the
  Diaspora; the days, five in all, following the Yom Tov days of the pilgrimage
  festivals, which have been ordained as
  Yomim Tovim by the Talmudic Sages

YOTZER HAMEOROS
  lit. Creator of the light givers; blessing
  recited during daily morning service
YOVEL
  the Jubilee year
ZMAN CHEIRUSEINU
  the time of our freedom, i.e., Passover
ZMAN MATTAN TORASEINU
  the time of the giving of our Torah, i.e.,
  Shavuos
ZOHAR
  1. splendid brilliance; shining light; 2.
  the principle work of Kaballah,
  authored by the Tanna Rabbi Shimon
  bar Yochai
Z'VUV
  fly